CONTRACT MANAGEMENT BODY OF KNOWLEDGE (CMBOK)

4th Edition

Updated by Margaret G. Rumbaugh, CPCM, Fellow

Contract Management Body of Knowledge (CMBOK)
Fourth Edition

©2013 National Contract Management Association
All rights reserved. Published 2013.
Printed in the United States of America.
ISBN-13: 978-0-9700897-7-9
01202016

contents

contents

The National Contract Management Association (NCMA) was formed in 1959 to foster the professional growth and educational advancement of its members. It is a membership-based professional society whose leadership is composed of volunteers. The NCMA office has a full-time staff to support its members' needs. The NCMA Staff Directory provides information about the office departments responsible for different services. NCMA is located at 21740 Beaumeade Circle, Suite 125; Ashburn, VA 20147. The office is open between the hours of 8:30 a.m. and 5:00 p.m. (EST).

This document supersedes the National Contract Management Association's (NCMA) *Contract Management Body of Knowledge (CMBOK)*, third edition, published in 2011.

The fourth edition of the *CMBOK* expands, refines, and reorganizes the information presented in previous editions. It provides further definition of the field of contract management, the framework for the body of knowledge, the practices outlined, the definitions (lexicon), and the processes of contract management. It provides procedural steps that apply to the contract management process in general, as well as specialized areas and those that are unique to either federal or commercial contracting. In addition, it includes recommended curricula for contract management degree programs.

Readers should note that the *CMBOK* does not purport to define the body of knowledge, but rather to serve as a compendium and guide to the body of knowledge that has been developing and evolving over the past five decades. Furthermore, this body of knowledge is not static. The guide must, necessarily, develop and evolve as the contract management profession matures. It nevertheless constitutes a valuable source for information on the competencies and knowledge areas required for success in the profession.

preface

acknowledgements

Acknowledgements are made to previous authors and contributors of earlier editions of the *CMBOK* and *Annotated Guide to the CMBOK*. Acknowledgements and thanks go to the oversight group and independent reviewers for the 2013 edition, including:

Dr. Ralph M. Criss, CPCM
John Dobriansky, CPCM, Fellow
Bill Kaplan, CPCM, Fellow
Rodney F. Matsushima, Fellow
Ina R. Merson, CPCM, Fellow
Dr. Rene Rendon, CPCM, CFCM, Fellow
Debra Scheider, CPCM
Larry Trowel, CPCM, CFCM
John W. Wilkinson, EdD, CPCM, CFCM, Fellow

The Contract Management Framework

chapter one

The Contract Management Framework

The Contract Management Profession

What constitutes a profession? Although individual responses to this question may differ, the U.S. Department of Labor has held that a profession has at least five distinct characteristics:

- A professional organization,
- A code of ethics,
- A body of knowledge,
- Research activities, and
- A credentialing arm.

The contract management profession has all five of these characteristics:

- A professional organization (the National Contract Management Association [NCMA], with news of the profession being published in *Contract Management* Magazine and monthly electronic newsletters);
- A code of ethics for the profession;
- A body of knowledge, which is updated continuously;
- A research publication (the *Journal of Contract Management*);
- A research arm (the Contract Management Institute [CMI]); and
- A viable and highly visible credentialing program (Certified Federal Contracts Manager (CFCM), Certified Commercial Contracts Manager (CCCM), and Certified Professional Contracts Manager (CPCM)).

In 1996, Frank Meneely defined the body of knowledge as:

> ...a conceptual framework that is systematized about a central theme and formulated through the process of definition, classification, and analysis with reference to the discovery of general concepts, theories, laws, and/or principles. The [body of knowledge] is the keystone of a profession and provides the baseline for the development of education and training materials and certification requirements for its membership. It encompasses both theory and practice.

Building on Meneely's definition and borrowing from the Project Management Institute's definition of the "project management body of knowledge," the *CMBOK* offers the following encompassing definition:

> The *CMBOK* is an inclusive term that describes the sum of knowledge for the profession of contract management. The complete body of knowledge concerning contract management resides both with the practitioners and those who, like academicians and governing bodies, apply and advance contract management. This body of knowledge includes both the generally accepted practices (such as business and finance) that are widely applied, as well as state-of-the-art practices (such as e-commerce and catalog aggregation).

The *CMBOK* has undergone a number of revisions over the past 15 years. In 1996, the *CMBOK* was revised and reorganized to make it more relevant and useful to the contracting profession. In 2001, the then-existing Contract Management Certification and Accreditation Board (CMCAB) appointed a *CMBOK* Committee. This committee was charged with investigating and subsequently updating the *CMBOK*. The original committee was responsible for the publication of the first edition of the *CMBOK*. Another committee added commercial content, and ongoing committee activities continually monitor the profession for changes to this primary document.

The second edition of the *CMBOK* included an updated lexicon of contracting terms for both federal and commercial areas. A series of charts patterned on a work breakdown structure (WBS) helped the reader understand the relationship among the elements of the *CMBOK*, as well as the similarities and differences among competencies associated with federal and commercial contract management. The dictionary complemented the charts and defined the terms used. The definitions take the guesswork out of discerning the meaning ascribed to each term.

In 2006, an *Annotated Guide to the CMBOK* further refined and reorganized the information presented in previous editions. The basic WBS pattern was retained, and the content was reordered into a series of chapters. Each chapter discussed a grouping of competencies essential for successful practice. The chapters were arranged from the general to the specific, and also attempted to stress the similarities between government and commercial contracting, as well as unique aspects of each.

Given that no body of knowledge is ever static, periodic reviews are necessary. What new areas of knowledge have emerged that must be mastered? What are the tasks that contract professionals perform on a regular basis and in what knowledge areas must they demonstrate competency? This analysis is generally accomplished via a job analysis, which identifies the tasks performed by contract management professionals as well as the knowledge areas required for performance. In 2009, NCMA empaneled a Job Analysis Task Force. With the assistance of Professional Examination Services (a company providing a full range of assessment and advisory services to organizations across a broad range of professions in support of professional licensure and certification, training, and continuing professional education), the task force was charged with creating a contemporary description of the work of contracts managers consisting of the major performance domains of practice, the tasks performed within the domains, knowledge content areas, and the knowledge used in each of these areas. The intent was to support the development of a structured description of contemporary contracts management practice as well as determine any updates needed for NCMA's Certification Program and the body of knowledge.

Professional Examination Services formulated these tasks and domains into a survey sent to a combination of certified and noncertified members. Those surveyed were asked to rate tasks and knowledge areas in terms of both frequency of use and importance to the practice of the profession. The survey results give us a snapshot of the practice of contract management and enable us to identify gaps in the body of knowledge or areas that should be more or less strongly emphasized. (The tasks and knowledge domains are provided in the Appendices.)

Of the over 300 respondents, 82 percent held an NCMA certification with 48 percent on the buyer side and 49 percent on the seller side. There was a clear distinction between pre- and post-award activities dependent on whether the respondent was on the buyer or seller side. The only knowledge domain where more than 15 percent of respondents spent more than half their time was the "Manage Contract" domain. Similarly, the most frequently used knowledge was in the post-award areas; however, nearly all respondents indicated the need for knowledge in other areas, even if they did not spend their practice time in those areas. Therefore, it can be said that the contracts professional must have a wide knowledge base and some level of familiarity with many subjects, even if his or her current environment does not require him or her to practice in those fields.

The dynamic nature of contract management continues to impact its body of knowledge. Building upon the findings of the 2009 Job Analysis Task Force, it was determined in 2013 to further refine and organize the *CMBOK*. All competencies have been made to be more effective. Also, some competencies have been combined to help bring an expanded understanding of the competencies. For instance, the "Service Contracts" competency now includes the "Performance-Based Acquisition" competency, the "Government Property" competency includes the "Property Administration" competency, and the "Standards of Conduct" competency includes the "Organizational Conflict of Interest" competency.

Purpose of the *CMBOK*

Contract management is a mature profession, but still growing. The purpose of this guide is to provide a common understanding of the terms used in the profession. As a basic reference, this document is neither comprehensive nor all-inclusive; rather, it seeks to provide a tutorial of the contract management process in commercial as well as U.S. government contracting.

This document is also used by NCMA as a basic reference about contract management knowledge and practices for its professional development programs, including NCMA's Certification Program.

What is a Contract?

A "contract" is an agreement between two or more parties, especially one that is written and enforceable by law. For a contract to be valid, both parties must indicate that they agree to the terms. This is accomplished when one party submits an offer that the other accepts within a reasonable time or a stipulated period. If the terms of the acceptance vary from those of the offer, that acceptance legally constitutes a counteroffer; the original offering party may then accept it or reject it. At any time before acceptance, the offer may be rescinded on notice unless the offering party is bound by a separate option contract not to withdraw. Only those terms expressed in the contract can be enforced; secret intentions are not recognized. For a contract to be binding, it must not have an immoral or criminal purpose or intent or be contrary to public policy. Since a contract is an agreement, it may be made only by parties with the capacity to reach an understanding.

Most contracts are "bilateral," consisting of reciprocal promises. Under bilateral contracts, each party has made a promise, has an obligation to perform, and has expectations that the other party will perform. An example is a contract where one party promises to provide services and the other party promises to pay an agreed-to amount of money to receive said services.

There are also "unilateral contracts," where only one party has made a promise and is obligated to perform. An example of this may be a contract that promises monetary reward to find a missing pet. No one is obligated by that contract to search for that pet, but if the pet is found, the party who promised the reward is obligated to pay a reward.

An "express contract" is one in which the terms of the contract are stated in words, either written or spoken, and assented to by both parties. An "implied contract," sometimes called "implied in fact," is one in which the terms of the contract are wholly or partly inferred from conduct or surrounding circumstance. "Quasi contracts," sometimes called "implied in law," are obligations imposed by law to prevent the unjust enrichment of one person at another's expense.

A legally binding contract must contain the following elements:

- It must involve two or more parties that have the capacity to contract;

- It must show agreement, including offer, acceptance, and mutual assent;

- It must show something of value changing hands between the parties to a contract, or other inducement that leads a person to make a promise;

- It must be for a legal purpose; and

- It must be in the correct form.

A contract can be partially or totally unenforceable. If a party to the contract does not have the capacity to contract (such as being underage or having a mental infirmity), a contract is unenforceable. An "illegal contract" is a type of unenforceable contract that violates public policy or statutes. A court will not intervene in the case of illegal contracts; however, the court may divide the contract into legal and illegal portions and consider only the illegal portions void. A contract can also be unenforceable in cases of misrepresentation, duress, undue influence, lack of written evidence of the terms of certain business-related contracts, and in some cases mistakes.

A contract is "executed" when all the parties have fully performed their contractual duties.

What is Contract Management?

"Contract management" is the process of managing contracts, deliverables, deadlines, and contract terms and conditions while ensuring customer satisfaction. Public agencies and private companies know that the purchasing process does not end when the contract is awarded.

Effective post-award contract management is essential to the seamless acceptance of supplies and services. Contract management impacts many areas within an organization and can significantly influence its budget, operations, customer service, and public image.

Procurement and contract management are actually mirror images of each other. Both professions describe the broader process of sales or acquisition between two parties. Some objectives of buyers and sellers are distinctly different, while others are surprisingly similar. A mutually beneficial contract can often be challenging to write. Buyers want the lowest price, whereas sellers want to maximize profit. Both, however, should strive to meet the quality, delivery, and performance expectations of each other. Working together, they form a group of professionals under the "procurement" umbrella.

Popular discussion often differentiates between "acquisition" and "procurement," with procurement often characterized as the mechanical or even clerical fulfillment of acquisition goals. Notwithstanding such periodic variations, this document considers "procurement" at the overarching level, encompassing the whole gamut of actions required to achieve programmatic or organizational goals. Procurement consists of evaluating and selecting suppliers based on availability, reliability, and price to obtain the highest quality products at the lowest price. Buyers conduct market research by attending trade shows and conferences and visiting suppliers' plants to examine products and stay abreast of industry trends. They must develop a working technical knowledge of the goods or services they buy. They often forge a strong working relationship with their supplier counterparts—the contract managers—to optimize the outcome for both parties.

The mission of a contract management organization may read as follows:

> The contract management organization's mission is to provide vision, leadership, and professional expertise within the total business team necessary to ensure, at the lowest cost consistent with the significance of the issue or matter, that:
>
> - Contracts with its customers are negotiated, managed, and communicated in a manner that satisfies the customers' needs and requirements;
> - Working with program and business management functions, the [organization] complies with contractual terms and conditions and applicable laws and regulations;
> - Contractual issues and risks are anticipated, avoided, or mitigated (if possible) and appreciated in making business decisions; and
> - Opportunities to advance or protect the [organization]'s legitimate interests are identified and appropriately pursued.
>
> To be fully effective, contract management services are best developed and provided through full integration and active participation in the business team from the first moment of the business process.

About the Contract Management Profession

"Contract management" is a specialized competency within the procurement profession, but it has a very broad perspective in terms of the responsibilities assigned to a contract manager. The job scope ranges from the administrative skills of managing, organizing, and planning to the excitement and challenge of negotiating a major contract. Both procurement and contract management demand competence in such areas as contract law, administration, accounting, psychology, management, and planning.

The Contract Management Institute (CMI) commissioned two studies on the contract management profession in 1999 and 2001. The first study, conducted by PricewaterhouseCoopers, analyzed the implications of current and future business requirements

on contract and business management professionals. An important objective of this research was to reach conclusions gleaned from the insights of active and inactive contract management professionals and others, such as educators, consultants, lawyers, and those working in various related disciplines. Some notable findings of the study included the following:

- Essential core activities of contract managers include structuring business arrangements, contract formation, contract execution, pursuit of innovative contracting or business approaches, decision-making, and building strategic relations.

- More than 80 percent of CMI's respondents believed that the contract professional's role was more time-sensitive, involved more responsibility, and was more team-oriented and more strategic. Contract managers have an increasingly important role to play in cross-functional or integrated process teams.

- In the future, business-related performance metrics would be used to assess practitioner effectiveness.

- Almost 93 percent of CMI's respondents agreed or strongly agreed that a specialized undergraduate degree in contracting/purchasing is the most desirable educational background. However, effective written and verbal communication skills are the most important current and future professional requirements. Analysis and negotiation skills were highly prized in the short term, but would be superseded by computer literacy and problem-solving skills. Business judgment is a competency valued highly, regardless of the time period.

- With respect to education and training opportunities, contract and business managers are largely responsible for guiding their own career development.

- The results showed a high correlation between salary levels and education.

The purpose of a second study commissioned by CMI, conducted by Stratecon, was to provide a better understanding of the performance metrics and performance evaluation systems by which organizations measured the performance of contract managers and purchasing professionals, as well as what standards might be appropriate to use in the future. The study showed that the contract management profession was evolving. Seventy-five percent of survey respondents agreed or strongly agreed that the contract management/purchasing function in their organizations was evolving into a strategic function that interacts with most aspects of an organization's business to include such activities as:

- Building strategic relationships internally and externally,
- Conducting strategic planning and sourcing,
- Collaborating on acquisition planning,
- Participating in cross-functional or integrated process teams,
- Pursuing innovative contracting or business approaches, and
- Making important decisions.

The top 10 metrics chosen by the overall population to evaluate the performance of contract management and purchasing professionals were:

1. Responsiveness,
2. Integrity and adherence to ethical standards,
3. Timeliness,
4. Written communication,
5. Verbal communication,
6. Human relations/interpersonal skills,
7. Problem-solving ability,
8. Education,
9. Internal customer service, and
10. Business judgment.

The 10 top metrics recommended for use in the future to evaluate the performance of contract management and purchasing professionals were:

1. Integrity and adherence to ethical standards,
2. Human relations/interpersonal skills,
3. Business judgment,
4. Decision-making,
5. External customer service,
6. Written communication,
7. Negotiation skills,
8. Customer focus,
9. Problem-solving ability, and
10. Responsiveness.

About NCMA

NCMA is devoted to education, training, research, study, and to a certification program that reflects the highest standards of professional achievement. Guided by a code of ethics, the association is committed to develop and provide programs, products, and services that nurture and enhance contract management competencies through leadership and business management partnering.

NCMA's Mission

NCMA's mission is to advance the contract management profession.

NCMA's Vision for the Profession

Contract management will be viewed by all organizations—public and private—as an essential business management function that directly contributes to organizational success. People will recognize contract management as a challenging and rewarding profession, and will prepare for and seek out positions in the profession. Universities will provide undergraduate and graduate degree programs and courses designed to prepare students for entry into or advancement in the contract management profession.

NCMA's Vision for the Organization

NCMA will lead in defining the standards and the body of knowledge for the contract management profession. NCMA will provide tools that enable the entry, development, and advancement of all contract management professionals. NCMA will be a model for not-for-profit individual membership organizations, recognized for innovation, effective and efficient operations, and agile and responsible governance.

NCMA's Value Propositions

NCMA provides the tools, resources, and leadership opportunities to enhance each member of the profession's performance, career, and accomplishments. NCMA provides the structure, name recognition, and products directly and through chapters to contracting professionals worldwide. NCMA provides employers ready access to skilled human capital, learning resources, best practices, standards, and metrics of the profession. NCMA also enables other entities, such as researchers, consultants, trainers, recruiters, advertisers, and universities, to gain broad access to defined segments of our community of practice and our body of knowledge for the purpose of advancing the profession and fulfilling their individual goals.

NCMA's Values

NCMA is committed to:

- Principled professional conduct and achievement, as dictated by our Code of Ethics;

- An open exchange of ideas in a neutral forum;

- A culturally and professionally diverse membership;

- Excellence in everything we do, especially our service to our members and the contract management community;

- Continuing education, training, and leadership opportunities through a network of local chapters;

- Remaining the preeminent source of professional development for contract professionals;

- Recognizing and rewarding professional excellence and superior individual achievement in support of the contract management profession;

- Demonstrated professional achievement through certification;

- Quality volunteer leadership; and

- Members' highly principled freedom of action and responsibility to the people and organizations they serve.

Thousands of professionals enhance their knowledge and leverage opportunities in purchasing, procurement, project management, and contract management with NCMA. Comprising individual members and professional groups from nonprofit, industry, and government, NCMA provides unique resources for the contracting community.

For more than 50 years, members have taken advantage of NCMA membership benefits to advance their careers. Practical, proven survival techniques and industry news help members stay informed about current contract management events. NCMA continues to provide vital information about the field through the association's prestigious publications, educational materials, and professional resources.

As in the past, over the next several years, previously unimagined technological changes will produce a new realm for virtually instantaneous business transactions. Over the next decade alone, what now seems farfetched in electronic commerce will

become commonplace. Even the most vivid imaginations cannot predict what may occur and affect the contract management profession, NCMA, and its membership. To help prepare for the vagaries of an uncertain future, NCMA continues to monitor the contract management profession and reflects the changing character of that profession in its Certification Program. One such change is the increasing tendency of contract professionals to no longer pursue what can be termed as "traditional career paths," where an employee enters a profession out of college and seeks upward mobility through increasingly higher levels within that same functional area. The new predominant career profile is a person enters a job out of college, and then moves laterally, or diagonally, seeking new challenges and opportunities in adjacent fields. This new progression is typified by:

- Increasing geographic and assignment mobility;

- Pursuing career-broadening experiences;

- Pursuing flexible work arrangements to accommodate lifestyle shifts;

- Working for multiple employers over the course of a career;

- Working in multiple professions;

- Entering, departing, and reentering a specific profession;

- Engaging, disengaging, and reengaging with the association serving the profession; and

- Accepting lower compensation and occasional backward or downward movements, seeking lesser responsibilities.

The term for this model has been referred to as "the career web" or "lattice," which is intended to convey the fact that traditional career paths may have been made obsolete (or perhaps just significantly less common). There is indeed a shift being observed across the global workforce, driven by generational expectations, globalism, and technology. Therefore, the challenge for NCMA is to help an individual understand his or her options within the career web, or to move effectively in a horizontal or diagonal manner between adjacent fields.

NCMA also demonstrates its commitment to the profession through the Contract Management Code of Ethics discussed as follows.

Contract Management Code of Ethics

Each member of the contract management profession accepts the obligation to continuously improve one's professional knowledge and job performance in the field of contract management and to abide by the letter and spirit of the ethical standards set forth as follows.

Each member of NCMA shall:

- Strive to attain the highest professional standard of job performance, to exercise diligence in carrying out one's professional duties, and to serve the profession to the best of one's ability;

- Conduct oneself in such a manner as to bring credit upon the profession, as well as to maintain trust and confidence in the integrity of the contract management process;

- Avoid engagement in any transaction that might conflict or appear to conflict with the proper discharge of one's professional duties by reason of a financial interest, family relationship, or any other circumstances;

- Comply with all laws and regulations that govern the contract management process in the jurisdictions in which one conducts business, including protection of competition-sensitive and proprietary information from inappropriate disclosure;

- Keep informed of developments in the contract management field, utilizing both formal training and ad hoc means, to continuously increase knowledge, skill, and professional competence;

- Share one's knowledge and experience openly to contribute to the development of other professionals, improve performance quality, and enhance public perception of the profession; and

- Not knowingly influence others to commit any act that would constitute a violation of this code.

Environmental Trends

In establishing the strategies and objectives we will pursue for the future of the profession and our association, we expect the following trends to impact the profession and the association (2011–2016).

> *The demand for contract management talent exceeds the supply.*

This has been the case since the early 2000s due to demands placed upon the acquisition workforce caused by significant increases in federal spending to deal with the wars on terror (2003–present), natural and unnatural disasters (i.e., Hurricanes Katrina and Sandy and the BP oil spill), and economic recovery investment (2008–present). Workforce demands have been further exacerbated by maturation and retirement of the baby boom generation, which is a key factor in the creation of the "bathtub effect"—a gap in talent to fulfill need (i.e., there are not enough individuals entering the workforce (water entering a bathtub) to meet the demand (a full bathtub) due to individuals exiting the workforce through horizontal employment or retirement (water exiting the bathtub through the drain)). Moreover, as there is no "front door" to the profession through traditional undergraduate degree programs that prepare individuals for entry into a profession, there is no ready stream of prepared talent to tap. Due to the extensive business process and legal and regulatory knowledge required to perform contract management tasks, new entries in contract management take up to three years to become functional. Due to many of these human capital challenges, training budgets have increased since 2008, and there has been a proliferation of intern programs to accelerate development of new talent.

> *The people doing contract management work are defining "career" differently.*

Whereas once professionals viewed their career progression as a linear path, ladder, or track (options for growth and advancement limited to within their field), they now view their careers as a nonlinear, multidimensional web or net, with many more opportunities for professional growth and advancement by branching off into parallel or adjacent careers. This phenomenon is in part driven by generational expectations, globalism, and technology. Today, workers move between as many as five and six careers over their life spans, as opposed to five or six jobs within a single career, as in past generations. Workers are also redefining retirement, treating it as a transition to different, more interesting or less stressful roles, rather than a complete exit from the workforce. Workers are also redefining mentoring relationships, from age-based (i.e., when an older worker mentors a younger worker) to role and skill-based mentoring (i.e., when a junior worker with Web-based skills mentors a senior worker). Workers are also increasingly mobile—geographically, interpersonally, and economically.

> *Changes in the U.S. federal legislative, regulatory, and budgetary environment will continue at a high pace for the foreseeable future.*

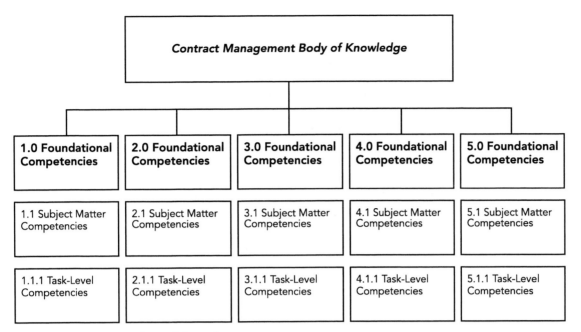

FIGURE 1. *CMBOK* Work Breakdown Structure

The volume of changes in legislation and regulations affecting the acquisition process has been extraordinary over the last several years, with major changes in the acquisition of major weapons systems, services, and information technology, including the planning and budgeting processes, as well as oversight. Many of the legislative changes were in response to audits finding problems with program cost overruns and schedule slips, as well as the proper use of contract tools to manage and oversee risk. There have also been issues about managing a blended workforce—one in which the government must perform certain functions and also effectively manage work done by contractors. Congressional pressure to spend federal monies with increased transparency, accountability, and oversight means agencies must provide better information faster. All of these factors are overlaid with global economic volatility and emerging world events requiring faster mobilization of acquisition involving more complex technology and logistics.

Objectives and Strategies

Responding to these external and internal forces, the association will strive to accomplish the following objectives during the succeeding five program years:

1. Develop and institutionalize an effective advocacy and outreach program that provides a neutral forum for the profession. The desired outcomes for this objective are public recognition that contract management is an essential business management function, and public recognition that NCMA is the preeminent neutral forum for contracting professionals.

2. Create standards for the profession that are widely recognized and adopted. The desired outcome for this objective is for NCMA's standards to be accepted across multiple domains (i.e., government, industry, and academia) as a framework for best practices.

3. Create programs and services to help people enter into and progress within the contract management profession. The desired outcome is for the contract management profession to be recognized as a career field in which education, professional development, and advancement opportunities exist for long-term practitioners as well as recent entrants into the profession. NCMA achieves this by creating programs and services to help people enter into and progress within the contract management profession.

4. Enhance and develop program delivery techniques to improve value for existing and potential members. The desired outcome for this objective is that NCMA will have multiple program and service delivery methods to maximize member value and engagement opportunities.

FIGURE 2. *CMBOK* Outline

Professional Certification

NCMA's first professional certification designation, the "Certified Professional Contracts Manager" (CPCM), was established in 1974. NCMA's leadership, understanding that NCMA needed to establish a method of recognizing professional achievement, worked closely with industry and government professionals to develop a comprehensive program. The CPCM represents a hallmark of professional achievement in the field of contract management.

The first CPCM exams were held across the country in 1976, with 23 successful candidates receiving the CPCM designation. Based on a set of stringent educational criteria and years of experience and service, some senior professionals were given a one-time opportunity to receive the CPCM designation without sitting for the examination.

The "Certified Associate Contracts Manager" (CACM) designation was added in 1980 to certify the mastery of the fundamentals of federal government contracting. In 2002, the CACM designation was renamed the "Certified Federal Contracts Manager" (CFCM) to more accurately describe its content and focus. All those who were awarded the CACM were automatically re-designated as CFCMs. Eventually, the "Certified Commercial Contracts

Manager" (CCCM) designation was developed to certify knowledge of the Uniform Commercial Code.

Although these designations were originally developed as methods of recognizing professional achievement among peers, both have evolved to be much more. Today, NCMA's professional designations and the standards behind them are widely recognized by both government and industry as a consistent measure of the skills and experience needed by successful contract managers. Across the nation, employment requisitions and advertisements are stating: "NCMA designation preferred." Government agencies are recognizing the value of certification when making promotion decisions. NCMA's designations are seen as a standardized hallmark of excellence across the contract management community.

NCMA's Certification Program

At the start of the new millennium, NCMA began to consider revising and revitalizing its certification program. From 2001 to 2008, the certification program was managed by a Contract Management Certification and Accreditation Board and the testing program consisted of several modules. Completion of certain modules led to a CPCM, CFCM, or CCCM.

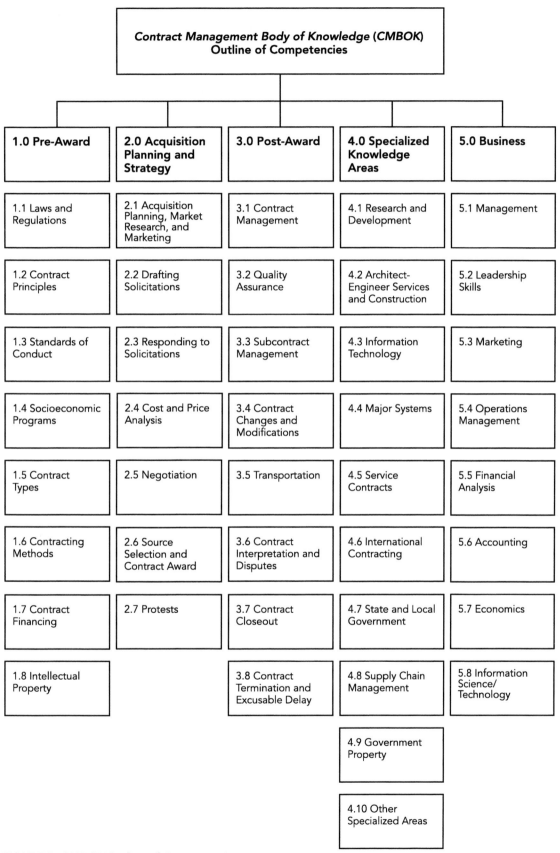

FIGURE 3. *CMBOK* Outline of Competencies

Today, NCMA has reduced the complexity of its premier certification program while retaining the stature of the credentials. The biggest change is the implementation of having only one exam per certification. The CPCM, CFCM, and CCCM are certifications awarded to candidates who meet rigorous standards, including experience, education, training, and knowledge. They are professional designations of distinction and carry the respect of their peers in the profession.

NCMA certifications are competency-based, legally defensible, and are based on psychometrically sound objective examination of knowledge. The NCMA professional certification program is designed to elevate professional standards, enhance individual performance, and distinguish those who demonstrate knowledge essential to the practice of contract management.

Eligibility Requirements

➢ *CPCM*

A candidate must have a degree from a regionally or Distance Education and Training Council (DETC)–accredited institution at a bachelor's level, five years of relevant experience, and 120 hours of continuing professional education. No waivers are given.

➢ *CFCM*

Eligibility for the CFCM requires a candidate to have a degree from a regionally or DETC-accredited institution at the bachelor's level, one year of relevant experience, and 80 hours of continuing professional education. Non-degreed candidates for the CFCM who have 10 years of verifiable contract management experience may request a waiver. Candidates lacking only the experiential and continuing education requirements may apply for the designation and take the examinations. Upon successful completion of the examinations, the candidate will be awarded the designation only when both experiential and continuing education requirements are met.

➢ *CCCM*

A candidate must have a degree from a regionally or DETC-accredited institution at the bachelor's level, one year of experience in the contract management field, and 80 hours of continuing professional education. Non-degreed candidates for the CCCM who have 10 years of verifiable contract management experience may request a waiver. Candidates lacking only the experiential and continuing education

requirements may apply for the designation and take the examinations. Upon successful completion of the examinations, the candidate will be awarded the designation only when both experiential and continuing education requirements are met.

The *CMBOK* Structure

The *CMBOK* may be organized into three major components:

* Foundational (or core) competencies,

* Subject matter competencies, and

* Job or task level skills.

The same structure can apply to both federal and commercial contract management. Foundational competencies are those general competencies needed for success regardless of job or role, while subject matter competencies relate to particular fields or subjects. Job or task level competencies involving performing specific tasks related to the work.

FIGURE 1 on page 9 illustrates the relationship of these competencies; FIGURES 2 and 3 on pages 10 and 11 are additional representations, with FIGURE 3 representing the actual structure of the *CMBOK*.

Additionally, the competency outline would be depicted more specifically as that shown in FIGURE 2.

The CMBOK: An Overview

The *CMBOK*: An Overview

Contract Life Cycle

Contracts have a defined beginning and end. The contract life cycle defines these parameters. The contract life cycle is broken down into several contract phases. The phases during the total life cycle can generally be categorized as:

- Pre-award (including acquisition planning),
- Contract award, and
- Post-award.

There is also consideration of special competencies required based on the requirement, contract type, and processes employed in the contract life cycle.

The pre-award phase actually begins with acquisition planning. Planning is an essential preliminary component to successfully completing virtually any effort. Acquisition planning is a critical first step in the contract life cycle. Competencies such as conducting market research, selecting the proper contract type, and formulating the acquisition strategy are all part of this phase.

Once the planning is completed, the next phase involves all of the work that leads up to an awarded contract. Some acquisitions are very simple, others are exceedingly complex, and the majority fall somewhere in the middle. This phase includes preparing requirements documents, evaluating proposals, conducting negotiations, and completing source selection.

The award phase is a transitional phase that goes from signing a contract to notifying unsuccessful vendors. The elements of the contract award phase include completing contract award, debriefing of unsuccessful offers, and addressing any mistakes in proposals or any protests or litigation.

Once the award phase is completed, the post-award phase begins. This involves all of the contract management functions known as "contract administration." The contract administration functions will vary greatly depending on the complexity of the contract. However, the basic premise remains the same. Is the seller delivering what the contract requires? The post-award phase includes the necessary contract administration activities in order to ensure performance and bring the contract to a successful conclusion. This includes executing contract modifications, addressing any issues arising during contract performance, and (upon completion of performance, invoicing, and payment) closing out the contract.

Contract Stakeholders

A contract is an agreement between two parties. Because of that, there are stakeholders on both sides of the contract. The party with the requirement, usually the initiating party in the contractual process, has several stakeholders who are directly affected by the contracting process.

The stakeholders begin with the organization that has the requirement for which a contract will ultimately be executed. This stakeholder is generally the end user of the item or service provided under the contract. There is also a program office that is responsible for defining the requirement in a manner that can be readily identifiable and that is clear and concise enough to allow for consistent understanding for all parties involved in the contracting process. The program office may be part of the end user's organization, but does not have to be. The finance office may be part of the program office and is responsible for identifying the funding to be used to buy the supply or service. Then there is the contracting officer, who is responsible for executing the contract and ensuring and enforcing contract terms and conditions, including performance or delivery.

The second set of stakeholders is the part of the organization receiving the contract and is tasked with providing the goods and/or services to the requiring organization. These stakeholders include the company or organization receiving the contract, including the group within that is tasked with providing the goods or services. The organization may not have the internal capability to provide the total requirements of the contract. In this case, some of the effort would be subcontracted and those subcontractors would also become contract stakeholders.

The organization providing the goods or services must have the financial capability to perform contractual requirements before delivering and receiving payment. That source of funding, whether internal or through creditors, is also a stakeholder in the contract process.

Organizational Influences

Organizational influences have a profound effect on the contracting process. These influences can be internal or external to the organization. Senior management in an organization directly influences the initiation of requirements that are ultimately fulfilled through the contracting process. This influence takes place in several ways.

For example, senior management may adjust or change company focus through strategic planning. This change in focus will commonly result in changing business processes and procedures. This results in new requirements for software, hardware, and can even cause a change in the qualifications of people working for the organization. These changing requirements are generally fulfilled or supported through the contracting process.

Evolving technology has an enormous impact on an organization. It affects business processes, which ultimately can affect organizational structure and enhance organizational performance. To take advantage of evolving technology and its benefits, an efficient and effective contracting process must be in place.

Other competitors can drive the need to maintain awareness of industry best practices and, where possible, develop best practices rather than continually implementing those already developed. Again, an efficient and effective contracting process is required to be an industry leader.

General Business Competencies

The duties and responsibilities of a contracting professional extend well beyond the specialized set of knowledge and experience unique to the profession. Current business and government organizational models are rapidly and continuously changing in pursuit of increased efficiency and decreased cost. Given the ongoing environment of rightsizing, outsourcing, Lean management, Six Sigma, continuous process improvement, balanced scorecards, transformation, and reinvention (just to name a few), one could argue that the people who work in this environment also have to change as well.

Contracting professionals, as well as other professionals in business and government, can no longer perform effectively in the isolation of specialized knowledge and experience. Most organizations rely, to greater or lesser degrees, on various forms of matrix-managed functions, project or program teams, permanent or temporary process improvement groups, and similar types of collaborative entities. These structures exist primarily to bring more attention to the idea that each segment of an organization, whether public or private, needs to make a positive contribution to the business of the business or the mission of the agency.

The team approach to the operation of business and government often results in a smaller and necessarily more proficient and agile staff. The knowledge required to be an effective contracting professional extends beyond the complex and dynamic contracting environment. A contracting professional must also (and some would argue first) be a business professional. One must have a clear understanding of the general functions of business and government and how those functions combine with and complement each other to achieve organizational goals.

General Contracting Competencies

A contract manager's skills are developed through continuing education and practice. A successful contract manager has developed skills in three main areas:

- Technical,
- Conceptual, and
- Human relations.

Technical skills are demonstrated by competently performing the tasks required, such as preparing and issuing solicitations, preparing bids and proposals, preparing or analyzing terms and conditions, or analyzing procurement requirements and supplier capabilities. Training for these skills can be accomplished in degree, certificate, professional continuing education, or specialized programs.

Conceptual skills relate to the manner in which the contract manager visualizes the contract's organization in terms of the agency's or company's goals. These skills involve the ability to see and use the "big picture" for greater organizational and personal success.

Human relations skills focus on the "people" aspect of contract management. Effective performance requires people to cooperate with each other even when the contract manager has little or no organizational control over them. Dealing with government and contractor representatives from a diverse range of disciplines requires strong relational and communication skills. Many contract managers consider competency in human relations to be the most important skill for the future of their jobs and careers.

The full *CMBOK* includes knowledge of generally accepted practices, which are widely applied to the practice of contract management. It also includes the knowledge of more innovative and advanced practices, which may be used less often. This knowledge is obtained, in part, by asking professionals in the contracting community—both public and private—and practitioners in the field what competencies and knowledge contract professionals need to do their jobs well.

Knowledge is also gained through a critical review of the myriad activities performed by contract managers. The diagram in **FIGURE 4** depicts the interrelationships and activities performed daily by contract managers in a corporation with notionally more than 300 people. A contract manager's activities include coordination with those personnel who think they need an item or service and continue through the development of a contract, its administration, and its ultimate successful completion and closeout. Along the way, the contract manager interacts with those who need the item or service, those who know and can describe the item or service, those who are the keepers of the finances, and all the people involved, as well as all the people who are in charge of those involved—the contract manager affects a wide circle.

FIGURE 4. Interrelationships of Contract Managers

The *CMBOK* Knowledge Areas/Outline of Competencies

chapter three

1.0 Pre-Award Competencies

The pre-award contract management competencies cover a variety of areas that impact contract management. A fundamental understanding of these areas is important before awarding and managing contracts, which is why they are in the "pre-award" category. The pre-award competencies cover eight topics that must be fundamentally understood before the contract management process begins. These competencies are relevant throughout the entire contract management life cycle and influence decision making. The competencies include:

- Laws and regulations (1.1),

- Contract principles (1.2),

- Standards of conduct (1.3),

- Socioeconomic programs (1.4),

- Contract types (1.5),

- Contracting methods (1.6),

- Contract financing (1.7), and

- Intellectual property (1.8). (*See* **FIGURE 1-0** on page 19.)

1.1 Laws and Regulations

At its core, the contracting profession is about the knowledge and application of laws and regulations. Contracts are legal documents that represent an agreement between the parties whose terms and conditions are legally binding and enforceable in various courts of law and other administrative bodies. As such, it is important for the contracting professional to have a good working knowledge of the laws, regulations, and other sources of guidance that define, to a large extent, the environment in which the contracting professional operates. These sources of law and guidance include:

- The Uniform Commercial Code (1.1.1);

- The Sarbanes-Oxley Act (1.1.2);

- Government contract law basics (1.1.3), including:

  o The government's budget process: authorization and appropriation;

- Laws and regulations relating to government contracts (1.1.4), including:

  o The Services Acquisition Reform Act,

  o The Federal Acquisition Reform Act,

  o The Government Management Reform Act,

  o The Federal Acquisition Streamlining Act,

  o The Government Performance and Results Act,

  o The Procurement Integrity Act,

  o The Competition in Contracting Act,

  o The Prompt Payment Act,

  o The Contract Disputes Act,

  o The Office of Federal Procurement Policy Act,

  o The Service Contract Act,

  o The Truth in Negotiations Act,

  o The Contract Work Hours and Safety Standards Act,

  o The Small Business Act,

  o The Federal Property and Administrative Services Act,

  o The Walsh-Healy Public Contracts Act,

  o The Miller Act,

  o The Buy American Act,

  o The Davis-Bacon Act,

  o The Anti-Deficiency Act,

  o *Public Law* 85-804 "Extraordinary Contractual Relief,"

  o The *Federal Acquisition Regulation* (*FAR*), and

  o Key government contracting concepts in the *FAR*;

- Laws and regulations related to international contracting (1.1.5), including:

  o U.N. Convention on Contracts for the International Sale of Goods,

  o The Arms Export Control Act,

  o The Foreign Corrupt Practices Act,

  o The *Export Administration Regulations*,

  o The *International Traffic in Arms Regulations*,

  o Free trade agreements,

  o The Foreign Assistance Act,

  o Anti-boycott regulations, and

  o Foreign laws and customs; and

- Case law (1.1.6). (*See* **FIGURE 1-1-1** on page 20.)

1.1.1 The Uniform Commercial Code (UCC)

The UCC is a comprehensive set of laws governing commercial transactions within the United States. The primary intent of the UCC is to provide

FIGURE 1-0. Pre-Award Competencies

a framework in which commercial organizations can conduct business across state or other jurisdictional boundaries with reasonable assurance that the same or similar rules apply. This concept of mutual understanding of commercial terms and practices is essential to an organization's ability to contract effectively.

It is important to note that the UCC, as a uniform law, must be adopted as law by each state separately. As a result, there are differences in the UCC from state to state. The UCC has been enacted in 49 of the 50 states—Louisiana has enacted most of the UCC, but differences in state law resulting from Louisiana civil law and the Napoleonic Code make complete adoption of the UCC difficult. Some states have not adopted all of the UCC's articles or have enacted modified versions of the UCC. Therefore, when the UCC applies to a transaction, the requirements of each state need to be separately considered as applicable.

The UCC is organized into parts, called "articles," and are listed in **FIGURE 1-1-2** on page 21.

The UCC is a primary source of guidance in the commercial contracting community. The UCC, as with any body of law, is subject to continual review, refinement, and revision in order to keep pace with changes in the business environment and technological advancements. Further, since the government contracting community uses some commercial

contracting practices, government contracting professionals should include the UCC and its impact on contracting policy, procedures, and commonly accepted practices in their skill set. (A more detailed table of contents for the UCC is provided in Appendix A.)

The underlying purposes of the UCC, as stated in Section 1-102 of the code, are:

- To simplify, clarify, and modernize the law governing commercial transactions;

- To permit the continued expansion of commercial practices through custom, usage, and agreement of the parties; and

- To make uniform the law among the various jurisdictions.

The overriding philosophy of the UCC is to allow people to make the contracts they want, but to fill in any missing provisions where the agreements they make are silent. Current law governing contracts for the sale of any kind of "goods" between two U.S. corporations is Article 2 of the UCC. The UCC applies to goods, but not services. Services contracts can become voluminous because there are no "missing provisions" or "gap filler" provisions under the UCC to protect buyers and sellers, so buyers and sellers create provisions that are suitable for their own needs. Article 2 is intended to be the sole source of law governing sales, supplemented by state law

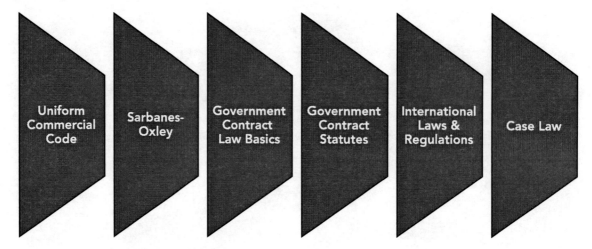

FIGURE 1-1-1. Laws and Regulations

only if not addressed by a provision within the UCC (see UCC § 1-103). Article 2 addresses such issues as contract formation, nonperformance, performance of contractual obligations, repudiation of contract, contract termination, the remedies for nonperformance, the cure rights of a party who fails to perform, the implicit and explicit warranties, the waiver or disclaimer of such warranties, and risk of loss.

1.1.1.1 Underlying Concepts in the UCC

The UCC has several underlying concepts that apply to contracts:

- A "merchant" is a person who deals in goods or otherwise holds itself out by occupation as having knowledge or skill peculiar to the practices or goods involved in the transaction or to which the knowledge or skill may be attributed by the person's employment (see UCC § 2-104).

- Every contract imposes an obligation of good faith in its performance or enforcement. "Good faith" means honesty in fact and the observance of reasonable commercial standards of fair dealing (*see* UCC § 2-103).

- There are formal requirements ("statute of frauds") for certain contracts. There must be a written record of any contract for the sale of goods of $500 or more in order for it to be enforceable. The written record may be considered sufficient even if it omits or incorrectly states a term agreed upon (*see* UCC § 2-201).

- The express terms of an agreement and any applicable course of performance, course of dealing, or usage of trade must be construed whenever reasonable as consistent with each other. If such a construction is unreasonable:

  o Express terms prevail over the course of performance, course of dealing, and usage of trade;

  o The course of performance prevails over the course of dealing and usage of trade; and

  o The course of dealing prevails over usage of trade (see UCC § 1-303).

1.1.1.2 Formation of a Sales Contract

A contract for the sale of goods with a price of $500 or more must be in writing to be enforceable. The written contract must contain sufficient detail to indicate that a contract for sale has been made between the parties and signed by the party against whom enforcement is sought or by his or her authorized agent or broker. Article 2 contains three requirements of the written contract:

- It must provide evidence that there was a contract for the sale of goods,

- It must be signed by the party to be charged, and

- It must specify a quantity.

A contract is enforceable as long as the above three requirements are included. Thus, the price, time, and place of payment or delivery; the general quality of the goods; or any particular warranties may be omitted. No other formal written requirement exists for there to be sufficient evidence of a valid transaction.

The Uniform Commercial Code Articles	
Article 1	General Provisions
Article 2	Sales
Article 2A	Leases
Article 3	Negotiable Instruments
Article 4	Bank Deposit
Article 4A	Funds Transfers
Article 5	Letters of Credit
Article 6	Bulk Transfers and Bulk Sales
Article 7	Warehouse Receipts, Bills of Lading, and Other Documents of Title
Article 8	Investment Securities
Article 9	Secured Transactions

FIGURE 1-1-2. Uniform Commercial Code

Even if it is not in writing, a contract can also be validated if there is "partial performance," as evidenced that goods have been accepted and payment has been made and accepted. This provides evidence that the contract actually exists. The party receiving the contract must give written notice of objection within 10 days after it is received or the contract could be enforceable.

A signed offer to buy or sell goods remains irrevocable for a reasonable period not to exceed three months or for the period stated in the offer. Acceptance of the offer may be made by any reasonable manner, including either shipment or a prompt promise to ship or the beginning of performance by an offeree.

In commercial transactions, the offeree (i.e., buyer) often uses boilerplate (i.e., standardized contract language) terms on which the offer is printed, such as a "request for quote" form. The offeror (i.e., seller) may use additional terms or different terms than the buyer. The UCC allows for those additional terms to be construed as proposals for additional terms to the contract. Such terms are incorporated into the contract unless the offer stated that the offer expressly limits the terms of the offer, the acceptance was expressly made conditional on agreement on different terms, the additional terms materially alter the offer, or an objection of the additional terms is sent within a reasonable time.

UCC Article 2-207 states:

> Subject to Section 2-202, if (i) conduct by both parties recognizes the existence of a contract although their records do not otherwise establish a contract, (ii) a contract is formed by an offer and acceptance, or (iii) a contract formed in any manner is confirmed by a record that contains terms additional to or different from those in the contract being confirmed, the terms of the contract are:
>
> a) Terms that appear in the records of both parties;
>
> b) Terms, whether in a record or not, to which both parties agree; and
>
> c) Terms supplied or incorporated under any provision of this act.

In addition to the express terms of the contract, there are other factors that can be relevant when interpretation of the contract is required. These include the following:

- "Course of performance"—refers to any acts in the performance of the contract by either party that are not objected to. These acts can be interpreted as consistent with the express terms.

- "Course of dealing"—a series of previous conduct between the parties to a particular transaction that can be regarded as establishing a common basis of understanding for terminology and conduct.

- "Usage of trade"—practices or methods of dealing that are regularly observed and justify an expectation that they will apply to the transaction in question.

(*CMBOK* competency 3.6 has additional information about contract interpretation.)

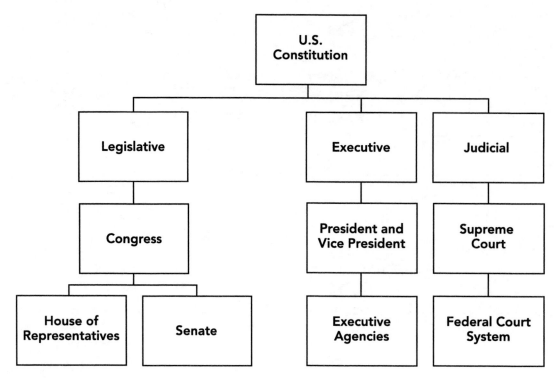

FIGURE 1-1-3. Federal Government Structure

1.1.1.3 Contract Modification

Under UCC rules, an existing contract can be modified without consideration, but the modification must satisfy the "statute of frauds" provision. A contract can be modified or rescinded only if done in writing on a form provided by the merchant and signed by the other party. Contract modifications must meet the test of good faith and cannot be used to escape performance obligations under the contract. A modification that does not meet the above requirements can be considered a waiver. (*See CMBOK* competency 3.4 for more information about contract changes and modifications.)

1.1.1.4 Performance

The general obligation of the seller under the contract is to transfer and deliver; the obligation of the buyer is to accept and pay in accordance with the contract. According to the UCC, the contract "imposes an obligation by the seller to use best efforts to supply the goods and by the buyer to use best efforts to promote their sale."

After the seller has manufactured the product, the seller may be unwilling to forward the product to the buyer until payment is received. Likewise, the buyer may be unwilling to pay until the buyer receives and inspects the product. The concept of "tender" entitles the seller, upon shipment, to the acceptance of goods and to payment according to the terms of the contract. It also entitles the buyer, upon payment, receipt of conforming goods. The seller's goods must conform in all respects to the terms of the contract or the buyer may reject the goods and not perform further. This is in addition to other rights the buyer may have. The concept of "tender" allows each party to be confident that the other party will perform so the seller and buyer can ship the product and make payment respectively.

The UCC states that acceptance of goods occurs when the buyer, "after a reasonable opportunity to inspect the goods, signifies to the seller that the goods are conforming or that he will take or retain them in spite of their nonconformity." Acceptance can also occur when the buyer fails to reject them or commits actions that are inconsistent with rejection.

The buyer has the right to reject the goods if they "fail in any respect to conform to the contract." The seller has a right to cure defects if the time for performance has not run out and the seller can cure

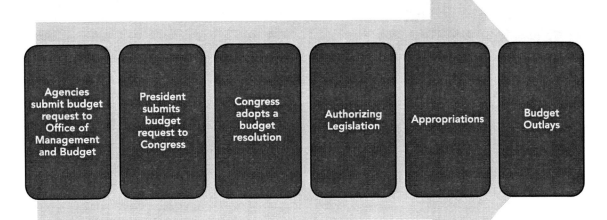

FIGURE 1-1-4. Federal Budget Process

the defects within that time, or the seller has reason to believe the buyer would accept nonconforming goods (in which case the seller can take a reasonable amount of extra time, beyond the time for original performance, in curing the defects).

In certain situations, a buyer may revoke a prior acceptance of nonconforming goods (as long as the buyer notifies the seller of revocation in a reasonable time after the buyer discovered or should have discovered the nonconformity) when the defect has substantially impaired their value. A prior acceptance can be revoked if acceptance was made on the reasonable assumption that the defects would be cured in a reasonable time but haven't been, acceptance was predicated on the seller's assurances of conformity, or the defect was difficult to discover before acceptance. In order for the revocation to be effective, the goods must be in the same condition they were in when they were delivered to the buyer except for changes caused by the defects themselves. A revocation puts the buyer in the same position as if the buyer had rejected the goods initially.

1.1.1.5 Implied Warranties
Under the UCC, every sale of goods gives rise to certain implied warranties, including:

- "Implied warranty of merchantability"—A warranty a merchant makes that guarantees that goods are reasonably fit for the general purpose for which they are sold; and

- "Implied warranty of fitness for a particular purpose"—A warranty for when a seller knows or has reason to know of a particular purpose for which some item is being purchased by the buyer, the seller is guaranteeing that the item is fit for that particular purpose, and if the buyer is relying on the seller's expertise to select suitable goods.

An implied warranty can be expressly disclaimed but has strict requirements in how it is disclaimed. The phrases "as is" or "with all faults" must appear distinctly in the contract in a different kind of print or font that makes it stand out. A disclaimer of the implied warranty of merchantability must use the word "merchantability." Contractual language can also limit the remedies available for breach of an implied warranty—e.g., capping recoverable damages or limiting the remedy to a replacement of a defective item.

1.1.1.6 Repudiation
"Repudiation" is the refusal, especially by public authorities, to acknowledge a contract or debt. In

Services Acquisition Reform Act (2003)	Federal Acquisition Reform Act (1996)	Federal Acquisition Streamlining Act (1994)	Government Management Reform Act (1994)	Government Performance and Results Act (1993)
Procurement Integrity Act (1988)	Competition in Contracting Act (1984)	Prompt Payment Act (1982)	Contract Disputes Act (1978)	Office of Federal Procurement Policy Act (1974)
Service Contract Act (1965)	Truth in Negotiations Act (1962)	Contract Work Hours and Safety Standards Act (1962)	Small Business Act (1958)	Federal Property and Administration Services Act (1949)
Walsh-Healy Act (1936)	Miller Act (1935)	The Buy American Act (1933)	The Anti-Deficiency Act (1870)	*The Federal Acquisition Regulation (FAR) (1984)*

FIGURE 1-1-5. Government Contract Laws and Regulations

the case of repudiation, a party can wait a commercially reasonable time for the repudiating party to perform or resort to any remedy for breach, even if it has notified the repudiating party that it is waiting for performance and urges it to retract the repudiation.

The repudiating party can retract the repudiation until its next performance is due unless, since the repudiation, the aggrieved party has cancelled or materially changed its position or the aggrieved party has indicated it considers the repudiation final. A retraction must be accompanied by "adequate assurances" within a reasonable time of the retraction.

Adequate assurances may be demanded in writing by any party when it has reasonable grounds for insecurity with respect to the performance of the other party. Until it receives such assurances, it may suspend its own performance. These adequate assurances would need to make a reasonable merchant believe the promised performance will be forthcoming.

When anticipatory repudiation substantially impairs the value of the contract, the innocent party may resort to any remedy, including suing immediately for breach, even if it is still negotiating with the repudiating party for performance or retraction. The innocent party can, if it so chooses, wait for a commercially reasonable time for the repudiating party to perform. Either way, taking some action now or waiting, the innocent party can suspend its own performance.

1.1.2 The Sarbanes-Oxley Act (SOX)

SOX (*Public Law* 107-204) was signed into law on July 30, 2002. The substance of the law is to create requirements to prevent companies from accounting for profits not realized in an effort to portray value where none exists. SOX has had a significant impact on the accounting practices of nearly all companies doing business in the United States. Indirectly, SOX has had a significant impact on contract management functions as well. A sales contract is typically the primary record underlying a revenue transaction. Before SOX, many large companies did not have standard practices for contract creation or management. Under SOX, firms could no longer carry a *laissez faire* attitude in how they created, recorded, and managed contracts. Since SOX was passed into law, a mini-industry for creation and implementation of contract management software systems has boomed, and many firms have devoted more attention to the contract management function than ever before in order to ensure SOX compliance.

SOX has had a disproportionate impact on commercial companies versus those that do business principally with the U.S. federal government. This is because companies who did substantial business with the government were already required to maintain a higher standard of contract management and cost accounting systems in order to comply with the *Federal Acquisition Regulation* and associated laws and regulations.

Contracts for the International Sale of Goods	The Arms Export Control Act (AECA)	The Foreign Corrupt Practices Act (FCPA)	Export Administration Regulation (EAR)
International Traffic in Arms Regulation (ITAR)	Free Trade Agreement	The Foreign Assistance Act	

FIGURE 1-1-6. International Laws and Regulations

Additional information about SOX can be found at **www.soxinstitute.org**.

1.1.3 Government Contract Law Basics

The U.S. federal government contracting process involves all three branches of the U.S. government:

- Legislative,
- Executive, and
- Judicial (see **FIGURE 1-1-3** on page 22).

Congress, as the legislative branch, enacts laws that impact the contracting process and provide funding. The agencies, as part of the executive branch, draft regulations implementing the laws, solicit offers, and award and administer contracts. The federal courts, representing the judicial branch, interpret legislation and sometimes resolve disputes. These three branches thus work together to preserve the system of checks and balances necessary for the U.S. government to function properly. Each has an integral function to serve in the procurement process.

Some may argue that as the sovereign, the U.S. government receives special consideration in the contracting process. Although certain conflicts exist between the government as lawmaker and the government as contracting party, the laws have been designed to ensure that there is no special treatment conferred to the government. The government must be treated as other contracting parties in order to maintain a fair and equitable business relationship and to protect those with whom the government deals. Nonetheless, as the sovereign, the government can and does specify exactly how it will conduct its business. This includes how it will use contracting to implement social policy, how it will allow a contract to be canceled (e.g., termination process), and how, when, and in which courts it can be sued. All of these are significant differences between government contracts and commercial contracts.

The origin of the government's authority to enter into contract comes from the U.S. Constitution and is subject to various statutes and regulations. Although the Constitution does not specifically refer to government contracts, the government has the implied power to use contracts to fulfill its responsibilities. For example, Article 1 § 8, Clause 18, gives the Congress the power to "[m]ake all laws which shall be necessary and proper for carrying into execution the foregoing powers and all other powers vested by this Constitution of the government of the United States, or in any department or officer thereof." The clause is called the "necessary and proper" clause and provides, by implication, the power for the government to enter into contracts to fulfill its obligations by providing and paying for the common defense and general welfare of the United States. Article I § 8, Clause 12, gives Congress the power to "raise and support armies." The constitution also plays a role in the federal budgeting process that is an important aspect of government contracting.

1.1.3.1 The Government's Budget Process: Authorization and Appropriation

Congress also has the authority to appropriate funds to federal agencies to fulfill their obligations (*see* **FIGURE 1-1-4** on page 23). Article I § 9 of the Constitution states: "No money shall be drawn from the Treasury, but in consequence of appropriations made by law...." This section is the basis of Congress' "power of the purse." It means that no debt may be paid out of public funds unless Congress has made an appropriation for that purpose.

Although the Constitution requires appropriation, the funds that are appropriated have limits imposed by the Anti-Deficiency Act. As the Anti-Deficiency Act states at 31 U.S.C. 665(a):

> No officer or employee of the United States shall make or authorize expenditure from or create or authorize an obligation under any appropriation or fund in excess of the amount available therein; nor shall any such officer or employee involve the government in any contract or other obligation, for payment of money for any purpose, in advance of appropriations made for such purpose, unless such contract or obligation is authorized by law.

Congress has extremely broad power to pass laws affecting the procurement process. Many of the laws are substantive (i.e., they describe how the process must be conducted). Examples of these laws would include:

- The Armed Services Procurement Act,
- The Federal Property and Administrative Services Act,
- The Competition in Contracting Act, and
- The Federal Acquisition Streamlining Act.

These acts are a primary means by which Congress grants contracting powers to an agency, as well as to place limitations on the way an agency exercises those powers. Congress also places limitations through authorization and appropriation acts.

Other laws Congress passes each year deal principally with fiscal matters. Each "pot of money" from Congress must pass two key gates. The first is an authorization act. This law authorizes the various congressional committees to propose appropriations within a defined ceiling. The second gate is the appropriation act, which makes the specified funds available to the agencies. Both acts must be followed by agencies. If a particular program is authorized but not funded (i.e., no appropriation made), the program cannot survive. Conversely, if funds are appropriated but the program is not authorized, it likewise cannot survive.

There are certain steps that must be made in the budgeting process. The first step requires agen-

cies to compile a budget from their various commands, installations, or field sites. This is presented to the Office of Management and Budget, which negotiates with the agencies—in concert with the president's desires—to compile a proposed federal budget. This federal budget is sent to Congress, which holds hearings and debates to finally settle on proper "authorized" and "appropriated" budgets for the various agencies. Once the acts become law by the president's signature, this budget is returned to the Office of Management and Budget, which then allocates it to the agencies, which then makes allotments and sub-allotments, as appropriate, to their various segments.

In recent years, the budget process has not always been smooth. When consensus on budget issues cannot be reached, continued government operations must be funded by a "continuing resolution," based on a proportion of the prior year's authorized and appropriated budget. While this avoids a potential government shutdown, it can have an extremely adverse impact on contracting, both in terms of performance as well as payment restrictions. Both contracting sides must be aware of the impact to contract requirements.

The funds appropriated by Congress are commonly restricted in two principle ways: 1) intended use and 2) time of availability. The executive branch has limited ability to reprogram funds to alter their intended use—and no authority to obligate funds beyond their period of availability (usually one year), generally referred to as "the color of money." However, obligating funds should not be confused with actually paying those funds to a contractor. An obligation occurs when the funds are specifically designated to a particular contract or grant by the actual "award" of the contract or grant. Congress requires that all obligations be recorded by some clear documentary evidence (see 31 U.S.C. 1501). Once obligated, however, it may be some time (sometimes years) before the work is completed and the contractor paid with those funds. Thus, expenditure occurs after the obligation.

If contracting officers are not clear whether a particular use of funds is proper, they can seek the guidance of the Government Accountability Office, a part of the legislative branch that will issue an opinion that is binding, since the Government Accountability Office has the authority to "settle all accounts" of the government (see 31 U.S.C. 3526).

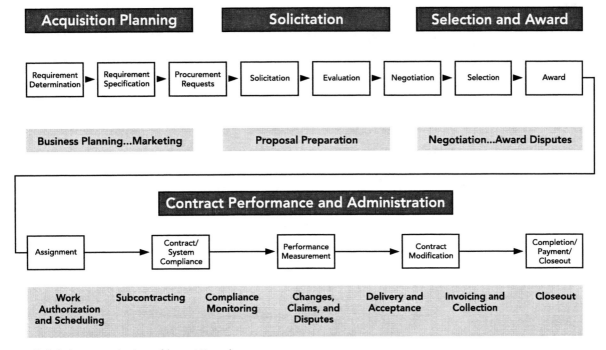

Requirement Determination → Requirement Specification → Procurement Requests → Solicitation → Evaluation → Negotiation → Selection → Award

Business Planning...Marketing

Proposal Preparation

Negotiation...Award Disputes

Contract Performance and Administration

Assignment → Contract/ System Compliance → Performance Measurement → Contract Modification → Completion/ Payment/ Closeout

| Work Authorization and Scheduling | Subcontracting | Compliance Monitoring | Changes, Claims, and Disputes | Delivery and Acceptance | Invoicing and Collection | Closeout |

Dark shade represents the phases of the acquisition cycle
Light shade represents sellers' activities during each phase

FIGURE 1-2-1. Acquisition Process

1.1.4 Laws and Regulations Relating to Government Contracts

As listed in **FIGURE 1-1-5** on page 24, the following are significant contract laws and regulations governing government contracts.

Services Acquisition Reform Act (SARA)

Passed in 2003, SARA (*Public Law* 108-136) established the civilian acquisition workforce training fund, the position of "chief acquisition officer" for civilian agencies, and the requirement for performance-based service contracts.

Federal Acquisition Reform Act (FARA)

FARA (*Public Law* 104-106 § 4101) states that full and open competition must be pursued in a manner that is consistent with the government's need to efficiently fulfill its requirements. It also accomplished the following:

- Introduced the concept of efficient competition to limit the competitive range,

- Revised the definition of "competitive range" to include only those proposals that are the most highly rated,

- Requires a pre-award debriefing for companies eliminated from the competitive range, and

- Simplified the commercial item exception to submitting certified cost or pricing data.

(Margaret G. Rumbaugh, *Understanding Government Contract Source Selection* (Management Concepts, Inc., 2010).)

Government Management Reform Act (GMRA)

Passed in 1994, the GMRA (Public Law 103-356) was designed to provide a more effective, efficient, and responsive government through a series of management reforms primarily for federal human resources and financial management.

The act requires each federal agency to:

- Submit to the Office of Management and Budget a single, audited financial statement for the preceding fiscal year, which includes performance measures of outputs and outcomes;

- Give a clear and concise description of accomplishments, financial results, and conditions; and

- Disclose whether and how the mission of the federal agency is being accomplished and what, if anything, needs to be done to improve either program or financial performance.

(Margaret G. Rumbaugh, *Understanding Government Contract Source Selection* (Management Concepts, Inc., 2010).)

Federal Acquisition Streamlining Act (FASA)

Passed in 1994, FASA (41 U.S.C.) changed over 200 existing statutes and shifted the emphasis in federal procurement to using commercial practices, empowering contracting officers to exercise business judgment and emphasizing the importance of past performance. FASA also accomplished the following:

- Established a preference for commercial item acquisition;

- Emphasized past performance in source selection;

- Introduced electronic systems in the procurement process;

- Eliminated regulatory requirements for simplified and commercial acquisitions;

- Requires requests for proposals to identify significant evaluation factors and subfactors and to state whether they are more, as, or less important than cost or price;

- Permits awarding contracts to other than the lowest-priced proposal (i.e., "best value"); and

- Requires timely debriefings.

(Margaret G. Rumbaugh, *Understanding Government Contract Source Selection* (Management Concepts, Inc., 2010).)

Government Performance and Results Act of 1993 (GPRA)

The GPRA (*Public Law* 103-62) puts the focus on program goals and improvements. The GPRA (also referred to as the "Results Act") is the foundation for refining requirements of FASA and (where applicable) the Information Technology Management Reform Act that link program needs, the budget, and acquisitions.

Procurement Integrity Act

Passed in 1988, this act (41 U.S.C. 432) tightened the reins on procurement officials and contractors alike by establishing new rules regarding ethical behavior for government and contractor personnel, including technical staff. It also accomplished the following:

- States that a person shall not, other than as provided by law, knowingly disclose contractor bid or proposal information or source selection information before the award of a federal agency procurement contract to which the information relates;

- Prohibits the government from releasing source selection information before contract award;

- Restricts procurement officials from seeking or accepting employment from contractors;

- Prohibits contractors from offering gratuities, gifts, or money to procurement officials; and

- Requires annual ethics training.

(Margaret G. Rumbaugh, *Understanding Government Contract Source Selection* (Management Concepts, Inc., 2010).)

Competition in Contracting Act (CICA)

Passed in 1984, CICA's (41 U.S.C. 253) requirement for "full and open competition" means that all responsible sources may submit proposals or bids. CICA also accomplished the following:

- Requires full and open competition unless certain exceptions apply,

- Identifies seven exceptions to full and open competition,

- Requires market research and acquisition planning,

- Requires that specifications foster full and open competition,

- Requires publicizing requirements to increase competition,

- Requires that significant evaluation factors be included in the request for proposals,

- Requires that award be based only on evaluation criteria stated in the request for proposals, and

- Permits award without discussion.

(Margaret G. Rumbaugh, *Understanding Government Contract Source Selection* (Management Concepts, Inc., 2010).)

Prompt Payment Act

Passed in 1982, this act (31 U.S.C. 3903) was enacted in order to ensure that companies transacting business with the federal government were paid in a timely manner upon submission of a proper invoice. The act provides for interest payments for late payments.

Level	Buyers	Sellers	Market Entry/Exit	Relative Pricing Power
Perfect Competition	Many independent	Many independent	Relatively easy	Pricing balance between buyers and sellers
Effective Competition	Limited independent	Limited independent	Relatively easy	Relative pricing balance between buyers and sellers
Oligopoly	Many independent	Few independent	Restrictions	Relatively greater pricing advantage to sellers
Oligopsony	Few independent	Many independent	Relatively easy	Relatively greater pricing power to buyers
Monopoly	Many independent	One	Restrictions	Considerable pricing power to sellers
Monopsony	One	Many independent	Relatively easy	Considerable pricing power to buyers
Bilateral Monopoly	One	One	Restrictions	Pricing power established by negotiation (as in sole source government negotiation)

FIGURE 1-2-2. Types of Competition (*derived from* Federal Acquisition Institute, *Contract Pricing Reference Guide, Volume 1, Price Analysis* (February 2012): 16)

Contract Disputes Act

Passed in 1978, this act (41 U.S.C. 601) states that all claims by a contractor against the government arising under a contract shall be in writing and shall be submitted to the contracting officer for a decision. Also, all claims by the government against a contractor arising under a contract shall be the subject of a decision by the contracting officer. Each claim by a contractor against the government arising under a contract and each claim by the government against a contractor relating to a contract shall be submitted within six years after the accrual of the claim.

Office of Federal Procurement Policy Act

Passed in 1974, this act (41 U.S.C. 401) established an agency to be known as the Office of Federal Procurement Policy (OFPP) within the Office of Management and Budget. The act also directs the administrator of OFPP to provide overall guidance and direction of procurement policy, and to the extent he or she considers appropriate, to prescribe policies, regulations, procedures, and forms that shall be followed by executive agencies in the area of procurement.

Service Contract Act (SCA)

Passed in 1965, the SCA (41 U.S.C. 351) states that every contract entered into by the United States or the District of Columbia in excess of $2,500— the principal purpose of which is to furnish services in the United States through the use of service employees—shall provide minimum wages based on the "prevailing wages" in that location. The wage determinations are maintained by the Department of Labor and can be found in the Wage Determination Online site at **www.wdol.gov**. This website provides a single location for federal contracting officers to use in obtaining appropriate (SCA) and Davis-Bacon Act wage determinations for each official contract action. The website is available to the general public as well.

Truth in Negotiations Act (TINA)

Passed in 1962, TINA (*Public Law* 87-653) was enacted for the purpose of providing for full and fair disclosure by contractors in the conduct of negotiations with the government. TINA also accomplished the following:

- Requires all executive agencies to get certified cost or pricing data in certain circumstances,

- Permits agencies to get a price reduction for defective cost or pricing data,

- Requires the presence of adequate price competition for exemption from submitting certified cost or pricing data, and

- Requires contracting officers to hold discussions with offerors in the competitive range.

(Margaret G. Rumbaugh, *Understanding Government Contract Source Selection* (Management Concepts, Inc., 2010).)

Contract Work Hours and Safety Standards Act

Passed in 1962, this act (40 U.S.C. 327) established a 40-hour work week and time-and-one-half for hours worked in excess of 40 hours.

Small Business Act

Passed in 1958, this act (*Public Law* 108-447; *Public Law* 85-536) states that it is the declared policy of the Congress that the federal government, through the Small Business Administration, acting in cooperation with the Department of Commerce and other relevant state and federal agencies, should aid and assist small businesses, as defined under the act, to increase their ability to compete in international markets by:

- Enhancing their ability to export;
- Facilitating technology transfers;
- Enhancing their ability to compete effectively and efficiently against imports;
- Increasing the access of small businesses to long term capital for the purchase of new plant and equipment used in the production of goods and services involved in international trade;
- Disseminating information concerning state, federal, and private programs and initiatives to enhance the ability of small businesses to compete in international markets; and
- Ensuring that the interests of small businesses are adequately represented in bilateral and multilateral trade negotiations.

Federal Property and Administrative Services Act

Passed in 1949, this act (40 U.S.C. 101) provides for an economical and efficient system for procurement and supply of personal property and nonpersonal services.

Walsh-Healy Public Contracts Act (PCA)

Passed in 1936, the PCA (41 U.S.C. 35) requires contractors engaged in the manufacturing or furnishing of materials, supplies, articles, or equipment to the U.S. government or the District of Columbia to pay employees who produce, assemble, handle, or ship goods under contracts exceeding $15,000 the federal minimum wage for all hours worked and time-and-one-half their regular rate of pay for all hours worked over 40 in a work week.

Miller Act

Passed in 1935, this act (40 U.S.C. 3131–3134) requires contract surety bonds on federal construction projects in domestic construction contracts over $150,000. This law requires a contractor on a federal project to post two bonds: 1) a performance bond and 2) a labor and material payment bond.

Buy American Act (BAA)

Passed in 1933, the BAA (41 U.S.C 10a) states that only such manufactured articles, materials, and supplies as have been substantially manufactured in the United States from articles, materials, or supplies mined, produced, or manufactured, as the case may be, in the United States, shall be acquired for public use.

Davis-Bacon Act (DBA)

Passed in 1931, the DBA (40 U.S.C. 276a) requires a minimum rate of wages for laborers and mechanics employed on public buildings of the United States and the District of Columbia by contractors or subcontractors for contracts over $2,000. The wage determinations are maintained by the Department of Labor and can be found in the Wage Determination Online site at **www.wdol.gov**. This website provides a single location for federal contracting officers to use in obtaining appropriate SCA and DBA wage determinations for each official contract action. The website is available to the general public as well.

The Anti-Deficiency Act

Passed in 1870, this act (31 U.S.C. 1341) and subsequent amendments prohibit federal employees from the following:

- Making or authorizing an expenditure from, or creating or authorizing an obligation under, any appropriation or fund in excess of the amount available in the appropriation or fund, unless authorized by law;
- Involving the government in any obligation to pay money before funds have been appropriated for that purpose, unless otherwise allowed by law;
- Accepting voluntary services for the United States, or employing personal services not authorized by law, except in cases of emergency involving the safety of human life or the protection of property; and
- Making obligations or expenditures in excess of an apportionment or reapportionment, or in excess of the amount permitted by agency regulations.

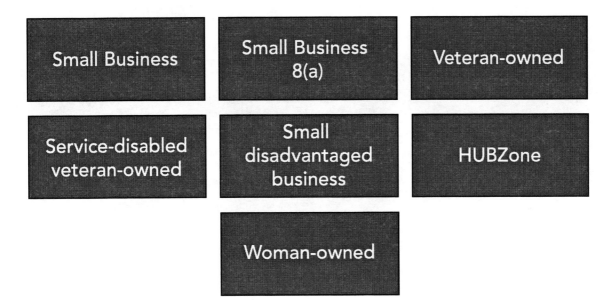

FIGURE 1-4-1. Types of Small Business

Public Law *85-804, "Extraordinary Contractual Relief"*

This law empowers the president to authorize agencies exercising functions in connection with the national defense to enter into, amend, and modify contracts, without regard to other provisions of law related to making, performing, amending, or modifying contracts, whenever the president considers that such action would facilitate the national defense. Executive Order 10789 authorizes the heads of the following agencies to exercise the authority conferred by *Public Law* 85-804 and to delegate it to other officials within the agency:

- The Government Printing Office,
- The Department of Homeland Security,
- The Tennessee Valley Authority,
- The National Aeronautics and Space Administration,
- The General Services Administration,
- The Department of Defense,
- The Department of the Army,
- The Department of the Navy,
- The Department of the Air Force,
- The Department of the Treasury,
- The Department of the Interior,
- The Department of Agriculture,
- The Department of Commerce,
- The Department of Transportation,
- The Department of Energy (for functions transferred from other authorized agencies), and
- Any other agency that may be authorized by the president. (*See Federal Acquisition Regulation* 50.101-1.)

The Federal Acquisition Regulation (FAR)

The statutes previously noted and others are implemented in the *FAR*. The regulation establishes uniform policies and procedures for executive agencies to award and manage government contracts. Thus, the *FAR* is the principal source of contracting guidance within the federal government.

The *FAR* has been in place since April 1, 1984. The *FAR* system was developed in accordance with the Office of Federal Procurement Policy Act, as amended by Public Law 96-83 and Office of Federal Procurement Policy policy letter 85-1, dated August 19, 1985. The *FAR* system consists of the *FAR* and various agency acquisition regulations that supplement the *FAR*. The *FAR* is prepared, issued, and maintained jointly by the secretary of defense and the administrators of the General Services Administration (GSA) and the National Aeronautics and Space Administration (NASA) via two councils, who must agree to all revisions proposed by either council. The Defense Acquisition Regulatory Council chair is appointed by the secretary of defense. Remaining council membership includes representatives from the military

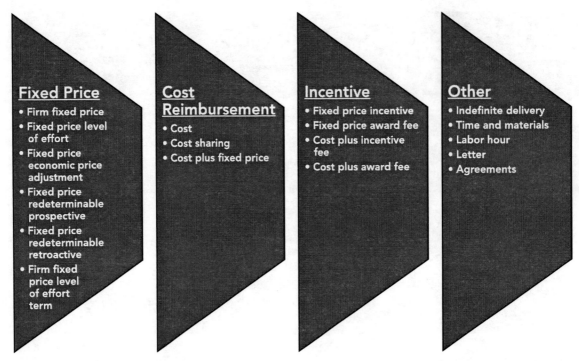

FIGURE 1-5-1. Contract Types

departments, the Defense Logistics Agency, and NASA. The Civilian Agency Acquisition Council chair is appointed by the administrator of GSA. Remaining council membership includes representatives from the Departments of Agriculture, Commerce, Energy, Health and Human Services, Homeland Security, Interior, Labor, State, Transportation, and Treasury; and from the Environmental Protection Agency, Social Security Administration, Small Business Administration, and the Department of Veterans Affairs.

The *FAR* is printed, published, and distributed by the *FAR* secretariat, which is controlled by GSA. A detailed table of contents for the *FAR* is provided in Appendix B.

Although the *FAR* was intended to be the single comprehensive source of procurement regulations, many executive agencies have extensive *FAR* supplements (e.g., the *Defense FAR Supplement* (*DFARS*), which is the Department of Defense's supplement to the *FAR*) and sub-supplements (e.g., the *Army FAR Supplement* (*AFARS*), which is the U.S. Army's supplement to the *DFARS*). In addition, there are Office of Management and Budget circulars, OFPP policy letters, Executive Orders, and the Code of Federal Regulations, as well as agency directives and instructions and agency handbooks and manuals.

All of the applicable statutes, regulations, and contract law basics must be used together to effectively manage federal government contracts. Relying solely on the *FAR* may not answer every contract manager's questions about contract law.

Key Government Contracting Concepts in the *FAR*

➢ Statement of Guiding Principles for the Federal Acquisition System (FAR 1.102)

The vision for the Federal Acquisition System is to deliver on a timely basis the best value product or service to the customer, while maintaining the public's trust and fulfilling public policy objectives. Participants in the acquisition process should work together as a team and should be empowered to make decisions within their area of responsibility. The Federal Acquisition System will:

- Satisfy the customer in terms of cost, quality, and timeliness of the delivered product or service by, for example—

  o Maximizing the use of commercial products and services,

  o Using contractors who have a track record of successful past performance or who demonstrate a current superior ability to perform, and

  o Promoting competition;

- Minimize administrative operating costs;
- Conduct business with integrity, fairness, and openness; and
- Fulfill public policy objectives.

The acquisition team consists of all participants in government acquisition, including not only representatives of the technical, supply, and procurement communities, but also the customers they serve and the contractors who provide the products and services. The role of each member of the acquisition team is to exercise personal initiative and sound business judgment in providing the best value product or service to meet the customer's needs. In exercising initiative, government members of the acquisition team may assume that if a specific strategy, practice, policy, or procedure is in the best interests of the government and is not addressed in the *FAR*, nor prohibited by law (statute or case law), Executive Order, or other regulation, that the strategy, practice, policy, or procedure is a permissible exercise of authority.

➢ Contracting Officer Authority and Responsibility (FAR 1.602-1–2)

Contracting officers have authority to enter into, administer, or terminate contracts and make related determinations and findings. Contracting officers may bind the government only to the extent of the authority delegated to them. Contracting officers shall receive from the appointing authority clear instructions, in writing, regarding the limits of their authority. Information on the limits of the contracting officers' authority shall be readily available to the public and agency personnel. No contract shall be entered into unless the contracting officer ensures that all requirements of law, executive orders, regulations, and all other applicable procedures, including clearances and approvals, have been met.

Contracting officers are responsible for ensuring performance of all necessary actions for effective contracting, ensuring compliance with the terms of the contract, and safeguarding the interests of the United States in its contractual relationships. In order to perform these responsibilities, contracting officers should be allowed wide latitude to exercise business judgment.

➢ Ratification (FAR 1.602-3)

"Ratification" is the act of approving an unauthorized commitment by an official who has the authority to do so (see FAR 1.602-3). "Unauthorized commitment" is a nonbinding agreement made by a government representative who lacks the authority to enter into the agreement on behalf of the government (see FAR 1.602-3). The government is not bound by unauthorized acts of its agents. The agent's unauthorized action may become binding, however, if the principal chooses to ratify the agent's act. A principal may ratify an unauthorized act of his or her agent only if the principal could have authorized the agent to act when the agent performed the unauthorized act.

Commitments that cannot be ratified may be subject to extraordinary contractual relief as authorized by *Public Law* 85-804, or may be subject to resolution by the Government Accountability Office under its account settlement authority.

➢ Standards of Conduct (FAR 3.101)

Government business shall be conducted in a manner above reproach and, except as authorized by statute or regulation, with complete impartiality and with preferential treatment for none. Transactions relating to the expenditure of public funds require the highest degree of public trust and an impeccable standard of conduct. The general rule is to strictly avoid any conflict of interest or even the appearance of a conflict of interest in government-contractor relationships. While many federal laws and regulations place restrictions on the actions of government personnel, their official conduct must, in addition, be such that they would have no reluctance to make a full public disclosure of their actions. (*See CMBOK* competency 1.3 for more information on standards of conduct.)

➢ Competition (FAR 6.101)

Contracting officers shall promote and provide for full and open competition in soliciting offers and awarding government contracts.

➢ Describing Agency Needs (FAR 11.002)

Agencies must specify needs using market research in a manner designed to—

- Promote full and open competition (see FAR Part 6), or maximum practicable competition when using simplified acquisition procedures, with due regard to the nature of the supplies or services to be acquired; and
- Only include restrictive provisions or conditions to the extent necessary to satisfy the needs of the agency or as authorized by law.

Descending Buyer Risk

- **Time and Materials**
- **CPFF**
- **CPAF**
- **CPIF**
- **Cost and Cost Sharing**
- **FIPF**
- **FFP w/EPA**
- **FFP**

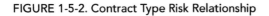

Ascending Seller Risk

- **FFP**
- **FFP w/EPA**
- **FPIF**
- **Cost and Cost Sharing**
- **CPIF**
- **CPAF**
- **CPFF**
- **Time and Materials**

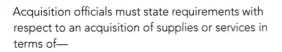

FIGURE 1-5-2. Contract Type Risk Relationship

Acquisition officials must state requirements with respect to an acquisition of supplies or services in terms of—

- Functions to be performed,
- Performance required, or
- Essential physical characteristics.

In addition, federal agencies should:

- Define requirements in terms that enable and encourage offerors to supply commercial items, or, to the extent that commercial items suitable to meet the agency's needs are not available, nondevelopmental items, in response to the agency solicitations;
- Provide offerors of commercial items and non-developmental items an opportunity to compete in any acquisition to fill such requirements;
- Require prime contractors and subcontractors at all tiers under the agency contracts to incorporate commercial items or nondevelopmental items as components of items supplied to the agency; and
- Modify requirements in appropriate cases to ensure that the requirements can be met by commercial items or, to the extent that commercial items suitable to meet the agency's needs are not available, nondevelopmental items.

1.1.5 Laws and Regulations Related to International Contracting

Several U.S. government agencies are involved with international contracting:

- The Department of Commerce,
- The Department of State,
- The U.S. Agency for International Development,
- The Department of the Treasury, and
- The Millennium Challenge Corporation (MCC).

For example, the Department of Commerce includes the Bureau of Industry and Security Export Enforcement, whose mission is to protect U.S. national security, homeland security, foreign policy, and economic interests through a law enforcement program focused on sensitive exports to hostile entities or those that engage in onward proliferation, prohibited foreign boycotts, and related public safety laws.

When contracting beyond the governmental limits of the United States, whether with foreign governments or foreign corporations, contracting professionals must be careful to ensure a complete understanding of the legal, regulatory, political, and social consequences of their actions (*see* **FIGURE 1-1-6** on page 25). Some of the more significant issues regarding international contracting include the following.

U.N. Convention on Contracts for the International Sale of Goods (CISG)

The purpose of the CISG is to provide a modern, uniform, and fair regime for contracts for the international sale of goods. Thus, the CISG contributes significantly to introducing certainty in commercial exchanges and decreasing transaction costs.

The adoption of the CISG provides modern, uniform legislation for the international sale of goods that would apply whenever contracts for the sale of goods are concluded between parties with a place of business in contracting states. In these cases, the CISG would apply directly, avoiding recourse to rules of private international law to determine the law applicable to the contract, adding significantly to the certainty and predictability of international sales contracts. (*See* **www.uncitral.org/uncitral/en/uncitral_texts/sale_goods/1980CISG.html**.)

FIGURE 1-6-1. Contracting Tools

The Arms Export Control Act (AECA)

The AECA (22 U.S.C. 2778) provides the authority to control the export of defense articles and services and charges the president to exercise this authority. Executive Order 11958, as amended, delegated this statutory authority to the secretary of state. The *International Traffic in Arms Regulations* implements this authority, and is described in further detail later in this chapter.

The Foreign Corrupt Practices Act (FCPA)

The FCPA (15 U.S.C. 78dd-1, et seq.) is primarily concerned with the issues of bribery and other corrupt payments, as well as record-keeping and accounting provisions to facilitate the review or audit of international transactions. The FCPA prohibits the payment or promise of payment of money or other items of value to foreign officials to influence or attempt to influence obtaining business, retaining business, or directing business to anyone. The record-keeping and accounting provisions require that reasonable record systems and accounting controls be present to ensure that all transactions and the disposition of assets are reflected. These requirements apply to domestic as well as foreign operations.

The Export Administration Regulations (EAR)

The *EAR* is issued by the U.S. Department of Commerce, Bureau of Industry and Security, under laws relating to the control of certain exports, re-exports, and activities. In addition, the *EAR* implements anti-boycott law provisions requiring regulations to pro-hibit specified conduct by U.S. persons that has the effect of furthering or supporting boycotts fostered or imposed by a country against a country friendly to the United States. Violations of these regulations can result in civil and criminal penalties for the entire organization and loss of the organization's exporting privileges in the future. It can also result in debarment from government contracting. It is important to be aware of the applicable *EAR* requirements when entering into a contract.

The International Traffic in Arms Regulations (ITAR)

The Department of State is responsible for the control of the permanent and temporary export and import of defense articles and services. According to the Department of State:

> [This responsibility] is governed primarily by 22 U.S.C. 2778 of the [AECA] and Executive Order 11958, as amended. The AECA, among these other requirements and authorities, provides for the promulgation of implementing regulations, the *International Traffic in Arms Regulations* (ITAR, 22 CFR 120-130). The *ITAR* is available from the Government Printing Office (GPO) either as an annual hardcopy publication of the Code of Federal Regulations (CFR) or as an e-document. The annual GPO publication includes all amendments to the *ITAR* made since the last annual printing.

(As per **www.pmddtc.state.gov/regulations_laws/itar.html**.)

Free Trade Agreements

A free trade agreement is a treaty between two or more countries that do not impose tariffs for commerce conducted across their borders. This doesn't mean capital and labor moves freely between them, and tariffs are still imposed upon nonmember countries. The idea is to open markets and provide opportunities for businesses to compete globally. (*Desktop Guide to Basic Contracting Terms*, seventh edition (Ashburn, Virginia: NCMA, 2012).)

The Foreign Assistance Act (FAA)

The FAA established the U.S. Agency for International Development and separated, for the first time, military and humanitarian foreign assistance, acknowledging "that a principal objective of the foreign policy of the United States is the encouragement and sustained support of the people of developing countries." The FAA lays out U.S. development policy and sets out the conditions under which U.S. foreign assistance is given. (*See* **www.humanrights. gov/2010/11/12/foreign-assistance-act-of-1961/**.)

Anti-Boycott Regulations

The U.S. Department of Commerce and the U.S. Department of the Treasury both enforce regulatory requirements to prevent U.S. companies from entering into foreign transactions that could be construed as supporting a foreign boycott against a country that is friendly to the United States. Violations can result in fines, imprisonment, and loss of their privilege to export.

Foreign Laws and Customs

In addition to ensuring compliance with applicable U.S. laws and regulations, U.S. firms pursuing or contemplating international contracting need to become knowledgeable regarding the myriad foreign laws, regulations, customs, and practices that may impact their ability or desire to conduct business in foreign countries. Particular care is required when dealing with or in foreign countries whose legal, political, business, and social systems are vastly different from our own.

Please refer to Section 4.6, "International Contracting," for more information about international contracting.

1.1.6 Case Law

Generally, contract principles come from case law and court decisions, which are summarized in the *Restatement of the Law, Second, Contracts*. The "*Restatement*" is a presentation of contract law by the American Law Institute. It is regarded as an authoritative reference and is relied upon in judicial opinions.

In addition to the *Restatement*, the UCC is the current legal guideline for commercial transactions. The UCC is a law drafted by the National Conference of Commissioners on Uniform State Laws Governing Commercial Transactions, and is applicable in nearly every U.S. state. While the *Restatement* and the UCC are not binding on federal government contracting, they provide useful examples to determine the rights and obligations of contracting parties and serve as a significant source of legal principles applicable to government contracts.

Contract managers should also be familiar with how various adjudicating bodies (boards and courts) resolve contractual conflicts. To become familiar with case law, contract managers should read relevant cases and articles to understand how these adjudicating bodies interpret contracts, protests, and disputes.

Researching case law in commercial contracting may vary depending on each contract. For example, many commercial contracts state: "This contract is made under and will be construed in accordance with the laws of [insert state name here] state." Commercial contract managers could research that state's case law as appropriate.

The award of U.S. federal government contracts may be protested to the Government Accountability Office. The protest is decided by the office of general counsel. Contract managers interested in learning more about the Government Accountability Office's legal decisions may research them at **www.gao.gov/ legal/index.html**. The Civilian Board of Contract Appeals decisions can be found at **www.cbca.gsa. gov** and the Armed Services Board of Contract Appeals decisions can be found at **www.asbca.mil**.

Case law decisions can also be found at the Court of Federal Claims. The Contract Disputes Act gives the contractor the option of appealing the contracting officer's final decision to the Court of Federal Claims. Contract managers may research these decisions at **www.uscfc.uscourts.gov/opinions-decisions-0**.

In addition to the Court of Federal Claims, the Court of Appeals for the Federal Circuit may hear cases

FIGURE 1-8-1. Intellectual Property Types

on appeal from Court of Federal Claims decisions. Contract managers may research cases in this forum at **www.cafc.uscourts.gov/opinions-orders/search/report.html**.

1.2 Contract Principles

"Contract principles" are the fundamentals of acquisition that all contracting professionals should understand. These principles are divided into two sections:

- "General concepts" (1.2.1), including:
  - o Principal and agency,
  - o Types of authority,
  - o Essential Elements of a contract,
  - o Market research,
  - o Competition,
  - o Fair and reasonable prices, and
  - o Ethics; and
- "Specific contract clauses" (1.2.2), including:
  - o Inspection and acceptance,
  - o *Force majeure*,
  - o Risk of loss,
  - o Repudiation,
  - o Warranties,
  - o Payment terms,
  - o Contract modification, and
  - o Termination.

The contract principles and specific clauses discussed in this *CMBOK* competency are those that are common to both government and commercial contracts. Detailed explanations will be provided in the applicable *CMBOK* section that relates to the topic.

1.2.1 General Concepts

FIGURE 1-2-1 on page 27 illustrates a typical acquisition process with the major phases depicted in dark-shaded boxes above individual buyers' steps shown in a process flow below. The light-shaded areas below the buyer's process steps are corresponding seller actions.

1.2.1.1 Principal and Agency

This concept is concerned with any principal-agent relationship; a relationship in which one person has legal authority to act for another. The authority-granting party (a company or government agency) is the principal. The party who receives authority from the principal to act on their behalf is called the agent. The principal is responsible for the acts of the agent and the agent's acts bind the principal. (*See* Cornell University Law School, Legal Information Institute, **www.law.cornell.edu/wex/agency**.)

The principal-agent relationship can result from an explicit appointment where the principal authorizes the agent to represent his or her interests and perform acts that bind the principal, or this relationship can result by implication where it is implied by the conduct of the parties. For example, in commercial contracts, contract managers may be agents of the companies for which they work. In the federal government, contracting officers are agents of the government explicitly addressed in their warrants.

Such relationships arise from explicit appointment or by implication. The relationships generally associated with agency law include:

- "Guardian-ward,"

- "Executor" or "administrator-decedent," and

- "Employer-employee."

A "universal agent" provides broad authority for an agent to act on behalf of the principal. A "general agent" is authorized to conduct a limited series of transactions involving a continuity of service and may be empowered to enter into contracts that are binding on the principal.

The power and authority of a "special agent" is limited to accomplishing a specific and limited assignment and does not have the power or authority to enter into contracts on behalf of the principal.

1.2.1.2 Types of Authority

In order to bind the principal, the agent must act within the authority granted by the principal. This authority may be one of the following four types:

- *Actual authority*—An agent's specific authority that the principal intentionally confers on the agent. It confers a power to the agent to affect legal relations of the principals with third persons.

- *Express authority*—Authority plainly granted, either verbally or in writing, to an agent by a

principal. It is direction provided to the agent by the principal to do specific actions.

- *Implied authority*—Authority given by a principal to an agent that is not actually expressed or otherwise communicated. This allows the agent to perform all the usual and necessary tasks to exercise the agent's expressed authority. The direction to do something is not provided expressly from the principal's words, but implied from what is understood as customary in the industry.

- *Apparent authority*—The appearance of being a principal's agent with the power to act for the principal. Corporations are liable for an employee's acts and promises to a third party if it appears to the third party that the employee has been granted authority by his or her corporate employer (principal) to do those acts that bind the corporation.

1.2.1.3 Essential Elements of a Contract

A contract is a promise or a set of promises for the breach of which the law gives a remedy, or the performance of which the law in some way recognizes as a duty. In order for a contract to be valid, it must contain these essential elements:

- Demonstration of mutual agreement through an offer and acceptance;

- Consideration (i.e., something of value—typically money);

- Legal purpose (a contract for an illegal act is not valid); and

- Capacity of the parties (the contracting parties must have the legal capacity to enter into a contract).

All four elements must exist for the contract to be valid. In addition to the essential elements of a contract, there are certain fundamental aspects or principles that are common to the contracting process, which include market research and competition.

1.2.1.4 Market Research

Market research is the process used for collecting and analyzing information about the entire market available to satisfy the minimum agency needs to arrive at the most suitable approach to acquiring, distributing, and supporting supplies and services. (*Desktop Guide to Basic Contracting Terms*, seventh edition (Ashburn, Virginia: NCMA, 2012).)

1.2.1.5 Competition

The competitive forces of the marketplace help to establish fair prices. Buyers tend to prefer competition to get better prices and quality; suppliers tend to prefer sole-source or limited competition for higher profits.

There are different types of competition that manifests itself in the behaviors in the pricing power of buyers and sellers, as illustrated in **FIGURE 1-2-2** on page 29.

Competition is important because it is widely acknowledged as the best way to encourage firms to offer a quality product at a reasonable price. In addition, competitive prices are one of the best ways to evaluate and justify price reasonableness.

The benefits of competition, however, go beyond a short-term price advantage. The competitive process helps buyers find the best solution to meet their needs. Some of the most important benefits of competition can be improved ideas, designs, and/or technology. (*See* General Accounting Office, "Federal Regulations Need to be Revised to Fully Realize the Purposes of the Competition in Contracting Act of 1984," GAO/OGC-85-14 (Washington, DC: General Accounting Office, August 1985): 1–2.) A fair market price is determined by supply and demand if there is perfect or effective competition, which brings us to the contract principle of fair and reasonable prices.

1.2.1.6 Fair and Reasonable Prices

Awarding contracts at fair and reasonable prices is the foundation of a good business relationship. Sellers have to determine a selling price that takes into consideration current economic and market conditions and provides a product or service with the quality the buyer needs. Buyers should expect to pay the fair market value of a product or service, considering similar competitive market conditions for deliverables with similar product, quality, and quantity requirements.

The buyer who insists on the lowest price may be disappointed in the resulting quality. To be fair to the seller, a price must be realistic in terms of the seller's ability to satisfy the terms and conditions of the contract. That means the total cost of providing the supplies or services are what would be incurred by a well managed, responsible firm using reasonably efficient and economical methods of performance,

plus a reasonable profit. (*See* Federal Acquisition Institute, *Contract Pricing Reference Guide, Volume 1, Price Analysis* (February 2012): 13.)

Thus, the fair and reasonable price determination is a subjective evaluation of what each party considers to be equitable considering terms and conditions, quality, delivery, or other areas important to the negotiation.

1.2.1.7 Ethics

Ethical conduct is important in any business relationship, and the same is true for both government and commercial contracts. Government agencies, for example, undergo required annual ethics training pursuant to the requirements of the Procurement Integrity Act. Similarly, government contractors have annual ethics training requirements.

Ethics in the commercial side is less defined, but not less important. Corporations have standards of conduct and expect their employees to comply with them. (Ethics and standards of conduct are discussed more thoroughly in *CMBOK* 1.3.)

In addition to the concepts discussed here in section 1.2.1, there are other contract principles with which contract managers should be aware. The specific contract clauses described in the next section are found in many commercial and government contracts.

1.2.2 Specific Contract Clauses

The contract clauses described in this section are those that are common to both commercial and government contracts. This section is not intended to be an all-encompassing discussion of the terms and conditions surrounding these contract clauses. Rather, the intent is to make the reader aware of common elements and provide basic information for further research if desired.

1.2.2.1 Inspection and Acceptance

Inspection involves examining (including testing) supplies and services to determine if the supplies and services meet the contract's requirements. Inspection may also extend to raw materials, components, and intermediate assemblies. Acceptance occurs when the buyer inspects the goods and signifies that the goods conform to the contract's requirements or fails to reject the delivery. (*See* UCC 2-606.) Both government and commercial contracts should have specific inspection and acceptance clauses to avoid disputes after delivery.

1.2.2.2 Force Majeure

Force majeure is a French term that refers to an unexpected or uncontrollable event that upsets the plan or releases one from obligation. It literally means "superior force." An example of such a superior force is an act of God such as a flood, epidemic, or unusually severe weather. Government contracting uses the phrase "excusable delay" to convey the same meaning. To be an excusable delay in government contracting, the failure to perform must be beyond the control and without the fault or negligence of the contractor. (*See* FAR 52.249-14, "Excusable Delays.")

1.2.2.3 Risk of Loss

The contracting parties should establish in advance who bears the risk of loss under certain circumstances. The party who has title to the goods when the loss occurs has no impact on liability for risk of loss.

Typically, risk of loss does not pass to the buyer until the buyer accepts the goods under a "sale on approval" contract. The buyer bears the risk of loss when the seller delivers the products to the transportation carrier unless the contract requires the seller to deliver the goods to a specific destination. In that case, the buyer has the risk of loss when the goods are delivered to the transportation carrier. (*See* UCC 2.509.)

Generally, the party who has control of the goods or the right to control those goods also has the risk of loss. (*See* Bradford Stone, *Uniform Commercial Code in a Nutshell* (St. Paul, Minnesota: West Publishing Company, 1989): 59.)

1.2.2.4 Repudiation

Repudiation occurs when one contracting party (A) gives the other contracting party (B) reason to believe that they (party A) will not perform the contract through an action or statement. When repudiation occurs, contracting party B may then pursue a remedy against contracting party A for breach of contract. (*See* UCC 2-610.)

1.2.2.5 Warranties

As described in CMBOK 1.1, the UCC provides implied warranties of merchantability and fitness for a particular purpose. Express warranties should be in writing in the contract and specifically state what the product will or will not do. Express warranties should also state the repair/replacement policy if applicable.

1.2.2.6 Payment Terms

Since consideration (something of value) is a required element for a contract, payment terms should be stated in the contract. The payment terms should identify where and how the seller receives payment. For example, the clause may state the timing of invoices such as monthly, upon delivery, upon acceptance, or some combination, as well as the address to send invoices. Payment terms may also include a prompt payment discount if the buyer pays the seller within a stated time period.

1.2.2.7 Contract Modification

Many contracts, both government and commercial, undergo changes throughout performance. Contract terms should specify how and when changes may occur and if there are any restrictions on a party's authority to require a contract change. For example, in government contracts, only the contracting officer has the authority to require a contract change.

1.2.2.8 Termination

Commercial contracts may be terminated for cause if one party breaches the contract, such as nonperformance by the seller or nonpayment by the buyer. Commercial contracts may also be terminated by mutual agreement, but that is not the case in government contracting.

In government contracting, only the government may terminate the contract for convenience or default. Default termination is analogous to the commercial "termination for cause." Convenience termination is a uniquely government concept.

1.3 Standards of Conduct

The Merriam-Webster dictionary defines "professional" as 1) characterized by or conforming to the technical or ethical standards of a profession and 2) exhibiting a courteous, conscientious, and generally businesslike manner in the workplace. Thus, following ethical standards is an important part of being a professional. So, then what are "ethics?" The Merriam-Webster dictionary defines "ethics" as 1) the discipline dealing with what is good and bad and with moral duty and obligation and 2) a set of moral principles or a theory or system of moral values. (*See* **www.merriam-webster.com/dictionary**.) As discussed in Chapter One, the Department of Labor states that a code of ethics is a characteristic of a profession.

The requirement of ethical standards is an important element of any profession. There are laws and regulations that require ethical conduct—corporations have codes of conduct and so do federal, state, and local government agencies. These written documents may have a variety of titles such as "Standards of Conduct," "Codes of Ethics," "Statements of Professional Responsibility," or "Standards of Ethical Conduct," and regardless of title, they require that employees conduct themselves ethically.

An essential element of any code of conduct requires a strong leadership foundation. Without senior leadership's commitment, the code of conduct is simply another piece of paper. The organization should also have established procedures to implement the standards of conduct. (*See* Dean Krehmeyer, "2009 Compliance and Ethics Forum Summary Report: Leading Thoughts and Practices," Business Roundtable Institute for Corporate Ethics (2010): 13.)

A typical code of conduct would include the following elements:

- The formalized, written document that presents the standards of conduct or code of ethics.

- An ethics compliance officer or manager to monitor and enforce the written standards. The ethics compliance officer or manager is frequently a senior staff executive with direct access to the senior executive in the organization.

- A formal training program for employees to provide recurring refresher training in ethics issues.

- An internal information system to respond to general questions and provide specific guidance to employees.

- A complaint system to receive, investigate, and respond to actual or perceived issues of non-ethical behavior. Some of these complaint systems also provide, either internally or internally and externally, information regarding the resolution of ethics complaints. They may also include information about specific actions taken with regard to confirmed ethics violations, though the identities of violators are sometimes not revealed for legal reasons.

- Address issues related to:
  o Conflicts of interest (organizational and personal),
  o Behavior toward competitors,
  o Confidential and proprietary information,
  o Gift-giving and receiving,
  o Making and receiving political contributions,
  o Levels of dedication and work effort required,
  o Encouraged behavior,
  o Discouraged or prohibited behavior, and/or
  o Supplier relationships.

Standards of conduct can sometimes be codified as law when passed by Congress and signed by the president, such as the Ethics in Government Act of 1978 and the Procurement Integrity Act of 1988. For federal government employees, there are also Executive Orders that establish standards of conduct for federal government officers and employees. The Sarbanes-Oxley Act (see CMBOK 1.1) requires most publicly held U.S. companies to post their code of conduct on their public website. With that in mind, the next section reviews key points about ethics.

1.3.1 Ethics

Laws, regulations, and policy documents, such as standards of conduct, provide an authoritative, formalized, written set of guidelines that require certain actions, prohibit others, and define broad goals or desired traits for the proper way to conduct business. Ethics provides an environment of structures, people, concepts, and values that enables an organization, and the individuals in it, to operate in a manner that conforms to the basic norms of society and business.

An excellent working definition of *ethics* was provided in the April 2004 edition of *Contract Management* Magazine (*see* Margaret G. Rumbaugh, "Ethical Decision-Making: Issues for Contract Managers and Educators," *Contract Management* Magazine (April 2004): 34–35):

> Ethics are standards by which one should act based on values. Values are core beliefs such as duty, honor, and integrity that motivate attitudes and actions. Not all values are ethical principles.... Ethical principles are values that relate to what is right and wrong and thus take precedence over non-ethical values when making ethical decisions.

Although ethical conduct can be viewed as both the means and the end, there is also a practical application and benefit associated with high ethical standards and conduct: Ethics is good for business and the government. Business flourishes in an environment of profitability and sustainability. Government functions best in an environment of service to the governed, efficiency, and trust. Ethics is a critical component to both the business and government models.

For example, the Defense Industry Initiative was formed in 1986 as a result of several procurement scandals and is a nonpartisan, nonprofit association of responsible U.S. defense companies committed to conducting business affairs at the highest ethical level and in full compliance with the law. Members are the professional ethics officers, CEOs, and senior officials of 90 top defense and security companies serving the U.S. military. Members have also committed to establish written codes of business ethics and to train employees to comply with the codes. The Defense Industry Initiative is committed to ensuring a culture of ethical conduct within every company that provides products and services to the U.S. armed forces. (*See* **www.dii.org**.)

Government and business organizations generally recognize that ethics-related issues can have a positive or negative impact both internally and externally. They also realize that internal and external influences can have positive as well as adverse impacts on the best-planned ethics compliance system. Therefore, organizations that take ethics seriously seek to instill and influence high ethical standards in their own employees and with other firms and organizations with which they do business. Additionally, they seek to make their clients or customers, as well as the general public, aware of the significant role that ethics plays as a means to foster goodwill and a positive image.

The issue of personal ethics, as opposed to the issue of organizational ethics previously discussed, is naturally more philosophical than fact-based. Though an organization can implement and maintain a very aggressive and far-reaching ethics function or program, the value of such a program can be easily diminished or severely damaged by the action or inaction of individuals throughout the organization. Personal ethics—i.e., knowing the "right" thing to do, and doing it—is therefore a significant issue. Personal ethics is of particular significance in the contracting profession due to the fiduciary nature of the contracting function, the requirement to build good working relationships both internally and externally, and the effect that contracting can have on an organization's bottom line and/or public image.

One's sense of personal ethics is in no small part defined by one's life experiences. Though not bound exclusively to one's past, what has occurred before often influences what may occur in the future. It is important that, as individuals, we clearly understand the ethical challenges that our profession sometimes presents to us and that we clearly understand corporate or agency requirements or policy related to such challenges. We must then bring our life experiences, as well as societal norms, into the equation to determine if a particular course of action is right or wrong. In some cases, these decisions are so simple that they are made automatically. In other cases, they can be the source of great anxiety and turmoil. Regardless, true professionalism requires that we continuously verify the "true north" of our "ethical compass" and that all our words and deeds proceed along that "right," ethical direction. For more information, please refer to John W. Polk's article, "Ethics and Compliance in the Corporate Jungle," from the September 2010 issue of *Contract Management* Magazine. NCMA members are obligated to adhere to the "Contract Management Code of Ethics."

Thus, ethical behavior includes both personal and organizational ethics. Another area where there are both personal and organizational ethical considerations is a conflict of interest.

1.3.2 Conflict of Interest

Both corporations and individuals need to be aware of the potential for conflicts of interest in certain business situations. This section describes the importance of avoiding conflicts of interest.

1.3.2.1 Organizational Conflicts of Interest (OCIs)

An OCI exists when the nature of the work to be performed under a proposed contract may, without some restriction on future activities, result in an unfair competitive advantage to the contractor or impair the contractor's objectivity in performing the contract work. (*Desktop Guide to Basic Contracting Terms*, seventh edition (Ashburn, Virginia: NCMA, 2012).) An OCI also exists when, because of other activities or relationships with other persons, a person is unable or potentially unable to render impartial assistance or advice to the government, the person's objectivity in performing the contract work is or might be otherwise impaired, or a person has an unfair competitive advantage. (*Ibid.*)

In order to mitigate OCIs, many organizations establish "mitigation plans," which include elements such as the following (*derived from* Diane K. Whitmoyer, "Managing Organizational Conflicts of Interest," *Contract Management* Magazine (June 2004): 16):

Disclosure of Relevant Information

Several agencies require offerors to disclose all information relative to an OCI determination. This requirement tends to dictate that companies have systems in place to be able to screen not only new work against contracts already in place containing OCI provisions, but also new solicitations with OCI provisions that might conflict with future plans of other parts of the business.

Firewalls

The written agreement between the conflicted entities usually relies on a combination of procedures and physical security to establish organizational "firewalls" to avoid potential, real, or perceived OCIs from affecting the business activities of either party.

Confidentiality Agreements

Employees are required to execute special confidentiality agreements with penalties for noncompliance ranging from disciplinary action up to termination. Confidentiality agreements require the employee to notify a high-ranking corporate official should any person not working on the contract attempt to solicit information or influence the work being performed under the contract.

Separation of Personnel

Eliminating communication between personnel from the conflicted entity and the organization can effectively eliminate the potential for bias.

Divestiture of a Company

A new company can be created with a completely separate board of directors.

Removal of Conflict

Often, staff members have been supporting a particular program or agency for most of their careers, and their particular expertise and knowledge would have dire consequences for the program should their efforts be interrupted. In these cases, the affected individual(s) can be hired by another, non-conflicted entity to perform the same work. However, the buyer must be careful to keep the employees "whole" (from a salary and benefits perspective).

Work-Switch

Depending on who has the conflict, work can be switched between the prime and the subcontractor.

1.3.2.2 Personal Conflicts of Interest (PCIs)

Corporations and agencies also have policies to protect their organization from PCIs. For example, a company policy might state that employees must not have any conflicts of interest that could adversely influence their judgment, objectivity, or loyalty to the company in conducting business activities and assignments. The company recognizes that employees may take part in legitimate financial, business, charitable, and other activities outside their jobs, but any potential conflict of interest raised by those activities must be disclosed promptly to management. (*See* 3M Business Policies, "Conflict of Interest Policy," *available at* **http://solutions.3m. com/wps/portal/3M/en_US/businessconduct/bc-main/policy/policies/protect3m/conflictofinterest.**)

The federal government's general rule is "to avoid strictly any conflict of interest or even the appearance of a conflict of interest in government-contractor relationships." (*As per* FAR 3.101-1.) Corporations also suggest that employees avoid the appearance of a conflict.

The existence of a PCI may give the appearance of an unfair advantage or preferential treatment in the course of business. Employees are expected to act in their employer's best interests at all times and to exercise sound judgment that is not conflicted by personal interests or divided loyalties. A conflict of interest exists if your circumstances would lead a reasonable person to question whether your motivations are aligned with the organization's best interests.

1.4 Socioeconomic Programs

Socioeconomic programs are designed to benefit particular groups. They represent a multitude of program interests and objectives unrelated to procurement objectives. Some examples of these are preferences for small businesses and for American products, required sources for specific items, and minimum labor pay levels mandated for contractors.

The following socioeconomic programs are described in this section:

- Small business programs (1.4.1),
- Other socioeconomic programs (1.4.2),
- Application of labor laws to federal government acquisitions (1.4.3),
- Workplace and environmental considerations (1.4.4),

- Privacy and freedom of information (1.4.5), and

- Foreign acquisition (1.4.6).

1.4.1 Small Business Programs

It is the policy of the U.S. federal government, as stated in FAR Part 19, to provide the maximum possible acquisition opportunities to small business, veteran-owned small business, service-disabled veteran–owned small business, historically underutilized business zone (HUBZone) small business, small disadvantaged business, and women-owned small business concerns. These businesses must also have the maximum practicable opportunity to participate as subcontractors in the contracts awarded by any executive agency, consistent with efficient contract performance. The Small Business Administration (SBA) counsels and assists small business concerns and assists government contracting personnel to ensure that a fair proportion of contracts for goods and services are placed with small businesses.

Government contracting professionals are responsible for effectively implementing the small business programs, including achieving program goals. The Small Business Act requires each agency with contracting authority to establish an Office of Small and Disadvantaged Business Utilization. For the Department of Defense, in accordance with the National Defense Authorization Act for Fiscal Year 2006 (Public Law 109-163), the Office of Small and Disadvantaged Business Utilization has been redesignated as the Office of Small Business Programs.

1.4.1.1 Small Business Policies

Small businesses must have an equal opportunity to compete for all contracts that they can perform to the extent that is consistent with the government's interest. Federal government contracting officers shall, when appropriate:

- Divide proposed acquisitions, except construction, into reasonable, small lots to permit offers on less than the total requirement;

- Plan acquisitions so that more than one small business may do the work, if the work exceeds the amount for which a surety may be guaranteed by SBA against loss;

- Ensure that delivery schedules are established on a realistic basis that will encourage small business participation; and

- Encourage prime contractors to subcontract with small businesses. (*As per* FAR 19.202-1(d).)

Contracting professionals should make every reasonable effort to find additional small business concerns, unless existing lists are excessively long.

1.4.1.2 Small Business Set-Asides

A small business set-aside reserves an acquisition exclusively for small businesses. A small business set-aside may be open to all small businesses. A small business set-aside may relate to a single acquisition or a class of acquisitions and may be total or partial. For federal government contracts, all acquisitions within a certain dollar range are automatically set-aside for small business. Small business set-asides may be withdrawn by the contracting officer if award would be detrimental to the public interest (e.g., paying more than a fair market price).

1.4.1.3 Types of Small Businesses

Small Business

A "small business" is a concern, including its affiliates, that is independently owned and operated, not dominant in the field of operation in which it is bidding on government contracts, and qualified as a small business under the criteria and size standards contained in Title 13, Part 121, of the Code of Federal Regulations (CFR) (*see* **FIGURE 1-4-1** on page 31).

Small Business 8(a)

An "8(a) small business" is a small business operating in conjunction with SBA's Business Development Program, authorized by Section 8(a) of the Small Business Act (15 U.S.C. 637(a)). Fundamentally, SBA acts as a prime contractor for other government agencies and issues subcontracts to 8(a) firms. SBA sometimes delegates contract execution authority to the requiring agency. 8(a) contracts may be awarded competitively or noncompetitively.

Veteran-Owned Small Business

A small business qualifies as a "veteran-owned small business" if not less than 51 percent of the business is owned by one or more veterans or, in the case of publicly owned businesses, not less than 51 percent of the stock is owned by one or more veterans. In addition, the management and daily business operations of the concern must be controlled by one or more veterans.

Service-Disabled Veteran–Owned Small Business

A "service-disabled veteran–owned small business" is a veteran-owned small business in which the 51 percent veteran stipulation refers to veterans with a disability that is service-connected. As with veteran-owned small businesses, the management and daily business operations of the concern must be controlled by one or more veterans.

Small Disadvantaged Business

A "small disadvantaged business" is a small business that has received certification as a small disadvantaged business consistent with 13 CFR Part 124.

HUBZone Small Business

A "HUBZone" is a small business that operates in a historically underutilized business zone that is in an area located within one or more qualified census tracts, qualified non-metropolitan counties, or lands within the external boundaries of an Indian reservation. The business must also appear on the "List of Qualified HUBZone Small Business Concerns" maintained by SBA.

Women-Owned Small Business (WOSB)

In order to be considered a WOSB, a small business concern must be at least 51-percent directly and unconditionally owned by, and the management and daily business operations of which controlled by, one or more women who are citizens of the United States (13 CFR Part 127). The purpose of the WOSB program is to ensure small business concerns owned by women have an equal opportunity to participate in federal contracting and to assist agencies in achieving their WOSB participation goals. It is a program that authorizes contracting officers to limit competition to eligible economically disadvantaged WOSB concerns for federal contracts assigned a North American Industry Classification System (NAICS) code in an industry in which SBA has determined that WOSB concerns are underrepresented in federal procurement. WOSB concerns are eligible for federal contracts once they are assigned a NAICS code in an industry in which SBA has determined that WOSB concerns are substantially underrepresented.

An "economically disadvantaged women-owned small business (EDWOSB) concern" is a subcategory of WOSB and is a small business concern that is at least 51-percent directly and unconditionally owned by, and the management and daily business operations of which controlled by, one or more women who are citizens of the United States and who are economically disadvantaged in accordance with 13 CFR Part 127. It automatically qualifies as a WOSB concern eligible under the WOSB program.

1.4.2 Other Socioeconomic Programs

Federal contracting professionals need to be aware of and comply with federal laws and policies that have some form of socioeconomic implication. Commercial contracting professionals whose organizations perform under federal contracts are also often bound by these laws and policies, which are normally included as terms and conditions in government contracts. Some of the significant socioeconomic programs include the following.

1.4.2.1 Indian Incentive Program

Government policy states that Indian organizations and Indian-owned economic enterprises, including Alaskan Natives, shall have the maximum practicable opportunity to participate in performing contracts awarded by federal agencies. The policy also provides for incentive payments to Indian-owned economic enterprises that perform as subcontractors.

1.4.2.2 Disaster or Emergency Assistance Activities

When contracting for disaster or emergency assistance services following a major disaster or emergency, the government provides a preference to organizations, firms, or individuals residing or doing business in the area affected by the disaster or emergency. Such services can include debris clearance, distribution of supplies, or reconstruction.

1.4.2.3 Historically Black Colleges and Universities and Minority Institutions

The government promotes the participation of historically black colleges and universities and minority institutions in federal procurement, in compliance with Executive Order 12928, particularly for the types of services normally acquired from higher educational institutions.

1.4.2.4 Diversity

There are also programs designed to encourage a diverse workforce or education and training group, such as programs that prohibit employment or workplace discrimination based on race, color, religion, sex, national origin, age, or disability. More recent additions to federal socioeconomic provisions relate to human trafficking (2009) and immigration (2012). These additions pose additional requirements on federal government contractors and subcontractors.

1.4.2.5 Human Trafficking

According to *Federal Acquisition Regulation* 22.1703:

The United States Government has adopted a zero-tolerance policy regarding trafficking in persons. Additional information about trafficking in persons may be found at the website for the Department of State's Office to Monitor and Combat Trafficking in Persons' at http://www.state.gov/g/tip. Government contracts shall—

(a) Prohibit contractors, contractor employees, subcontractors, and subcontractor employees from—

   (1) Engaging in severe forms of trafficking in persons during the period of performance of the contract;

   (2) Procuring commercial sex acts during the period of performance of the contract; or

   (3) Using forced labor in the performance of the contract;

(b) Require contractors and subcontractors to notify employees of the prohibited activities described in paragraph (a) of this section and the actions that may be taken against them for violations; and

(c) Impose suitable remedies, including termination, on contractors that fail to comply with the requirements of paragraphs (a) and (b) of this section.

There is also an Executive Order prohibiting human trafficking that was signed in September 2012 (*available at* **www.whitehouse.gov/the-press-office/2012/09/25/ executive-order-strengthening-protections-against-trafficking-persons-fe**). It states, in part:

> As the largest single purchaser of goods and services in the world, the U.S. government bears a responsibility to ensure that taxpayer dollars do not contribute to trafficking in persons. By providing our government workforce with additional tools and training to apply and enforce existing policy, and by providing additional clarity to government contractors and subcontractors on the steps necessary to fully comply with that policy, this order will help to protect vulnerable individuals as contractors and subcontractors perform vital services and manufacture the goods procured by the United States.

1.4.2.6 Employment Eligibility

Statutes and Executive Orders require employers to abide by the immigration laws of the United States and to employ in the United States only individuals who are eligible to work in the United States. The E-Verify program provides an Internet-based means of verifying employment eligibility of workers employed in the United States, but is not a substitute for any other employment eligibility verification requirements. Federal government contractors must enroll as federal contractors in E-Verify and use E-Verify to determine the employment eligibility of all new hires working in the United States. (*See* FAR 22.18.)

1.4.3 Application of Labor Laws to Federal Government Acquisitions

Labor laws are frequently a matter of concern for contracting professionals, particularly as they relate to service contracts. As a matter of policy, the government seeks to maintain sound relations with both industry and labor and usually remains impartial concerning disputes between labor and contractor management. Some of the significant issues and policies related to the application of labor laws include:

- Restrictions on the use of convict labor;

- The requirement to pay at least the prevailing wage rate for construction contracts subject to the Davis-Bacon Act;

- The requirement for equal employment opportunity, equal employment opportunity for veterans, nondiscrimination because of age, professional employee compensation, and employing workers with disabilities;

- The requirement to pay overtime for work in excess of 40 hours per week, as governed by the Contract Work Hours and Safety Standards Act;

- The provisions of the Walsh-Healy Public Contracts Act, which require various stipulations regarding minimum wages, maximum hours, child labor, convict labor, and safe and sanitary working conditions for certain types of supply contracts;

- The provisions of the Service Contract Act of 1965 regarding minimum wages and fringe benefits, safe and sanitary working conditions, and notification to employees of the minimum allowable compensation for contracts covered by the act;

- The prohibition against acquiring products produced by forced or indentured child labor or trafficking in persons; and

- Various laws, Executive Orders, and policies that deal with equal employment opportunity, age discrimination, veteran's preference, providing employment opportunities for the disabled, and other related matters. (*See* FAR Part 22 for more information.)

1.4.4 Workplace and Environmental Considerations

The government implements various workplace and environmental policies through the acquisition process. Additional information is found in FAR Part 23, but includes the following.

1.4.4.1 Drug-Free Workplace

Contractors with noncommercial contracts over the simplified acquisition threshold have to take specified steps—including establishing an ongoing drug awareness program—providing published statements to its employees prohibiting the manufacture, distribution, dispensing, possession, or use of controlled substances, as well as taking appropriate action against employees who violate the policies.

1.4.4.2 Energy Conservation

Some contracts contain clauses that help implement government policies to acquire goods and services that promote energy and water efficiency, advance the use of renewable energy products, and help foster markets for emerging technology.

1.4.4.3 Hazardous Materials

The Occupational Safety and Health Administration (OSHA), part of the Department of Labor, is responsible for issuing and administering regulations that require government activities to apprise their employees of:

- All hazards to which they may be exposed,

- Relative symptoms and appropriate emergency treatment, and

- Proper conditions and precautions for safe use and exposure.

State programs must meet or exceed federal OSHA standards for workplace safety and health. Sometimes contractors are required to provide information to the government regarding hazardous materials that may be introduced into the workplace as a result of performing a government contract.

1.4.4.4 Recovered Materials and Biobased Products

Government policy on using products containing recovered materials and biobased products considers cost, availability of competition, and performance. Federal agencies shall purchase these products or require in the acquisition of services the delivery, use, or furnishing of such products. These regula-

tions apply to Environmental Protection Agency or U.S. Department of Agriculture–designated items. (*See* FAR 23.4.)

1.4.4.5 Ozone-Depleting Substances

Government policy strives to minimize the procurement of materials and substances that contribute to the depletion of stratospheric ozone, and gives preference to the procurement of alternative products that reduce overall risks to human health and the environment.

1.4.4.6 Green Procurement

The federal government and some states have green procurement policies. For example, the Pennsylvania Department of General Services Green Procurement Policy states that analysis is required on each material and service during the bid process to determine what "green" options are available. When an environmentally preferable product (EPP) is comparable, the statement of work or specifications is restricted to the EPP option. (*See* **www.portal.state.pa.us/portal/server.pt/community/green_procurement/5247**.)

Executive Order 13423 requires federal government contractors to establish a program to promote cost-effective waste reduction in all operations and facilities covered by a contract that has the "Waste Reduction Program" clause (FAR 52.223-10). The contractor's programs shall comply with applicable federal, state, and local requirements, specifically including Section 6002 of the Resource Conservation and Recovery Act (42 U.S.C. 6962, *et seq.*) and implementing regulations (40 CFR Part 247).

1.4.5 Privacy and Freedom of Information

The Privacy Act of 1974 (5 U.S.C. 552a) and the Freedom of Information Act (*Public Law* 89-554, 80 Stat. 383) have implications that sometimes affect government contracts. When a contract requires a contractor to design, develop, or operate a system of records on individuals, the contracting agency is required to apply the requirements of the Privacy Act to the contractor and its employees. The Freedom of Information Act generally provides that information contained in government records be made available to the public. There are some exceptions to the general rule that apply to acquisitions. For example, proposals submitted in response to a competitive solicitation may not be released under the Freedom of Information Act. Also, there are exceptions that relate to classified information, trade secrets, confidential commercial or financial information, and other matters. (*See* FAR Part 24 for more information.)

1.4.6 Foreign Acquisition

Certain acquisition regulations apply when purchasing foreign supplies, services, and construction materials, as well as for contracts performed outside the United States. Regulations implement the Buy American Act, Trade Agreements Act, and other laws and regulations that will be discussed in this section.

For example, the Buy American Act restricts buying supplies that are not domestic end products for use within the United States. A foreign end product may be purchased if the contracting officer determines that the price of the lowest domestic offer is unreasonable or if another exception applies. (*See* FAR Part 25 for more information.)

The Trade Agreements Act provides the authority for the president to waive the Buy American Act and other discriminatory provisions for eligible products from countries that have signed an international trade agreement with the United States, or that meet certain other criteria, such as being a "least-developed country." The president has delegated this waiver authority to the U.S. trade representative. In acquisitions covered by the World Trade Organization Government Procurement Agreement, free trade agreements, or the Israeli Trade Act, the U.S. trade representative has waived the Buy American Act and other discriminatory provisions for eligible products. Offers of eligible products receive equal consideration with domestic offers. (*See* FAR 25.4 for more information.)

1.5 Contract Types

"Contract types" refer to specific pricing arrangements or contracting methods used to structure the contract. They are specific business arrangements that govern the buyer-seller relationship. These business arrangements deal specifically with how the seller manages cost. Contract types also determine how cost and/or performance risk is allocated between the parties. Both commercial and government contracts use a variety of contract types.

This section describes the following contract types:

- Fixed-price contracts (1.5.1),
- Cost-reimbursement contracts (1.5.2),
- Incentive contracts (1.5.3), and
- Other contract types (1.5.4)

There are three primary contracting methods:

- Fixed-price,
- Cost-reimbursement, and
- Incentive.

Fundamentally, the three families of contracts are based on risk to both the buyer and seller. The more risk the seller has (such as untried technology, vague specifications, etc.), the less likely the seller will be to accept a fixed-price contract. Conversely, the more specific the requirement, the less likely the buyer will be to accept a cost-reimbursement contract type. But these three primary styles are not the only contract types. **FIGURE 1-5-1** on page 32 also illustrates other contract types. The "other" contract types do not fit into any of the other three categories, but are important nonetheless.

FIGURE 1-5-2 on page 34 illustrates the risk relationship of the various contract types for both the buyer and seller. It is interesting to note that the contract type with the most risk for one party is the contract type that has the least risk for the other party.

Selecting the contract type is generally a matter for negotiation and requires the exercise of sound judgment. Negotiating the contract type and negotiating prices are closely related and should be considered together. The objective is to negotiate a contract type and price (or estimated cost and fee) that will result in reasonable contractor risk and provide the contractor with the greatest incentive for efficient and economical performance. Typically, the contract file should include documentation to show why the particular contract type was selected.

There are many factors to consider when negotiating a contract type, including the following:

- Price competition,
- Price analysis,
- Cost analysis,
- Combined contract types,
- Type and complexity of the requirement,
- Urgency of the requirement,
- Period of performance,

- Adequacy of the contractor's financial system,

- Seller's technical capability and financial responsibility,

- Concurrent contracts,

- Extent and nature of subcontracting, and

- Acquisition history. (*See* FAR 16.104.)

1.5.1 Fixed-Price Contracts

"Fixed-price" refers to a style or group of contracts that require a firm pricing arrangement established by the parties at contract award. Fixed-price contracts typically include:

- Firm-fixed-price (1.5.1.1);

- Firm-fixed-price, level of effort (1.5.1.2);

- Fixed-price with economic price adjustment (1.5.1.3); and

- Fixed-price redetermination (prospective (1.5.1.4)/retroactive (1.5.1.5)).

1.5.1.1 Firm-Fixed-Price

As the name implies, firm-fixed-price contracts require a price that is not subject to any adjustment based on the contractor's actual cost to perform the contract. This contract type places the maximum performance risk on the contractor as well as full responsibility for all costs and the resulting profit or loss. It provides strong incentives for the contractor to control costs and perform effectively and imposes a minimum administrative burden on the contracting parties. The level of risk assumed by the contractor is often reflected in the contract price. (*See* FAR 16.202-1.)

1.5.1.2 Firm-Fixed-Price, Level of Effort

This type of contract requires the contractor to provide a specified level of effort, typically stated in number of hours, over a defined period of time, on work that can be described only in general terms. In return for the specified level of effort, the contractor is paid a fixed dollar amount. (*See* FAR 16.207.)

1.5.1.3 Fixed-Price with Economic Price Adjustment

Fixed-price with economic price adjustment contracts provide for upward and downward revision of the stated contract price on the occurrence of specified contingencies. There are three general economic price adjustments:

- Adjustments based on established prices—The price adjustments are based on increases or decreases from an agreed-upon level in published or otherwise established prices of specific items or contract end items.

- Adjustments based on actual costs of labor or material—The price adjustments are based on increases or decreases in specified costs of labor or material that the contractor actually experiences during contract performance.

- Adjustments based on cost indexes of labor or material—The price adjustments are based on increases or decreases in labor or material cost standards or indexes that are specifically identified in the contract. (*See* FAR 16.203.)

1.5.1.4 Fixed-Price Redetermination (Prospective)

These types of fixed-price contracts combine a firm-fixed-price for an initial period of deliveries or performance and a prospective redetermination (at a stated time or times during performance) of the price for subsequent periods of performance. (*See* FAR 16.205.)

1.5.1.5 Fixed-Price Redetermination (Retroactive)

These types of fixed-price contracts combine a fixed ceiling price and a retroactive price redetermination after completion of the contract. The redetermined price cannot exceed the original ceiling price. (*See* FAR 16.206.)

1.5.2 Cost-Reimbursement Contracts

In cost-reimbursement contracts, the buyer pays allowable, allocable, and reasonable costs incurred in the performance of a contract to the extent that such costs are prescribed or permitted by the contract. These contracts establish an estimate of total cost to obligate funds and establish a ceiling that the contractor may not exceed (except at its own risk) without the buyer's approval. Cost-reimbursement contracts typically include:

- Cost contracts (1.5.2.1),

- Cost-sharing contracts (1.5.2.2), and

- Cost-plus-fixed-fee contracts (1.5.2.3). (*See* FAR 16.301.)

1.5.2.1 Cost Contracts

A cost contract is the least-complicated type of cost-reimbursement contract. It reimburses appropriate costs without fees. (*See* FAR 16.302.)

1.5.2.2 Cost-Sharing Contracts

In a cost-sharing contract, the buyer pays some of the contractor's allowable costs with no allowances for fees. Both the buyer and the seller share the costs. Cost-sharing contracts are used when both the buyer and the seller will derive some benefit from the contracted effort, and that benefit is sufficient enough that both parties are willing to share the costs and the benefits. (*See* FAR 16.303.)

1.5.2.3 Cost-Plus-Fixed-Fee Contracts

In a cost-plus-fixed-fee contract, the buyer reimburses the seller for appropriate costs associated with contract performance and pays a fixed fee that is negotiated at the outset. The fixed fee does not vary with actual cost, but may be adjusted as a result of changes made in the work performed under the contract. (*See* FAR 16.306.)

1.5.3 Incentive Contracts

Contracts containing various forms of incentives may be appropriate when there is a desire or need to provide additional motivation to a contractor/seller to attain specific acquisition objectives that would be unlikely without the incentives. Such objectives might be improved delivery, improved technical performance, improved cost management, or some other significant parameter. (*See* FAR 16.4.)

Incentives generally fall into the following four categories:

- Cost incentives (1.5.3.1),
- Performance or quality incentives (1.5.3.2),
- Delivery incentives (1.5.3.3), and
- Multiple incentives (1.5.3.4).

1.5.3.1 Cost Incentives

Cost incentives normally take the form of a profit or fee adjustment based on a formula. Cost incentives are intended to motivate the seller to effectively manage costs. Generally, cost incentives must be required before including other types of incentives in a contract.

1.5.3.2 Performance or Quality Incentives

Performance or quality incentives may be appropriate when the contractor can attain a level of performance or quality over the requirement and provides a desirable enhanced benefit to the buyer. These incentives should be designed to relate profit or fee to results achieved by the seller compared to specified targets.

1.5.3.3 Delivery Incentives

Delivery incentives are included when receiving the goods or services faster is important to the buyer. The value of the incentive, however, should not exceed the benefit received for the faster delivery.

1.5.3.4 Multiple Incentives

Include multiple incentives when there is sufficient justification to motivate the seller to strive for outstanding results in multiple areas simultaneously. Multiple incentives sometimes require the seller to make trade-off decisions among the incentives to achieve the maximum beneficial result. The buyer should be aware of the potential problems inherent in providing multiple incentives and closely monitor these situations to ensure that the primary goals of the acquisition are not compromised.

Contract incentives can also be used in both fixed-price and cost-reimbursement contracts to create the following types of contracts:

- Fixed-price incentive contracts (1.5.3.5),
- Fixed-price award fee contracts (1.5.3.6),
- Cost plus incentive fee contracts (1.5.3.7), and
- Cost plus award fee contracts (1.5.3.8).

1.5.3.5 Fixed-Price Incentive Contracts

A fixed-price incentive contract requires an initial fixed price and also permits adjusting profit and establishing the final contract price using a formula that compares the relationship of total final negotiated cost to total target cost. The final price is subject to a price ceiling, which is negotiated at the outset. There are two basic forms of fixed-price incentive contracts: 1) fixed-price incentive (firm target), and 2) fixed-price incentive (successive targets).

Fixed-Price Incentive (Firm Target)
A fixed-price incentive (firm target) contract specifies a target cost, a target profit, a price ceiling, and a profit adjustment formula.

Fixed-Price Incentive (Successive Targets)
A fixed-price incentive (successive targets) contract requires an initial target cost, an initial target profit, and an initial profit adjustment formula. The targets and the formula are used to establish the firm target profit, including a ceiling and floor for the firm target

profit, the production point at which the firm target cost and firm target profit will be renegotiated, and a ceiling price that is the maximum that may be paid to the seller. (*See* FAR 16.403.)

1.5.3.6 Fixed-Price Award Fee Contracts

A fixed-price award fee contract is sometimes used when it is difficult to include other incentives because seller performance cannot be measured objectively. A fixed-price award fee contract establishes a fixed price and includes profit (or base fee) paid for satisfactory contract performance. It also establishes an award fee that can be earned by the seller in addition to the fixed price based on the results of periodic evaluations of the seller's performance against an award fee plan. (*See* FAR 16.404.)

1.5.3.7 Cost Plus Incentive Fee Contracts

A cost plus incentive fee contract is a cost-reimbursement contract that also provides for an initially negotiated fee, which can be adjusted later by using a formula based on the relationship of total allowable costs to target costs. (*See* FAR 16.405-1.)

1.5.3.8 Cost Plus Award Fee Contracts

A cost plus award fee contract is a cost-reimbursement contract that also provides for an award fee pool that the contractor may earn in whole or in part during performance, based on the results of periodic evaluations of the contractor's performance against an award fee plan. (*See* FAR 16.405-2.)

1.5.4 Other Contract Types

1.5.4.1 Indefinite Delivery Contracts

There are three types of indefinite delivery contracts:

- Definite quantity,
- Indefinite quantity, and
- Requirements.

Definite Quantity Contracts

These contracts are generally used to purchase a definite quantity of goods or services, with an indefinite schedule for deliveries or performance.

Requirements Contracts

These contracts are generally used to purchase all required quantities of specified goods or services needed by a buying organization for a specified period of time. (*See* FAR 16.5.)

Indefinite Quantity Contracts

Indefinite delivery/indefinite quantity (IDIQ) contracts provide for the purchase of an indefinite quantity of goods or services for a fixed period of time. The indefinite quantity provisions sometimes include a guaranteed minimum quantity and normally include a maximum quantity. Deliveries or performance is scheduled by placing orders with the contractor. Examples of variations of IDIQ of contracts include:

- Delivery order contracts, which are IDIQ contracts generally used to purchase goods; and

- Task order contracts, which are IDIQ contracts generally used to purchase services.

Delivery or performance is accomplished by placing orders with the contractor.

1.5.4.2 Governmentwide Agency Contracts (GWACs) and Multi-Agency Contracts (MACs)

GWACs and MACs are federal contracts for goods or services issued by one federal contracting entity, but available for use by many or all federal contracting entities. (*See* FAR 16.5.)

1.5.4.3 Time-and-Materials (T&M) Contracts

T&M contracts are used to buy goods or services based on direct labor hours and the cost of materials required for contract performance. The labor hour rates are negotiated between the parties for each type or category of labor required. Each fixed hourly labor rate is a composite rate that includes wages, overhead, general and administrative expense, and profit. A T&M contract may be used when it is not feasible to accurately estimate the extent or duration of the work or to anticipate costs with any reasonable degree of confidence. T&M contracts that do not require the contractor to provide materials are also referred to as "labor hour contracts." (*See* FAR 16.6.)

1.5.4.4 Labor Hour Contracts

A labor-hour contract is a variation of the T&M contract, differing only in that materials are not supplied by the contractor. (*See* FAR 16.602.)

1.5.4.5 Letter Contracts

A letter contract is normally a brief, written, preliminary contractual instrument that authorizes a contractor to begin performance immediately. Letter contracts are used to initiate performance when performance is required, but there is insufficient time to negotiate a more formal, complete contract. (*See* FAR 16.603.)

1.5.4.6 Basic Agreements

A "basic agreement" is a written instrument of understanding, negotiated between a buyer and a seller, that contains terms and conditions that will apply to future contracts between the parties during the term of the agreement. A basic agreement contemplates separate future contracts that will incorporate, by reference or attachment, the appropriate terms and conditions negotiated in the basic agreement. A basic agreement itself is not a contract. (*See* FAR 16.702.)

1.5.4.7 Basic Ordering Agreements

A "basic ordering agreement" is similar to a basic agreement, but may also include terms and conditions intended to describe the types of goods and services that may be ordered in the future, to define pricing methods that will apply, or to define ordering or delivery procedures. A basic ordering agreement itself is not a contract. (*See* FAR 16.703.)

1.6 Contracting Methods

"Contracting method," "contracting methodology," and "acquisition method" are terms that refer to the processes used to solicit, request, or invite bids, quotes, or offers with the intent to award a contract.

This section describes the following contracting methods and contracting tools:

- Sealed bidding (1.6.1),

- Negotiation (1.6.2),

- Simplified acquisition (1.6.3), and

- Contracting tools (1.6.4), including:

  o Federal Supply Schedules,

  o Electronic commerce,

  o Modular contracting,

  o Auctions and reverse auctions,

  o Request for information,

  o Sales contract,

  o Framework pricing arrangement,

  o Performance-based contract,

  o Gap fillers,

  o Pre-qualification, and

  o Broad agency announcements.

1.6.1 Sealed Bidding

"Sealed bidding" is an acquisition method in which the buyer issues an invitation for bids (IFB). The IFB is publicized by distributing it to prospective bidders from a bidder's list the buyer maintains. Typically, the IFB is posted in a publicly accessible place.

The *FAR* states that contracting officers must use sealed bidding when:

- Time permits the solicitation, submission, and evaluation of sealed bids;

- The award will be made on the basis of price and other price-related factors;

- It is not necessary to conduct discussions with the responding offerors about their bids; and

- There is a reasonable expectation of receiving more than one sealed bid.

The federal government posts the IFB on the FedBizOpps website (**www.fbo.gov**). Buyers should allow sufficient time between issuing the IFB and the public bid opening to allow prospective bidders adequate time to prepare and submit bids.

An IFB should describe the buyer's requirements clearly, accurately, and completely. Unnecessarily restrictive specifications or requirements that might unduly limit the number of bidders are discouraged for most organizations and prohibited for the federal government. The invitation includes all documents (whether attached or incorporated by reference) necessary to submit a complete bid. The federal government requires that agencies use a fixed-price contract, or in some situations a fixed-price with economic price adjustment contract, for sealed bidding. (*Excerpted from* Margaret G. Rumbaugh, *Understanding Government Contract Source Selection* (Management Concepts, Inc., 2010.)

Bids received before the opening date and time should be kept in a secure location. All bids are opened publicly on the date and time specified in the IFB. In order to be considered for award, the bids must comply with the requirements in the IFB, unless the IFB permitted alternate bid submission. (*See* FAR 14.401.)

1.6.1.1 Two-Step Sealed Bidding

"Two-step sealed bidding" combines two competitive methods and is sometimes used to obtain the benefits of sealed bidding when adequate specifications, requirements, or descriptions are not available. The first step consists of the solicitation for submitting technical proposals, which are evaluated on technical merits only. The second step involves submitting sealed price bids only by those bidders who submitted acceptable technical proposals in the first step. (*See* FAR 14.5.) The solicitation tool normally used for two-step sealed bidding is the request for technical proposals (RFTP). RFTPs are used to pre-qualify bidders relative to their technical capacity to perform.

1.6.2 Negotiation

"Negotiation" is a contracting method that can be used to solicit proposals either competitively or noncompetitively, and may include discussions or negotiations. Negotiation is a flexible process where the buyer issues a solicitation called a "request for proposal" (RFP) that includes a statement of work, evaluation criteria, and relevant terms and conditions, among other information. The offerors responding to an RFP submit proposals by the date and time specified in the RFP. After the buyer receives proposals from offerors, the buyer evaluates the proposals in accordance with the evaluation criteria stated in the RFP. After evaluation, the buyer may award a contract based on the initial proposal submission (award without discussions), provided that the RFP stated that award without discussions might occur. If buyers need more information from sellers before making an award decision, then the parties enter into a negotiation that typically affords offerors an opportunity to revise their offers before final evaluation and contract award.

1.6.2.1 Single/Sole-Source Negotiation

"Single-source negotiation," also known as "sole-source negotiation," refers to contracting with a single provider in lieu of competitive contracting. Single/sole-source negotiation usually occurs because the provider is the only source of the product or service required (or the business relationship with the provider is of strategic importance to the buying organization) and is normally based on a long-term relationship built on mutual trust.

1.6.2.2 Unsolicited Proposal

An "unsolicited proposal" is a proposal from a prospective contractor to provide goods or services without a prior formal or informal solicitation from a contracting office. According to the *FAR*, a valid unsolicited proposal must:

- Be innovative and unique;

- Be independently originated and developed by the offeror;

- Be prepared without government supervision, endorsement, direction, or direct government involvement;

- Include sufficient detail to permit a determination that government support could be worthwhile and the proposed work could benefit the agency's research and development or other mission responsibilities;

- Not be an advance proposal for a known agency requirement that can be acquired by competitive methods; and

- Not address a previously published agency requirement. (*As per* FAR 15.6.)

Readers may consult FAR 15.602 for more information about the federal government's policies on unsolicited proposals.

1.6.3 Simplified Acquisition

"Simplified acquisition" is a less rigorous method for entering into relatively low dollar threshold contracts. Simplified acquisition is used to reduce administrative costs and remove any unnecessary burdens on potential suppliers. Simplified acquisition is also used to provide socioeconomically favored groups an opportunity to do business with the buyer in a less-structured way. Typically, there is a maximum dollar threshold to use simplified acquisitions. These dollar thresholds may vary between organizations. The federal government's simplified acquisition threshold is stated at FAR 2.101. Simplified acquisition usually occurs without the elaborate and formal solicitation techniques required by sealed bidding and negotiation.

The buyer issues a request for quotations (RFQ) in simplified acquisition. The response to an RFQ is a quotation. *See* the next sub-section on RFQs for more information.

Credit cards are often used for even smaller dollar value acquisitions ("micropurchase"). The federal government uses the term "purchase cards" instead of credit cards. The federal government's micropurchase threshold is defined at FAR 2.101.

1.6.3.1 Request for Quotations (RFQ)

The RFQ is a solicitation document used when a specification or statement of work already exists and the buyer needs to get information from potential sellers about price and delivery. The RFQ differs from the RFP in that an RFQ is not an offer. (*See* FAR 2.101.) The resulting purchase order is either an offer or a counter offer. (*See* Richard Christou, *Drafting Commercial Agreements*, third ed. (London: Sweet & Maxwell, 2005): 104.)

It is important to note that a quotation is not an offer and, consequently, the buyer cannot accept a quote to form a binding contract. When the buyer issues an order in response to a supplier's quotation, it does not establish a contract. The order is an offer by the buyer to the supplier to buy certain supplies or services upon specified terms and conditions. A contract is established when the supplier accepts the offer by either signing the purchase order or through performance.

1.6.4 Contracting Tools

Contracting tools are resources available to support the contracting methods previously described. For example, electronic commerce may be used to issue a sealed bidding (IFB) or negotiated solicitation (RFP). (*See* **FIGURE 1-6-1** on page 35)

1.6.4.1 Federal Supply Schedules (FSS)

The FSS program is directed and managed by the General Services Administration (GSA). The FSS program provides federal agencies, as well as some state and local governmental agencies, with a streamlined process for obtaining commonly used commercial goods and services. Fundamentally, the supply schedules are a series of pre-negotiated IDIQ contracts that can be used by authorized sources to issue orders for required goods or services.

1.6.4.2 Electronic Commerce

"Electronic commerce" refers to a group of automated processes that can be used to accomplish business transactions using the Internet. In the federal sector, the contracting officer must make available through FedBizOpps (**www.fbo.gov**) solicitations synopsized through FedBizOpps, including specifications and other pertinent information determined necessary by the contracting officer. Transmissions to FedBizOpps must be in accordance with the interface description *available at* **www.fbo.gov**.

GSA's Acquisition Systems Division is responsible only for the operation and maintenance of the FedBizOpps system and website. The content of any notice published on FedBizOpps is the sole responsibility of the agency that has issued the notice.

Electronic commerce has advanced to include mobile phones. This new form of electronic commerce is called "M-commerce." For Internet merchants, this means one e-commerce site can be accessed and used by customers on every type of device: computers, smart phones, and tablets.

Electronic commerce involves using computer networks to improve organizational performance. Some of the organizational performance gains possible with electronic commerce include:

- Increasing profitability,
- Gaining market share,
- Improving customer service, and
- Delivering products faster.

Electronic commerce is more than ordering goods from an online catalog; it involves all aspects of an organization's electronic interactions with its stakeholders—the people who determine the future of the organization. (*Derived from* Richard T. Watson (ed.), "Electronic Commerce: The Strategic Perspective," *available at* **http://globaltext.terry.uga.edu/userfiles/pdf/electronic%20commerce.pdf**.)

1.6.4.3 Modular Contracting

Modular contracting is an acquisition strategy that breaks a large "grand design" program into discrete components that are easier to manage. The Information Technology Management Reform Act (Pub. L. 104-106, also known as the Clinger-Cohen Act) increases modular contracting techniques when buying major IT systems. Section 5202 of this law directs federal agencies to use modular contracting "to the maximum extent practicable" in the acquisition of major IT systems. Following Clinger-Cohen, the president issued Executive Order 13011, which instructed agencies to apply modular contracting "where appropriate" and "to the maximum extent practicable." (*See Guide for Modular Contracting* (GSA Office of Governmentwide Policy, Emerging Information Technology Policies Division, Washington, DC, 1998).)

Modular contracting is intended to reduce program risk and to incentivize contractor performance while meeting the government's need for timely access to rapidly changing technology. Consistent with the agency's IT architecture, agencies should, to the maximum extent practicable, use modular contracting to acquire major systems of IT. Federal agencies may also use modular contracting to acquire non-major systems of IT.

When using modular contracting, an acquisition of a system of IT may be divided into several smaller acquisition increments that:

- Are easier to manage individually than would be possible in one comprehensive acquisition;

- Address complex IT objectives incrementally in order to enhance the likelihood of achieving workable systems or solutions for attainment of those objectives;

- Provide for delivery, implementation, and testing of workable systems or solutions in discrete increments, each of which comprises a system or solution that is not dependent on any subsequent increment in order to perform its principal functions;

- Provide an opportunity for subsequent increments to take advantage of any evolution in technology or needs that occur during implementation and use of the earlier increments; and

- Reduce risk of potential adverse consequences on the overall project by isolating and avoiding custom-designed components of the system. (*See* FAR 39.103.)

1.6.4.4 Auctions and Reverse Auctions

"Auctions" are sales transactions in which goods or services are offered and sold to the highest bidder. The price is not negotiated but is set by competitive and open bidding. In the article, "How to Compete in a Reverse Auction" in the May 2007 issue of *Inc. Magazine*, author Max Chafkin states:

> During a "reverse auction," a customer allows suppliers only a short window of time to bid down the price on their products or services. The practice was pioneered by automotive and aerospace buyers, which used reverse auctions to procure commodity parts. Today, many large companies use them to buy everything from paper clips to their employee health care plans.

1.6.4.5 Request for Information (RFI)

An RFI may be used as a part of market research to gather information from vendors in the marketplace.

RFIs are sometimes issued to determine the availability of products and services, and to gather market information on capabilities to perform when more casual forms of market research do not produce the desired results. An RFI might request information about a company's supplies and services to determine if the company is qualified to participate in a future acquisition. Many buyers use the Internet to obtain such information from potential suppliers and written RFIs are issued less frequently.

1.6.4.6 Sales Contract

A "sales contract" is a business arrangement in which all elements of the transaction are determined and defined between the parties at the time of contract formation, including mutual assent, exchange of consideration, capacity to contract, and legal purpose.

1.6.4.7 Framework Pricing Arrangements

A "framework pricing arrangement" is a contract that is definitive in all respects except pricing. The agreement or contract specifies a predetermined index, formula, algorithm, or method (the framework) for the calculation of price at the point of sale. Framework agreements are typically used when the buyer knows they are likely to have a need for particular products or services, but are unsure of the extent or schedule, so framework agreements are commonly set up to cover things like office supplies, IT equipment, consultancy services, and repair and maintenance services.

1.6.4.8 Performance-Based Contract

A "performance-based contract" is a contract that is structured around the purpose of the work to be performed, or the goal to be achieved, as opposed to either the manner in which the work is to be performed or a broad, imprecise statement of work. The requirements for performance-based contracts should be clear, complete, and objective, with measurable outcomes.

Performance-based service contracts are described in more detail in *CMBOK* 4.5.3 and FAR 37.6.

1.6.4.9 Gap Fillers

Contracts may have gaps or lack of continuity in the terms and conditions. This is possible when the parties use different forms with different terms, also called a "battle of forms" (see UCC 2-204). Article 2 of the UCC includes "gap filler" provisions. Such "gap fillers" are other sources of pertinent information that may be used to fill a gap when a contract fails to adequately address something. The UCC is frequently used as a gap filler, as are memoranda of understanding, letter contracts, and other agreements (when appropriate).

1.6.4.10 Prequalification

"Prequalification" refers to a buyer's announcement of interest, including criteria for selecting companies or specific products that meet predetermined requirements. Such prequalification may be documented in a qualified bidders list or a qualified products list. For example, a qualified products list identifies those products that have been examined, tested, and have satisfied all applicable qualification requirements. (*See* FAR 2.101.)

1.6.4.11 Broad Agency Announcements

A "broad agency announcement" is a general announcement of an agency's research interests, including criteria for selecting proposals and soliciting the participation of all offerors capable of satisfying the agency's needs. (*See* FAR 2.101.)

1.7 Contract Financing

"Contract financing" is a way to obtain the funds necessary for performing the contract, including payment methods, loan guarantees, advanced payments, progress payments, and contract funding. The advantages of contract financing include increasing competition, assisting small businesses, reducing contractor risk, and expediting performance. Contract financing issues are important in both the commercial and government contracting environments.

1.7.1 Commercial Contract Financing

Financing in commercial contracting includes:

- Obtaining loans and lines of credit from financial institutions,

- Obtaining advance funding of accounts receivable or funding of purchase orders from private firms, or

- Obtaining funds from venture capitalists.

It may also include negotiating favorable payment clauses, such as a sizable down payment or milestone payments as the work progresses.

Commercial contract financing could also include such methods as:

- Commercial advance payments made before performance begins,

- Commercial interim payments made after some work starts, and

- Partial delivery payments made after receiving and accepting some of the total work to be performed.

1.7.2 Government Contract Financing

In some cases, successfully completing a government contract may require the government's assistance with some form of contract financing. For example, contract financing might be appropriate in a multimillion-dollar contract that requires the contractor to make substantial initial investments in labor, materials, and production costs. In cases where the government determines that some type of contract financing is appropriate, it usually takes one of two forms, 1) private or 2) government.

According to FAR Part 32, when a contractor requests financing, the government contracting officer is to consider the following order of preference for methods of contract financing:

1. Private financing,

2. Customary contract financing other than loan guarantees,

3. Loan guarantees,

4. Unusual contract financing, and

5. Advance payments. (*See* FAR 32.106.)

Private financing without government guarantee includes loans from financial institutions, sale of bonds or stocks, and loans from family members or other private sources. However, the contractor should not be required to obtain private financing at unreasonable terms or from other agencies. In addition, under assignment of claims provisions, a financing institution can receive payments directly from the government in consideration for making a private loan to a contractor. (*See* FAR 32.8.)

Progress payments may be either customary or unusual. Customary progress payments are those made under the general guidance of FAR 32.501-1. There are different rates for large and small businesses and there is a limit on the percentage of work accomplished that is subject to customary progress payments. Any other progress payments are unusual and must have prior authorization from the head of the contracting activity. (*See* FAR 32.501-2.)

If a contractor applies for a conventional loan to finance a government contract, the private financial institution involved may submit an application for a loan guarantee to the Federal Reserve Bank in its district. The Federal Reserve Bank acts as a fiscal agent and transmits the application to the guaranteeing agency. The president has designated seven agencies as guaranteeing agencies:

- Department of Defense,
- Department of Energy,
- Department of Commerce,
- Department of the Interior,
- Department of Agriculture,
- General Services Administration, and
- The National Aeronautics and Space Administration.

The guaranteeing agency makes a determination of eligibility in accordance with the applicable FAR provisions. If the loan guarantee is approved, the private financial institution makes the loan and collects interest from the contractor, the guaranteeing agency guarantees the loan, and the Federal Reserve Bank acts as the "intermediary" or fiscal agent that processes the paperwork between the private financial institution and the contractor. (*See* FAR 32.3.)

"Advance payments" are advances of money by the government to a contractor. They are not measured by performance; they are made in anticipation of performance. Advance payments are the least-preferred method of contract financing and generally should not be authorized if other types of financing are reasonably available to the contractor in adequate amounts. Loans and credit at excessive interest rates or other exorbitant charges, or loans from other government agencies, are not considered reasonably available financing. Contractors may apply for advance payments before or after the award of a contract. If advance payments are approved, a special bank account may be required. Interest is usually charged on the advance payments and any interest earned is refundable to the government. (*See* FAR 32.4.)

1.7.2.1 Other Financing Methods

Other government contract financing methods may include the following:

- Progress payments may be based on costs incurred as work progresses under the contract.

- Loan guarantees are made by Federal Reserve Banks on behalf of designated guaranteeing agencies to enable contractors to obtain financing from private sources.

- Progress payments based on a percentage or stage of completion. Payments must be commensurate with work accomplished.

- Performance-based payments are made for work that meets the performance objectives.

1.7.3 Small Business Financing

Federal, state, and local governments offer a wide range of financing programs to help small businesses start and grow their operations. These programs include low-interest loans, venture capital, and scientific and economic development grants. State and local economic development agencies, as well as numerous nonprofit organizations, provide low-interest loans to small business owners who may not qualify for traditional commercial loans.

Loan applications typically require information such as a business plan, credit report, income tax returns, bank and financial statements, and other legal documents such as articles of incorporation and licenses. (*Refer to* **www.sba.gov**.)

1.8 Intellectual Property

"Intellectual property" refers to property developed from creations of the mind such as inventions and literary and artistic works. (*Refer to* "What is Intellectual Property?" World Intellectual Property Organization, Publication No. 450(E), June 2003.) Intellectual property rights include any or all of the following: patent, trademark, copyright, trade secret, trade name, service mark, and the like. Contracting professionals should be aware of the various forms of intellectual property, the need for intellectual property that may be part of contract requirements, and the limitations on the use of intellectual property imposed by law.

Typical examples of intellectual property include the following:

- Patent (1.8.1),
- Copyright (1.8.2),
- Trademark and servicemark (1.8.3),
- Technical data (1.8.4),
- Licensing (1.8.5),
- Royalties (1.8.6),
- Trade secret (1.8.7),
- Shop rights (1.8.8), and
- Nondisclosure agreement (1.8.9). (*See* **FIGURE 1-8-1** on page 37.)

1.8.1 Patent

A patent is a government grant of exclusive rights to an inventor that prohibits others from making, using, or selling an invention. The current term for patents is generally for 20 years. (Desktop Guide to Basic Contracting Terms, seventh edition (Ashburn, Virginia: NCMA, 2012.) Patents are issued by the U.S. Patent and Trademark Office (USPTO). U.S. patent grants are effective only within the United States, U.S. territories, and U.S. possessions. What is granted is not the right to make, use, offer for sale, sell, or import, but the right to exclude others from making, using, offering for sale, selling, or importing the invention. Once a patent is issued, the patentee must enforce the patent without the aid of the USPTO (*as per* **www.uspto.gov/patents/resources/general_info_concerning_patents.jsp#**).

As per the USPTO, there are three types of patents:

- Utility patents,
- Design patents, and
- Plant patents.

1.8.1.1 Utility Patents

"Utility patents may be granted to anyone who invents or discovers any new and useful process, machine, article of manufacture, or composition of matter, or any new and useful improvement thereof." (**www.uspto.gov/patents/resources/general_info_concerning_patents.jsp#**.)

1.8.1.2 Design Patents

"Design patents may be granted to anyone who invents a new, original, and ornamental design for an article of manufacture." (**www.uspto.gov/patents/resources/general_info_concerning_patents.jsp#**.)

1.8.1.3 Plant Patents

"Plant patents may be granted to anyone who invents or discovers and asexually reproduces any distinct and new variety of plant." (**www.uspto.gov/patents/resources/general_info_concerning_patents.jsp#**.)

1.8.2 Copyright

As per the U.S. Patent and Trademark Office:

Copyright is a form of protection provided to the authors of "original works of authorship" including literary, dramatic, musical, artistic, and certain other intellectual works, both published and unpublished. The 1976 Copyright Act generally gives the owner of copyright the exclusive right to reproduce the copyrighted work, to prepare derivative works, to distribute copies or phonorecords of the copyrighted work, to perform the copyrighted work publicly, or to display the copyrighted work publicly.

The copyright protects the form of expression rather than the subject matter of the writing. For example, a description of a machine could be copyrighted, but this would only prevent others from copying the description; it would not prevent others from writing a description of their own or from making and using the machine. Copyrights are registered by the Copyright Office of the Library of Congress.

(**www.uspto.gov/patents/resources/general_info_concerning_patents.jsp#**.)

1.8.3 Trademark and Servicemark

As per the U.S. Patent and Trademark Office:

A trademark is a word, name, symbol, or device that is used in trade with goods to indicate the source of the goods and to distinguish them from the goods of others. A servicemark is the same as a trademark except that it identifies and distinguishes the source of a service rather than a product. The terms "trademark" and "mark" are commonly used to refer to both trademarks and servicemarks.

Trademark rights may be used to prevent others from using a confusingly similar mark, but not to prevent others from making the same goods or from selling the same goods or services under a clearly different mark. Trademarks that are used in interstate or foreign commerce may be registered with the USPTO.

(www.uspto.gov/patents/resources/general_info_concerning_patents.jsp#.)

1.8.4 Technical Data

Federal Acquisition Regulation (*FAR*) 27.401 defines *data* as "recorded information, regardless of form or the media on which it may be recorded." As per the "Rights in Data—General" clause found at FAR 52.227-14, *technical data* is defined as:

> [R]ecorded information (regardless of the form or method of the recording) of a scientific or technical nature (including computer databases and computer software documentation). This term does not include computer software or financial, administrative, cost or pricing, or management data or other information incidental to contract administration. The term includes recorded information of a scientific or technical nature that is included in computer databases.

Rights to use technical data developed by a contractor may vary depending on the source of funds used to develop the item, component, process, software, or software documentation.

1.8.4.1 Data Rights

In any contract that may involve the production of scientific or technical data, the rights to those data must be clearly ascribed. Generally, a "rights in data" clause will protect the government's right to use and distribute—without limitation, free from payment or royalties, and with immunity against lawsuits for copyright infringement or misuse of data—any data produced under a contract funded by the government. (*See* FAR 27.4.)

"Limited rights data" means data other than computer software that embody trade secrets or are commercial or financial and confidential or privileged, to the extent that such data pertain to items, components, or processes developed at private expense, including minor modifications. (*See* FAR 52.227-14, "Rights in Technical Data—General.")

All contracts that require data to be produced, furnished, acquired, or used in meeting contract performance requirements must contain terms that delineate the respective rights and obligations of the government and the contractor regarding the use, reproduction, and disclosure of that data. Data rights clauses do not specify the type, quantity, or quality of data that is to be delivered, but only the respective rights of the government and the contractor regarding the use, disclosure, or reproduction of the data. Accordingly, the contract shall specify the data to be delivered.

There are different kinds of data rights in government contracts that are defined as follows.

Limited Rights

"Limited rights" means the rights of the government in limited rights data as set forth in a "Limited Rights Notice."

Limited Rights Data

"Limited rights data" means data other than computer software that embody trade secrets or are commercial or financial and confidential or privileged, to the extent that such data pertain to items, components, or processes developed at private expense, including minor modifications. (Agencies may, however, adopt the following alternate definition: "Limited rights data" means data (other than computer software) developed at private expense that embody trade secrets or are commercial or financial and confidential or privileged.)

Restricted Computer Software

"Restricted computer software" means computer software developed at private expense and that is a trade secret, is commercial or financial and confidential or privileged, or is copyrighted computer software, including minor modifications of the computer software.

Restricted Rights

"Restricted rights" means the rights of the government in restricted computer software as set forth in a "Restricted Rights Notice."

Unlimited Rights

"Unlimited rights" means the rights of the government to use, disclose, reproduce, prepare derivative works, distribute copies to the public, and perform publicly and display publicly, in any manner and for any purpose, and to have or permit others to do so. (*See* FAR 27.401.)

1.8.5 Licensing

A license permits the usage of software, patents, trademarks, or technology by another entity without transferring ownership rights. The sale of a license permits the use of patents, trademarks, or other technology to another entity. A license covering a patent, technical or proprietary data, technical assistance, know-how, or any combination of these may be granted by a U.S. firm to a foreign firm or government to produce, co-produce, or sell an article or service within a given sales territory. An "exclusive license" grants this right without competition from any other licensees or from the licensor. For a "non-exclusive" license, competition may be permitted with other licensees and/or the licensor. Licensing involves the many procedures administrative agencies perform in conjunction with issuing various types of licenses. (*Desktop Guide to Basic Contracting Terms*, seventh edition (Ashburn, Virginia: NCMA, 2012).)

A licensing agreement represents a partnership between an intellectual property rights owner (i.e., "licensor") and another individual or entity authorized to use such rights (i.e., "licensee") in exchange for an agreed payment (i.e., "fee" or "royalty"). There are different types of licensing agreements, including:

- Technology license agreement,
- Trademark licensing and franchising agreement, and
- Copyright license agreement.

Typically, these agreements are part of a contract since many rights are involved and not just one type of intellectual property right. (*Derived from* "Licensing of Intellectual Property Rights; a Vital Component of the Business Strategy of Your SME," World Intellectual Property Organization, *available at* **www.wipo.int/ sme/en/ip_business/licensing/licensing.htm**.)

1.8.6 Royalties

According to USLegal.com:

> A royalty is a percentage of gross or net profit or a fixed amount per sale to which a creator of a work is entitled that is agreed upon in a contract between the creator and the manufacturer, publisher, agent, and/or distributor. Inventors, authors, movie makers, scriptwriters, music composers, musicians, and other creators contract with manufacturers, publishers, movie production companies, producers, and distributors to be paid royalties in exchange for a license to manufacture and/or sell the product.

(**http://definitions.uslegal.com/r/royalties/**.)

For example, Microsoft invented the Windows operating system for personal computers as a means of managing files and performing operations. Computer manufacturers such as Dell and IBM pay a royalty to Microsoft in exchange for being allowed to use the Windows operating system in their computers.

1.8.7 Trade Secret

According to *Black's Law Dictionary*, a trade secret is a "formula, process, device, or other business information that is kept confidential to maintain an advantage over competitors." (*Black's Law Dictionary*, ninth edition (2009).) Such information may include:

> …a formula, pattern, compilation, program, device, method, technique, or process…that 1) derives independent economic value, actual or potential, from not being generally known or readily ascertainable by others who can obtain economic value from its disclosure or use, and 2) is the subject of reasonable efforts, under the circumstances, to maintain its secrecy.

(*Ibid.*)

The Trade Secrets Act (18 U.S.C. 1905) provides criminal penalties for the unauthorized disclosure of confidential commercial information.

1.8.8 Shop Rights

"Shop rights" are the right of an employer to use, without payment of royalties, an invention conceived by an employee in the course of employment or through the use of the employer's facilities if the employee was not hired to perform such work.

1.8.9 Nondisclosure Agreement

A "nondisclosure agreement" is a legally binding document setting forth the conditions under which proprietary information is offered, received, used, and protected between two or more parties. A nondisclosure agreement may also be called a "confidentiality agreement." A typical nondisclosure agreement will contain a provision that requires confidentiality. For example, the party receiving the proprietary information or intellectual property agrees:

- Not to make, use, or sell the disclosed information without first entering into an agreement with the other party to do so;
- Not to disclose the information received to any third party without the other party's prior written consent;

- Not to duplicate, copy, or replicate in any manner the information and materials provided; and

- To return any and all materials and information related to the disclosed information to the other party within a stated period of time.

2.0 Acquisition Planning and Strategy Competencies

The acquisition planning and strategy competencies cover the beginning of the acquisition cycle from planning to protest. These competencies review important considerations and decisions that are necessary to form a successful contract. Contract managers need to understand the importance of these strategic decisions and their impact on the resulting contract. Many problems of contract performance and administration can be avoided during this acquisition strategy phase.

In this set of competencies, the following acquisition planning and strategy competencies will be examined:

- Acquisition planning, market research, and marketing (2.1);

- Drafting solicitations (2.2);

- Responding to solicitations (2.3);

- Cost and price analysis (2.4);

- Negotiation (2.5);

- Source selection and contract award (2.6); and

- Protests (2.7).

FIGURE 2-1-1 on page 62 illustrates all of the acquisition planning and strategy competencies.

2.1 Acquisition Planning, Market Research, and Marketing

2.1.1 Acquisition Planning

"Acquisition planning" is the process by which efforts of all personnel responsible for an acquisition are coordinated and integrated through a comprehensive plan for fulfilling the buyer's need in a timely manner at a reasonable cost. It includes developing the overall strategy for management of the acquisition. Acquisition planning includes all the activities and events required for both buyers and sellers to prepare for, negotiate, and form a binding contractual arrangement. (*See* FAR 2.101.)

Planning is an essential preliminary component to successfully completing virtually any effort. In the government and business environments, planning is required to apply scarce resources to the goal-directed activity necessary to accomplish the mission or functions of the organization. As it relates to the contracting profession, planning in general and acquisition planning in particular is a function that begins at the point when a customer expressed a need for goods or services, or delivered a requirement to the contracting office.

Acquisition planning is a collaborative effort that requires input from the entire acquisition team, including technical, program management, finance/budget, legal personnel, and the customers they serve. The objective is to satisfy the customer in terms of cost, quality, and timeliness while minimizing administrative operating costs. (*See* FAR 1.102-2.)

Planning should begin as early in the development process as possible, before the traditional first customer contact, and should have an inward as well as outward focus, particularly as it relates to an important acquisition planning tool—market research.

2.1.2 Market Research

In the expanded role of a business professional, the contract manager should consider implementing a comprehensive market research process. Not only should he or she determine the degree to which external sources could meet requirements, but also look within the organization for information that might be valuable to anticipate future requirements. Thus, market research has both internal and external components.

2.1.2.1 Internal Market Research

For contracting professionals to be of maximum value to the management team and to the overall organization, they must know the "business of the business," including the mission of the buyer's organization generally and the goal of the acquisition at hand specifically. The contracting professional needs to know who the organization's internal and external customers or stakeholders are, what the organization's goals are, and what structures, processes, and procedures are in place to accomplish the goals. Fundamentally, the contracting professional needs to become immersed in the organization's activities and plans to the maximum extent possible. This level of involvement can usually be accomplished by activities such as:

FIGURE 2-1-1. Acquisition Strategy Competencies

- Reviewing historical information on prior acquisitions to know who the internal customers are;

- Attending regular management meetings, including those of the internal customers;

- Receiving detailed briefings on the functions and processes of internal customers;

- Participating in short-term assignments of customer work units;

- Reading pertinent customer-oriented professional publications (magazines, journals, and online subscriptions);

- Serving on cross-functional process improvement teams, or similar ad hoc teams, addressing issues that may have little or nothing to do with contracting but provide information about the "business of the business"; and

- Sharing information on contracting issues and trends with other managers.

The basic goal of internal market research is to learn as much as possible about the organization; how it does business and how it has used goods and services acquired in the past. A secondary goal of internal market research is to develop good working relationships with the customer base. Understanding the internal customers is an important aspect to develop a collaborative team environment. Get

to know the customers and end-users of the supplies and services. Learn what is important to them and why so that these priorities can be incorporated into acquisition planning documents.

In addition to doing internal market research, contract managers should also be involved in external market research.

2.1.2.2 External Market Research

Conducting external market research is typically done after a requirement is defined or at least conceptualized. External market research may also be done without a specific requirement when the contract manager knows what the internal customer's preferences are as a result of internal market research (discussed previously). Whether it is used in response to a specific need or not, the external market research looks for useful information about capabilities and limitations in the commercial marketplace. The basic intent of external market research is to find information to help determine the best method to obtain required goods and services consistent with pertinent law, regulation, and/or corporate policy.

Just as the contracting professional can use internal market research to better understand and anticipate the actual and potential needs of the customer,

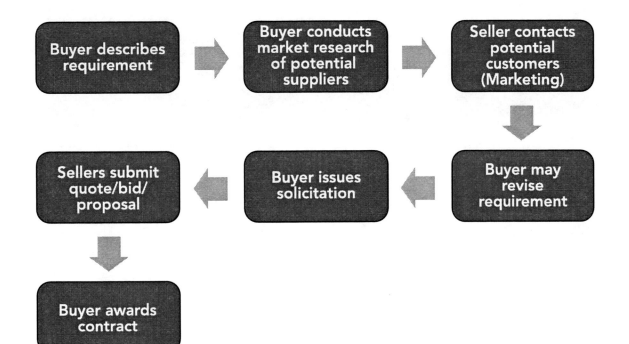

FIGURE 2-1-2. Market Research Cycle

external market research should be used to better understand the actual and potential capabilities of suppliers. Standard external market research techniques include:

- Reviewing historical information on similar prior acquisitions for related market research information;

- Reviewing pertinent professional news, trade, association, or industry publications;

- Contacting knowledgeable third-party sources of unbiased information regarding potential sources;

- Attending trade or professional association shows and exhibits;

- Contacting customers of potential sources for past performance information;

- Reviewing catalogs and other printed or electronic information published by potential sources;

- Contacting potential sources for specific capabilities information or briefings;

- Issuing requests for information; and

- Joining pertinent professional organizations and attending their meetings.

Though the amount of external market research conducted will vary according to the complexity of the anticipated effort and other issues, the results should be formally documented for current and future use. Buyers conduct market research to determine potential suppliers and suppliers look for potential customers through their marketing efforts.

FIGURE 2-1-2 illustrates a typical market research cycle. The cycle begins with the buyer's requirement and ends with the buyer awarding the contract. Throughout the process, the seller may contact potential customers who may have a need for their products and services. When sellers contact potential customers, it is also called "marketing." The federal government has strict rules about potential contractors contacting buyers after issuing a solicitation.

2.1.3 Marketing

Marketing for a business involves positioning the company to satisfy the market's needs. There are four critical elements in marketing, commonly called the "four P's":

- "Product"—The right product to satisfy the needs of the target market.

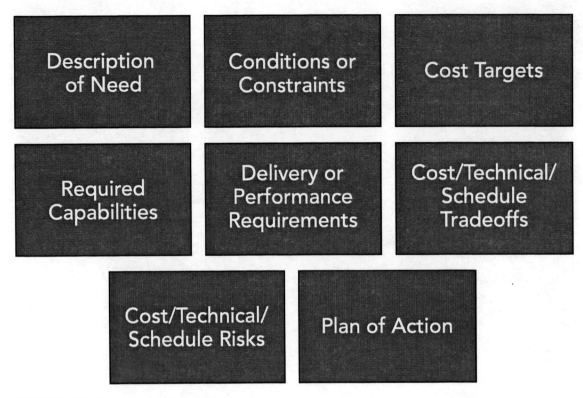

FIGURE 2-2-1. Acquisition Plan Contents

- "Price"—The right product offered at the right price.
- "Place"—The right product at the right price available in the right place to be bought by customers.
- "Promotion"—Informing potential customers of the availability of the product, its price, and its place.

Each of the four P's is a variable companies control in creating the marketing mix that will attract customers to their business. Marketing involves how to use these variables to be profitable.

"Product" refers to the goods and services offered to customers. The product should meet the needs of a particular target market. Product attributes include:

- Quality,
- Features,
- Options,
- Services,
- Warranties, and
- Brand name.

"Price" refers to how much a company charges for their product or service. Pricing should cover cost per item and include a profit margin. Pricing should be a balance between merely covering costs and earning exorbitant profits. The former make it impossible to grow and the latter could price the company out of the market.

"Place" refers to the distribution channels used to get the company's product to their customers.

"Promotion" refers to the advertising and selling part of marketing. It is how the company lets customers know what they have for sale. The purpose of promotion is to get customers to understand what the product is, what it can be used for, and why customers want to buy it. The objective is to let customers know that the company's product satisfies the customer's needs.

The four P's should work together in the company's marketing mix. Customer research is a key element in building an effective marketing mix. Companies should know the target market and competitors to offer a product that will appeal to customers and avoid costly mistakes. (*Refer to* Cole Ehmke, Joan Fulton, and Jayson Lusk; "Marketing's Four P's: First

Steps for New Entrepreneurs"; Purdue University; Purdue Extension EC-730 (March 2007).)

2.2 Drafting Solicitations

"Drafting solicitations" refers to the processes employed and the means used to solicit, request, or invite bids or offers that will normally result in issuing a contract. Buyers develop a comprehensive plan to fulfill their product and service requirements in a timely manner at a reasonable price. This process involves developing an overall strategy for the purchase (acquisition strategy or methodology), including conducting market research, developing a strategy, drafting the solicitation, and selecting a supplier. Sellers develop and execute a strategy for winning a contract that includes marketing strategies, pricing strategies, and responding to the solicitation.

This section describes the following competencies:

- The acquisition plan (2.2.1),
- Documenting requirements (2.2.2),
- Other considerations (2.2.3), and
- Publicizing requirements (2.2.4).

2.2.1 The Acquisition Plan

The acquisition plan should reflect a collaborative effort involving significant stakeholders. The level of detail provided in the acquisition plan will vary depending on the anticipated dollar value, level of complexity, degree of significance, and other appropriate factors. A written plan may not be required for simple, straightforward, low dollar value purchases. In the absence of a written plan, contract managers should ensure that there is a common understanding and consensus among the stakeholders regarding the acquisition methodology. When required, written acquisition plans should clearly explain all pertinent issues relating to the acquisition as detailed in **FIGURE 2-2-1** on page 64 and described as follows:

- *A description of the need to be satisfied*—The description should be concise, yet complete enough to explain:
  - o What the need is,
  - o How it came to be needed at the current time,
  - o Any pertinent history of related prior acquisitions, and

  - o How they were acquired.

- *An explanation of conditions or constraints that relate to the proposed acquisition*—These conditions or constraints might include:
  - o The need for compatibility with existing or future equipment or systems;
  - o Implementation constraints caused by space, personnel, or other limitations;
  - o Budget constraints, particularly as they relate to lease vs. purchase decisions; and
  - o Other known constraints that could influence cost, schedule, capability, or performance issues.

- *The established cost targets for the acquisition, with sufficient explanation to support the targets*—This section should include discussions of the following issues, as appropriate:
  - o The make-or-buy decision,
  - o Estimated life cycle costs,
  - o Design-to-cost,
  - o Should-cost analysis, and
  - o Other cost issues determined to be of significance.

- *The required capabilities or performance to be acquired*—This section should address such issues as speed, accuracy, reliability, ease of use, and other pertinent performance characteristics when acquiring goods. When acquiring services, the required performance standards or knowledge requirements that are required to provide the services should be discussed. This section should also explain how the goods or services being acquired relate to and will satisfy the need.

- *Delivery or performance period requirements*—This section should provide the required delivery date(s) or the required period of performance, as well as an explanation for why the dates or periods were selected. If an emergency or urgent condition exists that has influence on the delivery or performance requirements, explain that relationship, as well as the incremental impact that the emergency may have on cost considerations.

- *Trade-offs related to the previously defined plans for cost, technical performance, capability, and schedule requirements*—Explain the following:
  - o What trade-off issues are likely to occur,
  - o The degree to which a trade-off decision may

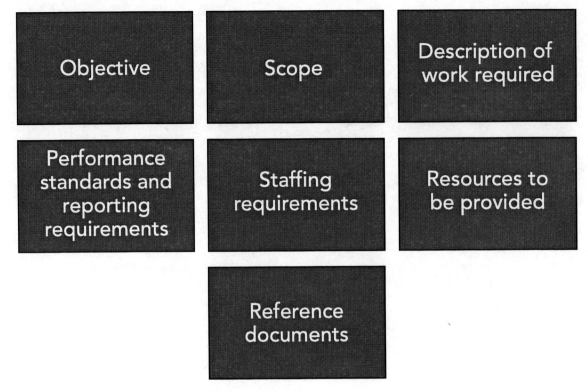

FIGURE 2-2-2. Typical Statement of Work Contents

imp8act other plan components, and

o How trade-offs may impact the overall acquisition plan.

- *A discussion of the level of risk associated with the technical, cost, schedule, and other pertinent aspects of the plan*—This discussion should clearly define the following:

  o The anticipated risks;

  o The strategies or actions planned or taken to eliminate, reduce, or mitigate risk to an acceptable level; and

  o The likely consequences that might result from failure to achieve goals.

- *The contracting plan of action*—Taking into consideration all of the pertinent plan components previously mentioned, the contracting plan of action should address such issues as:

  o Proposed sources that can provide the required goods or services including, for government agencies, consideration of the various socioeconomic programs prescribed;

  o The degree to which the acquisition will be subject to competition;

  o The contract type(s) proposed for use;

o The source selection process, including an explanation of how the evaluation factors relate to the achievement of the goals of the acquisition;

o How the contract will be administered after issuance;

o Milestones or target dates for completion; and

o Any other pertinent issues of concern. (*See* FAR 7.105.)

The need for acquisition plans differs in the public and private sectors. In the public sector, such plans are normally required for significant or complex acquisitions. In the private sector, such plans may be created as the result of corporate policy or as a matter of professionalism or convenience. Regardless of whether they are required or desired, acquisition plans provide valuable information regarding the initial intent of a proposed acquisition and a basic roadmap to check progress against during the acquisition cycle.

2.2.2 Documenting Requirements

Preparing requirements, also referred to as "solicitation preparation," is arguably the single most important function in the acquisition cycle. Although

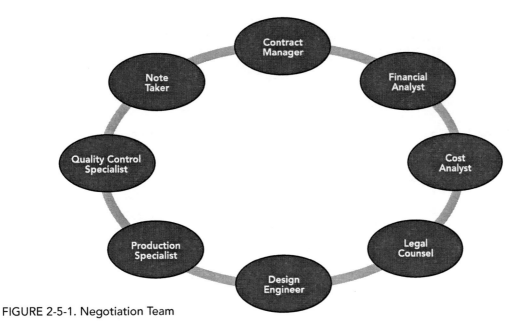

FIGURE 2-5-1. Negotiation Team

acquisition planning activities also have a significant impact on the success or failure of the proposed acquisition, requirements preparation usually provides the last major opportunity for contract managers to influence the solicitation package before potential suppliers see it. It is therefore important that contract managers, in collaboration with the customer and internal sources with specific expertise, write a solicitation package that accurately reflects the customer's needs and communicates those needs and other related information clearly and concisely to potential suppliers. The end goal should always be to satisfy the customer's need, at a fair price, with the minimum acceptable level of risk. This is an area in which contract professionals help the customer by sharing their knowledge of the marketplace, including business practices such as terms and conditions and inspection and acceptance criteria. The contract manager can work closely with the program office or primary customer and prepare a solicitation package that satisfies a majority of needs.

Some acquisitions are very simple, others are exceedingly complex, and the majority usually fall somewhere in between. The format and content of solicitation packages and the resulting contracts are often mandated by law, regulation, or corporate policy, such as the use of the "Uniform Contract Format" for government contracting professionals.

Regardless of the complexity, the solicitation package normally provides the following information:

- Statement of work,
- Contract type and method,
- Terms and conditions,
- Evaluation procedures,
- Instructions for preparing and submitting proposals, and
- Other relevant information.

2.2.2.1 Statement of Work (SOW)

The SOW is likely the single most important document in the solicitation package. The SOW is the document that describes the goods or services required in sufficient detail to provide potential offerors with a complete understanding of the requirement. Generally, there are three basic types of SOWs:

- Design,
- Performance, and
- Functional.

The differences among them relate to the degree to which the requirement is defined and explained, from specific to general. Each type of SOW has its own advantages and disadvantages, and SOWs often reflect elements of all three basic types in order to completely describe the requirement.

Design SOWs

A design SOW is most often used when the buyer requires a specific manufactured good. Design SOWs are extremely detailed, and usually define all required materials, production processes, and specifications such as size, shape, color, tolerances, etc. Design SOWs also frequently provide specific requirements related to quality, inspection, packaging, and related needs. The basic intent of a design SOW is to document the requirement with such specificity so any competent seller can provide the product, and that the end product will be exactly what the buyer required.

The degree of precision inherent in design SOWs also presents challenges for the contracting professional. Design SOWs may restrict the competitive process by imposing too many specifications that result in no-bid decisions from sellers that might otherwise be willing to provide the product. Design SOWs may also result in higher costs, since the seller may have to use materials and processes that are different from those used in the normal course of business. Additionally, the buyer assumes virtually total performance risk when contracting with design SOWs, since the seller is performing based on the buyer's design and specification requirements. As a result of these drawbacks, using a design SOW is commonly discouraged whenever a less restrictive type of SOW can be reasonably expected to provide the results required.

Performance SOWs

Performance SOWs are less restrictive than design SOWs. Performance SOWs define requirements in terms that relate to minimum acceptable standards or ranges of acceptable performance. A performance SOW may require a particular approach or a particular type of product, but it leaves most of the "how" decisions to the contractor. Performance SOWs are normally considered to enhance competition because they enable a contractor to use their company's strengths and creativity to satisfy the requirement.

Functional SOWs

The functional SOW is the least restrictive of the three basic SOW types. Functional SOWs describe requirements in terms of the end purpose, expected result, or final objective, rather than in terms of how the work effort is to be performed. Though the functional SOW may include needed quality standards or minimum essential characteristics, it focuses primarily on the "what" aspects of the requirement. Functional SOWs provide the contractor with the maximum degree of flexibility and innovation in determining how best to satisfy the buying organization's needs. It is for this reason that functional SOWs are the preferred type of SOW in most government and commercial contracting organizations.

Another alternative with some popularity is the "statement of objectives" (SOO). The SOO provides basic, top-level objectives of an acquisition and is provided in the request for proposal in lieu of a government-written SOW. It provides potential offerors the flexibility to develop cost-effective solutions and the opportunity to propose innovative alternatives. The disadvantage to using this approach is that significantly different technical solutions may be proposed, thus requiring additional evaluation time or specialized evaluation personnel. Performance-based service acquisition is discussed in more detail in *CMBOK* 4.5.

In practice, SOWs rarely fall neatly into one of these three types. Most SOWs reflect characteristics of at least two, if not all three SOW types in order to adequately describe the requirement.

2.2.2.2 Typical SOW Contents

Regardless of which type or types used, SOWs normally contain at least some of the elements detailed in **FIGURE 2-2-2** on page 66.

Objective

An "objective" is a brief statement of the goal to be achieved, the end product desired, or the basic purpose of the requirement.

Scope

The "scope" is a general statement defining the parameters or boundaries of expected actions, required performance, or products required. Scope statements can be viewed as the "fenced in area" in which the contractor performs.

Description of Work Required

The "description" is a sufficiently detailed explanation of what is required. The description often contains an explanation of interfaces that will impact the work effort, a history of how the required effort came to be needed, required place of performance, issues and problems that require resolution, and other pertinent information. To the maximum extent possible, the description should be outcome-focused, providing the contractor as much flexibility as possible for determining how to accomplish the work required to achieve the objective within the defined scope. When necessary, specific performance elements can be prescribed, but they should be kept to a minimum.

Performance Standards and Reporting Requirements

"Performance standards and reporting requirements" are an explanation of how the contractor's work effort will be evaluated in terms of quantity, quality, frequency, or other appropriate measures. The performance standards should clearly define the expected, required, or acceptable level of performance that will be anticipated from the contractor. The standards need to be achievable and measurable. Reporting requirements should explain how often and in what format any required progress or performance reports will be provided. Both performance standards and reporting requirements should be limited to the minimum necessary to achieve effective and efficient contract administration.

Staffing Requirements

If personnel with certain specific qualifications are required to perform the work (e.g., electrical engineer, Certified Public Accountant, etc.), these qualifications should be included. However, in most cases, the contractor should have the option to propose staffing levels and composition to accomplish the required work.

Resources to be Provided

Specify any space, equipment, materials, services, information, or other resources that will be provided to the contractor.

Appropriate Reference Documents

Provide a list of any pertinent reference documents that may have been discussed in the SOW, or that may be required by the contractor to ensure adequate performance or clarify contract requirements.

As previously mentioned, SOWs may be of varying lengths and levels of complexity, depending on the needs of the buying organization. While not all SOWs will necessarily contain all the elements noted in this section, each SOW should be constructed to provide a complete, clear, and concise description of the requirement. Well-constructed SOWs reduce risk, enhance competition, and help achieve organizational goals.

2.2.2.3 Contract Type and Method

The solicitation package should also define the contract type and method that the acquisition will use. An explanation of commonly used contract types and methods were presented earlier in *CMBOK* sections 1.5 and 1.6. As they relate to the solicitation package, the contract type and method used should complement the degree of complexity and risk associated with the overall SOW. The use of certain contract types and methods for specific types of acquisitions is sometimes required by law, regulation, or corporate policy. In other cases, the contract type and method used is a discretionary decision made by the contracting professional. Sometimes the contracting professional must blend more than one contract type into a solicitation, such as including both firm-fixed-price and time-and-material line items when appropriate. The choice of contract type and method is frequently a business decision, influenced by a variety of organizational and marketplace dynamics. The contracting professional should strive to ensure that the contract type and method chosen are:

- Consistent with the level of complexity and uncertainty inherent in the SOW;

- Reflect an acceptable level of risk-sharing between the buyer and seller;

- Conform to applicable law, regulation, or corporate policy; and

- Help promote the successful accomplishment of the contracting function and the overall goals of the organization.

2.2.2.4 Terms and Conditions

In addition to the SOW and contract type and method, terms and conditions are another component of the requirements package that helps define the business relationship between the buyer and seller and the rights and obligations of both parties to the contract. The primary function of terms and conditions is to eliminate or reduce the risk of contract ambiguity, which is often the source of disputes and misunderstandings. Most government and commercial contracting organizations include standard terms and conditions related to certain contract types in all solicitations and resulting contracts. In many cases, the selection of clauses that comprise the terms and conditions is an automated function that occurs within the buyer's contract writing software programs. In other cases, terms and conditions can be selected from a "shopping list" provided for the appropriate contract type. In still other cases, specific clauses must be crafted to meet an individual need, usually with the assistance of legal counsel and other professionals.

Though frequently referred to as "boilerplate," and though sometimes included in solicitations as little more than an afterthought, terms and conditions are another risk mitigating tool that contracting professionals can use to enhance the likelihood of success. Contract managers need to be able to work with both boilerplate and customized terms and conditions. Carefully reviewing the solicitation's terms and conditions can reveal gaps that could cause confusion, unnecessary terms and conditions that could adversely affect price or performance, or terms and conditions that conflict with each other. Terms and conditions should be reviewed to ensure that each one included serves a legitimate purpose, is required or provides a direct benefit to the acquisition in question, promotes an acceptable level of risk-sharing between buyer and seller, and does not impose unreasonable burdens on prospective offerors.

2.2.2.5 Evaluation Procedures

The solicitation package should clearly indicate the general procedures that the buyers will use to evaluate proposals and the decisions that they will make as the basis for an award. The method of acquisition normally determines the basis for the award. Using an invitation for bids requires that the selection be based on price or price-related factors. Using a request for proposal indicates a negotiated procurement where various factors, with potentially different degrees of relative significance, will serve as the basis for award. The evaluation procedures can influence, either positively or negatively, the quality of bids or proposals received from offerors. Buyers must take great care in determining evaluation factors—too few factors may result in receiving inadequate proposals that are impossible to evaluate; too many factors may result in receiving exceedingly complex proposals or none at all.

Though price will always be included as an evaluation factor, other factors—such as cost realism, technical excellence, management capability, past performance, and other relevant factors—can and should be included as appropriate. Each evaluation factor should be independent of the other factors, again to reduce the potential for confusion. It is also important to advise potential offerors of the relative significance of the evaluation factors to each other.

Though it is not required nor may it be desirable to provide all the details of the evaluation plan in the solicitation, it is important for potential offerors to understand how proposals will be evaluated, the factors that will make up the evaluation, and the relative importance of each evaluation factor to each other and to the overall acquisition.

2.2.2.6 Instructions for Preparing and Submitting Proposals

The final piece of the solicitation package is the instructions provided to potential offerors for preparing and submitting proposals. The purpose of the instructions is to help ensure that uniform (or nearly uniform) submissions are received from offerors to permit a fair and unbiased evaluation process. Offerors usually pay close attention to the instructions since failure to comply with them may result in a proposal not being considered. The instructions can be very specific or very general, depending on the needs of the buying organization.

Instructions usually contain:

- Information regarding page format and page number limitations,
- The order of topic presentation,
- Required content to be addressed,
- Whether separate technical and price proposals are required,
- If the award will be made with or without discussions,
- If verbal presentations will be required,
- The number of copies to submit,
- The media proposals that may be submitted on,
- The place to submit proposals to,
- The due date and time, and
- Similar types of information.

The contracting professional has to balance the need for the information required to be provided in the proposal with the costs offerors will incur in proposal preparation. The instructions should be constructed to enable the offerors to submit the best possible proposals while also ensuring that the information received in the proposals will provide the necessary data for a thorough and appropriate evaluation and award decision.

2.2.3 Other Considerations

Once the solicitation package has been completed, there are a number of techniques that the buyer can use to validate the solicitation package's completeness and accuracy before it is formally issued. Some of these techniques include an independent technical review obtaining marketplace comments and pre-solicitation notices and conferences.

2.2.3.1 Independent Technical Review

The solicitation package can be reviewed by technical experts, legal counsel, and other resources within the organization to ensure it is complete and accurate. Normally, this independent technical review team is composed of people who had no prior involvement with the solicitation package.

2.2.3.2 Obtaining Marketplace Comments

A draft of the solicitation package can be issued to potential offerors requesting review and comments or suggestions. This pre-release review sometimes yields useful suggestions for revision that might otherwise have been overlooked. However, the contracting professional needs to be aware of the possibility that potential offerors may use this opportunity for preliminary marketing purposes and may try to influence content changes in the solicitation that enhance their ability to successfully compete for the contract.

2.2.3.3 Pre-solicitation Notices and Conferences

Pre-solicitation notices and conferences can be used to help identify potential interested sources and can provide a forum to explain technical or complicated aspects of the solicitation. These efforts can sometimes separate the interested potential sources from the merely curious ones.

2.2.4 Publicizing Requirements

Issuing solicitation packages and the degree to which competitive proposals are sought often depends on the buying organization. Government contracting professionals are subject to a law- and regulation-based preference for fully competitive procurements. Though there are a number of authorized exceptions permitting less than full and open competition and sole-source acquisition, the general rule in government contracting is to seek the maximum level of meaningful competition whenever possible.

Commercial contracting professionals sometimes work in organizations that also have a preference for competitive acquisition. However, other commercial considerations—such as supply chain agreements, approved source lists, and other business decisions—can sometimes have an influence on the degree to which competition is pursued. When competition is a goal, the buying organization normally uses publicizing as a technique to ensure adequate competition.

2.2.4.1 Publicizing—Government Agencies

Government contracting organizations are normally required to post solicitation packages exceeding certain dollar thresholds for full and open competition on an official Internet website: **www.fbo.gov**. Though certain limitations can apply to these postings (including small business set-asides, restricting competition to firms that hold GSA Federal Supply Schedule contracts, and other discriminators), the fundamental intent of these postings at a single location is to provide a uniform source of information to the business community in pursuit of a required or desired level of competition.

Solicitation packages that do not exceed certain dollar thresholds are normally competed by selecting an appropriate number of potential offerors and issuing the solicitation to them. Though the number of firms solicited usually varies depending on the dollar value and complexity of the acquisition, the intent is to seek a level of competition that will reasonably result in the receipt of multiple proposals, which will produce a competitive award and will not cause undue administrative burden to the agency.

Some government agencies also advertise open solicitations on their official Internet websites, usually under a title such as "Business Opportunities," "Current Business Opportunities," "Doing Business With…" or a similar title.

2.2.4.2 Publicizing—Commercial Organizations

Commercial contracting organizations may advertise their requirements in newspapers, trade journals, professional publications, and similar media. They may also provide the solicitation to capable firms in their supply chain, or as the result of other business agreements. Commercial firms may also advertise business opportunities on their official Internet websites, in much the same manner as government agencies sometimes do.

Although the methods for publicizing active solicitation packages may vary, the basic purpose does not. When competition is required or desired, the solicitation should be advertised uniformly to ensure that the target market of potential offerors is aware of the opportunity. Additionally, some other concepts should be used to make the publicity effort more meaningful.

Solicitations should remain open or active for a period of time sufficient to permit potential offerors enough time to carefully and completely review and analyze all aspects of the requirement, make an informed bid/no-bid decision, and prepare and submit their best proposal. Though the contracting professional often faces internal pressures to reduce the acquisition cycle time, the length of time a solicitation remains open can have a direct impact on the number and quality of proposals received and the success or failure of the overall acquisition.

Contracting professionals should normally provide a period of time within the solicitation period for potential offerors to submit written questions and/or to attend pre-proposal conferences. These activities are often very valuable in clarifying the buyer's intent, as well as technical or other complex aspects related to the acquisition. These conferences can sometimes include a "walkthrough" when the contract will be performed at the buyer's location, or other pertinent information that could be of value to potential offerors.

The need for changes or amendments to a solicitation may become evident after responding to written questions or after a pre-proposal conference. When appropriate, the solicitation should be modified to reflect the necessary changes and the due date for proposals should be extended to provide offerors the opportunity to respond to the changes.

The degree to which solicitation packages are publicized usually has a direct impact on both the quality and quantity of competitive proposals received. The solicitation phase is often a target when trying to reduce acquisition cycle time, primarily because a reduction in the length of time a solicitation remains open has little or no immediate adverse impact on the buying organization. Contracting professionals need to remain aware, however, that an inadequate solicitation period often affects the overall quality of the acquisition.

2.3 Responding to Solicitations

The contracting methods described in *CMBOK* 1.6 explain different ways to prepare solicitations.

Sealed bidding, for example, has different rules than contracting by negotiation. Although there are differences in responding to the various solicitation types, there are also similarities. For example, solicitations, regardless of type, have due dates and require companies to provide pricing and technical information in order to make a contract award decision. This section explains ways to respond to these different solicitation types, and concludes with an overview of preparing unsolicited proposals in the absence of a formal solicitation.

Many companies conduct a "bid/no-bid" analysis to determine if they are going to pursue a contract. This analysis typically includes assessing the competition and the probability of winning. The company also needs to determine if it has the resources to prepare a competitive or winning bid/proposal. Some companies have a bid and proposal budget set aside to fund the bid/proposal writing process.

2.3.1 Responding to an Invitation for Bid (IFB)

Buyers issue an IFB using the sealed bidding method of acquisition. The IFB should state the buyer's requirements clearly and provide all of the documents necessary to submit a complete bid. The bidder should provide enough information for the buyer to make an award decision. Such information includes identifying the technical solution that meets the buyer's requirements. Since contract award is typically based on price or price-related factors, companies should be especially careful in pricing the bid.

The company submitting the lowest responsive and responsible bid wins the contract award. Thus, the bid must be responsive to the IFB's requirements and the bidder must be responsible to complete the work on time and within the budget.

2.3.2 Responding to a Request for Proposal (RFP) or Request for Quotation (RFQ)

Buyers issue an RFP or RFQ using the negotiated method of acquisition. Typically, the dollar value distinguishes one from the other method. The RFQ is usually a small dollar value acquisition, whereas an RFP is for larger dollar value acquisitions.

"Proposal preparation" refers to the activities and events required to submit an offer or quotation, usually in response to a solicitation. Proposal preparation includes defining the proposal team (including any teaming or subcontracting decisions), writing the proposal, and submitting the proposal. Typically, specific areas to focus on are the SOW, invoicing and payment, and the contract type.

It is always a good idea to start by addressing the evaluation factors and subfactors with the highest priority or weighting, as identified in the solicitation. Make clear that the company understands the agency's needs and explain how the company will meet the agency's requirements by providing specific details. Illustrations and graphics are effective ways to explain processes, cause and effect relationships, and management structure. A successful proposal not only responds to the requirements set forth in the RFP, but convinces the agency that it has done so better than any other proposal. When writing a proposal, the authors need to keep the customer and its requirement in mind at all times. Some agencies recommend that evaluators quickly skim the proposal before doing a detailed evaluation. The company must show the evaluator during this quick read that the proposal is clear, concise, organized, and easy to evaluate.

The proposal should not only meet the RFP's requirements, but also be:

- Clearly written, or the evaluators will not understand the company's win strategy;

- Well organized, or the evaluators will not know where to find important information;

- Concisely written, so evaluators are not confused by overly complicated language; and

- Supported with credible statements, or the evaluators will not believe the company's solution will work. (*Adapted from* Margaret G. Rumbaugh, *Understanding Contract Source Selection* (Management Concepts, Inc., 2010.)

2.3.3 Preparing an Unsolicited Proposal

If a company has a new and innovative idea it would like a buyer to consider, it may consider submitting an unsolicited proposal. Unsolicited proposals should be prepared without assistance or endorsement from the buyer.

Unsolicited proposals should include sufficient detail to allow the buyer to make a decision if it will benefit the buyer's organization. It should also identify technical information about the work, including any proprietary or data rights restrictions. There should also be a statement of the period of time that the proposal is valid. The federal government has specific rules about unsolicited proposals at FAR 15.6.

The audience for a proposal (solicited or not) usually includes both managers and engineers and they both evaluate proposals differently. For example, managers review proposals to see if the plan for solving the problem is cost effective, whereas engineers evaluate proposals to see if the plan is technically feasible. (*See* Pennsylvania State University, **www. writing.engr.psu.edu/workbooks/proposals.html**.)

2.4 Cost and Price Analysis

One of the primary functions of contract management professionals is the determination of fair and reasonable prices when negotiating new contracts and contract modifications. This determination can have both subjective and objective evaluation components. A fair and reasonable price is one that is deemed fair to both sides when considering areas such as terms and conditions, cost or price, quality, contract performance, and/or any other areas subject to negotiation. Other considerations include such things as the law of supply and demand and other statutory, regulatory, and judgmental factors.

Two techniques used to determine a fair and reasonable price are "cost analysis" and "price analysis." Price analysis is the process of examining and evaluating a prospective price without evaluation of the separate cost elements and proposed profit of the individual offeror. Cost analysis, on the other hand, is the review and evaluation of separate cost elements and profit or fee on a proposal as needed to determine a fair and reasonable price or determine cost realism. Reasonable costs are those costs that a prudent seller, under the constraint of competition, would recognize as justifiable in amount and that a prudent buyer would recognize as a fair cost of doing business.

2.4.1 Price Analysis

Price analysis is the preferred method in determining a fair and reasonable price. It is done under fixed-price contract types where the seller does not provide the buyer with the detailed cost breakdown of cost elements. When conducting price analysis, one does not have access to these different cost elements and the price reasonableness determination is made by comparing previous prices, published

Negotiation Objective for a Fixed-Price Contract		
	Minimum	Objective	Maximum
Unit Price	$	$	$

FIGURE 2-5-2. Negotiation Objective for a Fixed-Price Contract

price lists, or market prices. Price analysis is an evaluation of the "bottom line" and does not concern itself with the eventual costs to the supplier or its ultimate profit margin.

For some supplies and services, the laws of supply and demand determine a fair and reasonable price. In the federal government, adequate price competition is an important element in determining a fair and reasonable price using price analysis. A price is based on adequate price competition if two or more responsible offerors, competing independently, submit priced offers that satisfy the government's expressed requirement. Award will be made to the offeror whose proposal represents the best value where price is a substantial factor in source selection—and there is no finding that the price of the otherwise successful offeror is unreasonable. In addition, there should be a reasonable expectation, based on market research or other assessment, that two or more responsible offerors, competing independently, would submit priced offers in response to the solicitation's expressed requirement, even though only one offer is received from a responsible offeror.

Price analysis clearly demonstrates that the proposed price is reasonable in comparison with current or recent prices for the same or similar items, adjusted to reflect changes in market conditions, economic conditions, quantities, or terms and conditions under contracts that resulted from adequate price competition.

Some organizations use different methods of price analysis, including parametric estimating, which involves collecting and organizing historical information through mathematical techniques and relating this information to the work output being estimated. Another method is to conduct a price trend analysis using indexes. Economic escalation ("inflation") is a concept of how prices vary over time, such as consumer prices paid for cars or factory prices paid for tools or raw materials. The Bureau of Labor Statistics, Department of Commerce, has established price level indexes that provide a measure of price movement in comparison with prices in a base year.

2.4.2 Cost Analysis

Cost analysis is done on all contract types where the seller provides the buyer with detailed information about the proposed contract price. When conducting cost analysis, it is important to understand the different types of cost:

- *Direct costs*—those that are specifically identifiable with a contract requirement, including, but not restricted to, costs of material and/or labor directly incorporated into an end item;

- *Indirect costs*—those that are not directly identifiable with a specific cost objective, but subject to two or more cost objectives;

- *Fixed costs*—those that, for a given period of time and range of activity (called the "relevant range"), do not change in total but become progressively smaller on a per-unit basis as volume increases; and

- *Variable costs*—those costs that change with the rate of production of goods or performance of services.

Cost analysis also involves evaluating detailed cost elements, such as the following:

- *Labor hours*—human resources that may be either direct or indirect costs, depending on the circumstances. To analyze direct labor costs, one evaluates the hours and rates involved. The quantity and mix of labor types is important as well.

- *Materials*—include raw materials, subassemblies, or components incorporated into an end product. Sellers typically include a bill of materials that itemizes individual material elements, as well as their quantity and cost.

- *Profit*—the difference between total cost and revenue. It is the amount realized by a contractor after the cost of performance (both direct and indirect) is deducted from the amount to be paid under the terms of the contract. Profit is the motivator for efficient and effective contract performance.

Negotiation Objective for a Cost-Plus-Fixed-Fee Contract			
Cost Element	Minimum	Objective	Maximum
Direct	$	$	$
Indirect	$	$	$
Total Cost	$	$	$
Profit/Fee	$	$	$
Total Cost Plus Fee	$	$	$

FIGURE 2-5-3. Negotiation Objective for a Cost-Plus-Fixed-Fee Contract

The objective of cost analysis is to determine what it should cost to perform the contract requirements, given reasonable contractor economy and efficiency. One way the federal government does this is through certified cost or pricing data.

2.4.2.1 Certified Cost or Pricing Data

The Truth in Negotiations Act (TINA) requires federal government contractors to submit certified cost or pricing data in certain circumstances. Cost or pricing data are all facts that, as of the date of price agreement or, if applicable, an earlier date agreed upon between the parties that is as close as practicable to the date of agreement on price, prudent buyers and sellers would reasonably expect to significantly affect price negotiations. Cost or pricing data are factual, not judgmental, and are verifiable. While they do not indicate the accuracy of the prospective contractor's judgment about estimated future costs or projections, they do include the data forming the basis for that judgment. Cost or pricing data are more than historical accounting data; they are all the facts that can be reasonably expected to contribute to the soundness of estimates of future costs and to the validity of determinations of costs already incurred.

FAR 15.403-5 provides submission instructions for cost or pricing data and for submission of other than cost or pricing data to be included in the solicitation. Instructions will include:

- Whether or not cost or pricing data are required;

- That, in lieu of submitting cost or pricing data, the offeror may submit a request for exception from the requirement to submit cost or pricing data;

- Any information other than cost or pricing data that is required; and

- Necessary pre-award or post-award access to the offeror's records.

It is important to note that cost or pricing data by itself is not sufficient information to determine cost/price reasonableness or realism. A comprehensive explanation of the significant factors and assumptions must support the cost data developed. This data must be analyzed and evaluated before it can be considered fair and reasonable.

2.5 Negotiation

"Negotiation" is a communication process where two parties attempt to reach agreement. Negotiation does not need to be a process where one party "wins" at the other's expense. It is possible and preferable that both parties finish negotiations feeling that they have "won." Despite the fact that both parties have different interests, they have a common goal: to negotiate a fair and reasonable contract. Please refer to *CMBOK* 2.6 for more information about source selection using the negotiated acquisition method.

2.5.1 Preparation

Preparation is the most important step in the negotiation process. Buyers and sellers have unique advantages going into negotiations. Buyers know how much money is available and the amount and nature of competition. Sellers know the basis for cost estimates and where there is flexibility in their proposals. Nonetheless, both parties must plan for negotiations. Thorough preparations can lead to smooth negotiations, a good contract, fewer changes, and successful performance.

The first step in the preparation process is to understand the acquisition and each party's

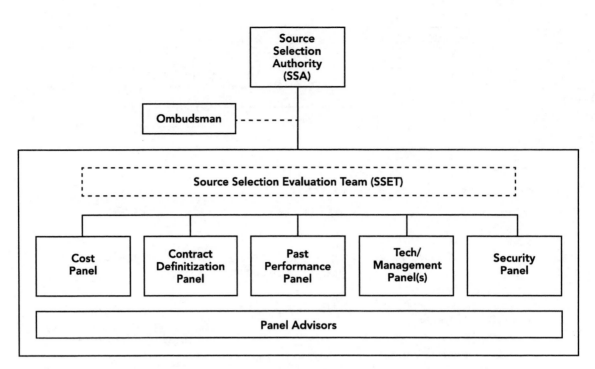

FIGURE 2-6-1. Sample Negotiated Source Selection Structure (*derived from* Margaret G. Rumbaugh, *Understanding Government Contract Source Selection* (Management Concepts, Inc., 2010)

critical objectives. Both parties must know what the requirement is, why it is needed, and whether it was bought before. Although it is not always possible for every negotiator to do an in-depth analysis of each acquisition, it is important to get to know as much as possible before beginning. Sellers must also understand the acquisition. They should know the purpose of the acquisition, the buyer's objectives, whether the buyer is the end-user (or if not, who is the end-user), and the end-user's needs.

2.5.2 The Negotiation Team

The negotiation team is typically comprised of members with different skills. Selecting team members depends on the nature of the acquisition and the experience that each member brings to the team. Team members on each side may include, but are not limited to:

- Contract manager,
- Financial analyst,
- Cost analyst,
- Legal counsel,
- Design engineer,
- Production specialist,

- Quality control specialist, and
- Note-taker. (*See* **FIGURE 2-5-1** on page 67.)

The negotiation teams for the buyer and seller designate a lead negotiator for their team, which is most often the contract manager, depending on the organization's customary practice and line of business. In the case of federal government contracting, the government's lead negotiator is always the contracting officer.

The best scenario occurs when team members have worked together on the acquisition since its early stages from solicitation to proposal submission. Negotiation can be a long process that takes several months, so it is important to put together a team that works well together. Each member of the team must understand and agree with the group's goal or the team will be ineffective. The group must function as a team, reporting to the lead negotiator. It is ineffective to have individuals who conduct side negotiations to protect their own interests. This will jeopardize the team's goals.

2.5.3 Negotiation Objectives

Each negotiation is different, even if the acquisition is for the something previously purchased. The

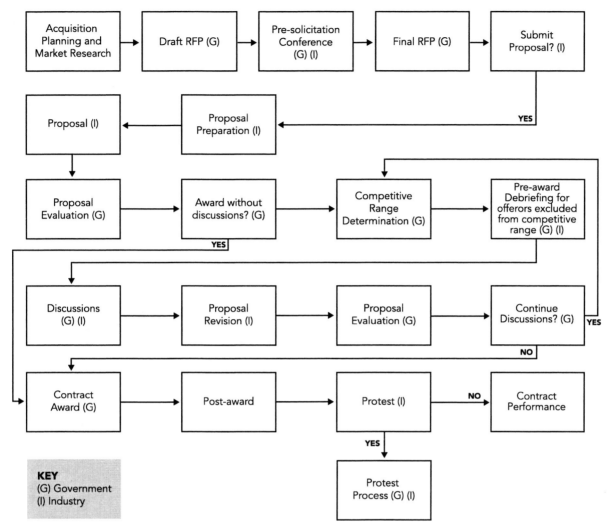

KEY
(G) Government
(I) Industry

FIGURE 2-6-2. **Sample Source Selection Process** (*derived from* Margaret G. Rumbaugh, *Understanding Government Contract Source Selection* (Management Concepts, Inc., 2010)

marketplace may be different, the delivery schedule may be different, and the economy may be different. All of these factors influence pricing decisions and negotiation objectives.

Establishing the negotiation objectives entails more than cost analysis and comparison. Most aspects of a solicitation are negotiable, such as the statement of work, contract type, delivery schedule, warranties, payment terms, terms and conditions, and/or reporting requirements. These aspects may be negotiable depending on the circumstances surrounding the acquisition.

Both buyers and sellers need to establish specific and realistic negotiation objectives. An objective of "the best price we can get" is neither specific nor realistic, as there would be no way of knowing

if the result was the best price. Establishing negotiation objectives is an ongoing process because the negotiation objectives will change as the situation changes.

Based on the requirement, proposed costs, delivery schedule, and risks involved, buyers and sellers prepare a negotiation objective based on the best information available. Since the circumstances change, the objective needs to be flexible. A way to ensure flexibility is to develop three positions in preparing an objective:

* The minimum,

* Objective, and

* Maximum.

By doing so, a range is established that permits movement one way or another depending on the situation. When the seller's objective overlaps the buyer's objective, both parties are satisfied with the final agreement.

FIGURES 2-5-2 and 2-5-3 on pages 74 and 75 illustrate forms to document a negotiation objective for a fixed-price contract and for a cost-plus-fixed-fee contract.

The amount for each position must be defensible. The negotiators must know the exact figures, the reasons for arriving at that number, and the means to justify those figures. Each party should document how they reached the amounts because as the facts surrounding the assumptions change, the positions will change.

The degree of competition, if any, also affects the relevance of negotiation objectives. If the acquisition is competitive, then the competitive forces of the marketplace set the price.

Discussing negotiation objectives during the management review also sets the stage for establishing basic strategies. Presenting pre-negotiation objectives and strategies helps the negotiators prepare for the negotiation by explaining the plan to upper management.

2.5.4 Negotiation Guidelines

Although both parties enter negotiations intending to reach agreement, the fact remains that they approach it from different perspectives. Lack of respect seriously reduces the possibility of reaching agreement. Respect for the individual and his or her authority is paramount to effective negotiations. Each side takes on certain risks when entering a contract, and it is important for the opposing side to not only recognize those risks, but to understand them as well. The first step in understanding is listening carefully to the other side's position and trying to understand it. The only way an agreement can be reached is for both parties to be flexible and compromise.

"Caucus" and "concession" are two techniques employed in negotiations. A caucus is used to break away from formal negotiations for the team to consider a point. When a counter-offer is made, negotiators use a caucus to confer with their team to consider all aspects of the counter-offer. A cau-cus is useful to discuss anything about the ongoing negotiation that you don't want the other team to hear. Negotiators may also caucus when a team member wants to bring to the negotiator's attention an important fact, if a fact needs to be checked with a team member, or if management approval is necessary in order to make a concession or counter-offer. Concessions are also necessary to the negotiation process. Entering into negotiations without an intention to concede any point will not result in a mutual agreement. Sometimes it is necessary to concede an item if your objectives can be met at the same time.

2.5.5 The Negotiation

Negotiators ask questions of the other party to obtain a common understanding and validate facts. The buyer initiates the process of validating assumptions, also known as "fact-finding." Fact-finding can be done through telephone calls, correspondence, and/or meetings. It can take place before the formal negotiation session or at the very beginning of the session, depending on the circumstances. Fact-finding may affect both parties' objectives. If an assumption for a negotiation objective is invalid or even slightly different, the basis for that objective also changes. Thus, conducting effective fact-finding is a vital element of successful negotiations.

The basic format of negotiations is question and answer. The buyer might begin by asking the seller to justify a proposed price or term, and the seller responds by describing their justification. Alternatively, the seller may ask the buyer about an item in the SOW, and the buyer responds by describing how that item fits into the program. Each agreement should be documented so that everyone knows that discussion on that item is considered "closed."

As multiple concessions bring the parties closer to the negotiation range, final agreement also becomes closer. Convincing the other party of your counter-proposal's reasonableness takes logic and salesmanship. Not only does one have to present the basis for why it is reasonable, but one also has to convince the other party that it is in their best interest to accept it.

As an agreement is reached, both parties must document it. The documentation must explain the facts upon which they based the agreement. The purpose of documentation is to establish that both parties accepted the final agreement.

Adjectival Evaluation Rating System	
Outstanding	A proposal that satisfies all of the government's requirements, with extensive detail indicating the feasibility of the approach and a thorough understanding of the problems. The proposal has numerous significant strengths that are not offset by weaknesses. The proposal has an overall low degree of risk.
Good	A proposal that satisfies all of the government's requirements, with adequate detail indicating a feasible approach and an understanding of the problems. The proposal has some significant strengths or numerous minor strengths that are not offset by weaknesses. The proposal has an overall low to moderate degree of risk.
Acceptable	A proposal that satisfies all of the government's requirements, with minimal detail indicating a feasible approach and a minimal understanding of the problems. The proposal has an overall moderate to high degree of risk.
Marginal	A proposal that satisfies all of the government's requirements, with minimal detail indicating a feasible approach and a minimal understanding of the problem. The proposal has an overall high degree of risk.
Unacceptable	A proposal that contains at least one major error, omission, or deficiency that indicates a lack of understanding of the problems. The approach cannot be expected to meet requirements or involves a very high risk. None of these conditions can be corrected without a major rewrite or proposal revision.

FIGURE 2-6-3. Sample Adjectival Evaluation Rating System

Although the narrative may have different formats or styles, the following list identifies some basic information that documentation should include:

- A description of the supplies or services to be purchased, quantities, and delivery schedule;

- The solicitation/proposal number;

- The parties involved, including complete names, addresses, and phone numbers;

- The acquisition history, including information gathered;

- The negotiation objectives and their justifications; and

- A negotiation summary, including:

  o Concessions made and their impact on negotiation objectives,

  o Major items discussed and the parties' positions and outcomes,

  o Use of and reliance on data (including but not limited to price and cost) submitted, and

  o A signed copy of the agreed-to final position.

Both parties keep this documentation in the contract file to explain the final agreement and why it is reasonable. It will allow other personnel who were not involved in the negotiations to track how the negotiators reached the final agreement.

2.6 Source Selection and Contract Award

Determining which company wins a contract is often referred to as the "source selection" and the term is also used to summarize all activities in the evaluation process. This section addresses the different methods of source selection and focuses on negotiated source selection because that method is more time consuming and complex. First, we review the different methods that align with the contracting methods described in *CMBOK* 1.6.

This section describes the following topics related to source selection and contract award:

- Simplified or small purchase acquisition (2.6.1),

- Sealed bidding (2.6.2),

- Negotiated source selection (2.6.3),

- Typical evaluation factors (2.6.4),

- Proposal evaluation techniques (2.6.5),

- Evaluation rating scales (2.6.6),

- Contract award (2.6.7), and

- Contract award practices unique to federal contracting (2.6.8).

2.6.1 Simplified Acquisition

Simplified acquisition source selection is the least complex method because the resulting contracts are less complex and less costly. Typically, simplified acquisitions are conducted at or below a stated dollar threshold. For example, the 2013 simplified acquisition threshold for government contracts is $150,000. State and local governments, as well as corporations, may have similar thresholds.

The basis for awarding a simplified acquisition contract is typically to obtain required supplies or services in a timely manner, and at a fair and reasonable price. Using a competitive process tends to establish fair and reasonable prices. The source selection decision should be documented for future reference.

2.6.2 Sealed Bidding

Source selection in sealed bidding is typically done using price or price-related factors stated in the invitation for bids and the lowest price wins the contract. In federal government contracting, the bids must also be responsive and responsible to be considered for contract award.

A bid is "responsive" when it complies in all material respects with the invitation for bids. Requiring such compliance ensures that bidders have equal footing in the source selection decision. (See FAR 14.301.) To be determined "responsible," a bidder must:

- Have adequate financial resources to perform the contract;

- Be able to comply with the required delivery schedule;

- Have a satisfactory performance record;

- Have a satisfactory record of integrity and business ethics;

- Have the necessary organization, experience, accounting, and operational controls and technical skills, or the ability to obtain them;

- Have the necessary production, construction, and technical equipment and facilities, or the ability to obtain them; and

- Be otherwise qualified and eligible to receive an award under applicable laws and regulations. (See FAR 9.104-1.)

Bids should accept all the terms and conditions of the invitation for bids and the awarded contract should not vary from the terms and conditions of the invitation for bids. The source selection decision should be documented in writing.

2.6.3 Negotiated Source Selection

Negotiated source selection is a more formal process that goes beyond conducting a negotiation. It involves numerous participants with defined roles and duties, as depicted in **FIGURE 2-6-1** on page 76 that illustrates a sample negotiated source selection structure.

The negotiated source selection process has several steps that depend on the nature of the acquisition. Some steps depicted in **FIGURE 2-6-2** on page 77 are not required for every source selection. The chart depicted in **FIGURE 2-6-2** shows a sample source selection process. Since every acquisition is unique, the sequence or number of events may be slightly different.

2.6.4 Typical Evaluation Factors

Evaluation criteria are the factors by which the proposals will be measured for compliance. The evaluation process should focus on the price, technical capabilities, management capabilities, and past performance requirements as set forth in the solicitation.

2.6.4.1 Price

Price (or cost) should always be an evaluation factor. In some cases, such as sealed bidding, price is the only factor. In negotiated procurements, price is always included, but may be of secondary or even lesser significance compared to other evaluation criteria.

2.6.4.2 Technical Considerations

Often required as a separate volume of the proposal, technical considerations relate to how well the offeror understands the requirement and how effective the offeror's proposed solution is in achieving the objectives of the acquisition.

2.6.4.3 Management Considerations

How the offeror intends to manage the work required under contract is often an important evaluation factor. When such information is required by the solicitation, appropriate evaluation factors should evaluate the proposed organization structure, management capability, experience and controls, and other pertinent factors.

2.6.4.4 Past Performance

Relevant information concerning how well an offeror has performed similar work in the past is often used as a significant evaluation factor. Offerors are normally required to submit past performance data that references other contracts they have performed that are similar in nature to the current requirement. When required by the solicitation, the evaluation plan must address how past performance issues will be evaluated, including the effect (usually neutral) of an offeror having little or no pertinent past performance. Evaluation factors for past performance normally require the evaluators or the contracting professional to attempt to verify the accuracy of past performance information submitted by an offeror. This is usually accomplished by contacting the sources provided by the offeror and obtaining answers to an established set of past performance questions. There are also government databases that compile past performance information (e.g., the Federal Awardee Performance and Integrity Information System (FAPIIS), the Contractor Performance Assessment Reporting System (CPARS), and the Past Performance Information Retrieval System (PPIRS)).

2.6.4.5 Relative Significance of Evaluation Factors

The evaluation plan should also address the relative significance of all evaluation factors to be used as a basis for selection, as well as the relative significance of price factors to non-price factors. This factor-ranking process is particularly important in negotiated procurements because the award is often made to some offeror of other than the lowest price. As with all other evaluation factors, the relative significance of the factors should have also been addressed in the solicitation.

2.6.4.6 Basis of Award

The federal government uses two different source selection methods for negotiated acquisition: 1) lowest price technically acceptable or 2) tradeoff. A lowest price technically acceptable proposal is one that offers the best price to the government after minimum technical requirements have been met. Proposals are evaluated for acceptability but are not ranked based on non-cost/price factors. The RFP must specifically state that award will be made on the basis of the lowest evaluated price as long as the proposal meets or exceeds the acceptability standard. All factors are evaluated using a "go/no-go" rating system.

Using the tradeoff source selection method allows an agency to select the most significant evaluation factors to emphasize: cost or price as well as non-cost factors such as technical or management. It also allows the government to award the contract to a company that did not submit the lowest price. The RFP using the tradeoff process must state whether all evaluation factors other than cost or price, when combined, are significantly more important than, approximately equal to, or significantly less important than cost or price. The perceived benefits of the higher-priced proposal must merit the additional cost, and the agency must document the rationale for making the tradeoff decision.

2.6.5 Proposal Evaluation Techniques

The intent of the evaluation process is to uniformly rate the quality and content of all proposals received against a clear set of pertinent criteria in order to arrive at an award recommendation decision that provides the maximum benefit to the buying organization. Several methods are often used to help ensure that the evaluation process is logical, unbiased, and defendable.

2.6.5.1 Evaluate Technical Aspects Separately

The solicitation package may have required the submission of separate technical and price proposals. However, even if separate proposal volumes were not required, the evaluation team should review technical considerations on their own merits. The proposals can be edited before review to eliminate any pricing information. Since there are defined evaluation criteria, and since price is always included as an evaluation factor, it is important not to allow the evaluation of one factor to be influenced by other evaluation factors at this stage.

2.6.5.2 Compliance Matrix

Organizations frequently use a prepared evaluation checklist or document to promote uniformity in the evaluation process. This checklist should contain a compliance matrix, which usually consists of:

- All evaluation factors and sub-factors;
- The rating scale to be applied;
- Weights to be applied to factors, if appropriate; and
- Room for evaluator comments.

The use of such a matrix can ensure that each proposal receives a thorough and comprehensive review.

Offerors often use a similar compliance matrix when preparing proposals to ensure they have addressed all pertinent requirements.

2.6.5.3 Independent Evaluation

Each member of the evaluation team should evaluate each proposal independently, without any input from other team members. Each member of the team brings unique experiences, knowledge, insights, perspectives, and expectations to the evaluation process. These personal differences should be viewed as assets that can be used to enhance the evaluation process. Though a consensus will eventually be required, the initial evaluation phase should normally be as uninhibited as possible. This preferred independence can be enhanced even further by removing the names of the offerors from the proposals, if it is possible to do so.

2.6.6 Evaluation Rating Scales

As previously noted, the evaluation checklist or documentation will usually include the rating scale, which is used to assign values to the factors evaluated in the proposals. Rating scales often take one of several forms.

2.6.6.1 Numeric Scales

Using numeric rating scales, evaluators assign a range of points (0–10, 0–25, 0–100, etc.) to each evaluation factor, with the highest possible rating equaling the sum of the maximum points available for each factor. Numeric scales most easily accommodate weighted evaluation factors. For example, if technical approach is twice as important as past performance, 20 total points can be allocated to technical approach and 10 points to past performance.

2.6.6.2 Color Scales

Many contracting professionals, most notably in the Department of Defense, use a color-based scale to evaluate proposals. Color scales are normally constructed with three, four, or five ranges. A three-range scale might consist of "Red" for "Unsatisfactory," "Yellow" for "Satisfactory," and "Green" for "Excellent." For four- and five-range scales, more colors and related scoring ranges are added. The rationale for assigning a particular color rating is usually provided in the source selection plan and instructions to evaluators.

2.6.6.3 Adjectival Scales

Adjectival scales are very similar to color scales, but they use adjectives indicating the value assigned.

As with color scales, adjectival scales usually have three, four, or five ranges and descriptions that often include: "Unsatisfactory," "Marginal," "Satisfactory," "Highly Satisfactory," and "Exceptional"; "Good," "Better," and "Exceptional"; etc. The evaluators must provide comments to support the ratings in a manner similar to that when using color scales. The table in **FIGURE 2-6-3** on page 79 is a sample of a typical adjectival evaluation rating system.

2.6.6.4 Compare Results and Reach Consensus

After each member of the evaluation team has completed their individual ratings, the team should come together and compare results. This process will often reveal significant differences in perceptions among team members concerning the relative quality of the proposals. These differences should be viewed as positive because they should require a spirited and collaborative deliberation process. Evaluation team members should avoid simply averaging individual scores, as this diminishes the benefits gained from the individual review process. Rather, each team member should both share and solicit information regarding how ratings were derived. The resulting consensus should be documented thoroughly, with the strengths and weaknesses of each proposal explained.

Proposal evaluation involves assessing the content of a proposal against established evaluation factors and determining whether the offeror will be able to perform the prospective contract successfully. Evaluators identify the relative strengths, deficiencies, significant weaknesses, and risks in each proposal and document their assessments. In so doing, evaluators must assess only what each offeror submits in its proposal.

2.6.7 Contract Award

The notification of award to the successful offeror should normally occur immediately after the conclusion of all source selection activities. Though the notification is usually made by issuing the contract, in some cases the award notification is made by separate correspondence or by a telephone call or e-mail, followed by the written contract or official correspondence. In any event, there should be little or no delay in making the award once the source selection process has been completed. In the case of contracts awarded by the government, congressional notification may be required in advance of notice to the successful offeror.

2.6.7.1 Preparing the Contract

The contract is prepared to document the terms of the agreement and the expectations of each party. The enforceability of the contract and the nature of the parties' obligations can be greatly affected by the form the contract is written in and the language used to express the agreement. Agreements made during preliminary negotiations may not be evident in the written contract and therefore be unenforceable. The terms and conditions within the contract will dictate its legal effect. Ambiguities in a written contract may cause differences in interpretation of the contract requirements. Internal conflict in the terms and conditions of a contract may lead to disagreement between the parties on which term should prevail. It is important to prepare a contract that accurately and concisely reflects the agreement between the two parties.

The contract is prepared using the appropriate format and terms and conditions for the type of contract being awarded and the type of organization awarding the document. The contract may contain standard contract language that has been formulated for the specific type of purchase or it may be necessary to write new contract language to fit the unique requirements of the contract. A great number of commercial contracts are form contracts. Commercial contracts for products, as a common practice in the everyday transactions under the Uniform Commercial Code, include the quantity of goods to be purchased, the time for performance, terms related to payment, delivery, passage of title, risk of loss terms, interest in goods, warranty, and returns of goods.

In the case of more complex requirements, a contract may include a statement of work, specifications, management plan, quality control plan, list of contract deliverables, licensing agreements, subcontracting plans, program and financial reporting requirements, and so on.

2.6.7.2 Notification

In addition to the prompt notification of the successful offeror, all unsuccessful offerors should be notified of their status immediately or very soon after award. In some cases, notification is provided to offerors who have been eliminated from competition before the award decision.

2.6.8 Contract Award Practices Unique to Federal Contracting

In the federal government contracting environment, there are several unique characteristics to making the contract award decision that are described as follows.

2.6.8.1 Pre-Award Notification

When an offeror has been eliminated from competition before an award decision has been made, the contracting officer should promptly notify the offeror in writing of their exclusion and the underlying reason for the decision. Pre-award notifications are normally made when elimination from further competition was made based on the offeror's exclusion from a predetermined competitive range or for other appropriate reasons. (*See* FAR 15.503.)

2.6.8.2 Post-Award Notification

Each unsuccessful offeror usually receives written correspondence from the contracting officer that notifies the offeror of their non-selection and provides additional information concerning:

- The number of offerors solicited, if known;

- The number of proposals received;

- The name and address of the successful offeror;

- A list of items, quantities, and unit prices in the award, or the total dollar value of the award if listing items is not practical; and

- The general reason(s) that the offeror's proposal was not selected for award, unless the price paid provides the obvious reason.

The contracting officer should take care not to reveal proprietary information, trade secrets, detailed financial breakdowns, or any other confidential or sensitive data related to the successful offeror's proposal or related to any other unsuccessful offeror's proposal when providing this notice to unsuccessful offerors. The contracting professional should also be aware that this notice often serves as the prelude to a request for a formal debriefing. (*See* FAR 15.503.)

2.6.8.3 Debriefing

Once notified, an unsuccessful offeror may request a formal debriefing. Normally, such a request should be received by the contracting officer within three days of the initial notification of non-selection or pre-award elimination. The types of information appropriate for sharing depend on whether the debriefing occurs pre-award or post-award.

FIGURE 3-1. Post-Award Competencies

Pre-Award Debriefing

An unsuccessful offeror may request a debriefing before contract award when the offeror has been notified of its elimination from the competitive range, or has otherwise been eliminated from further competition. The offeror may also elect to defer the debriefing until an award has been made. Under certain circumstances, the contracting officer may deny a request for a pre-award briefing in favor of a post-award debriefing. When conducted, pre-award debriefings are somewhat more restrictive than post-award debriefings. The debriefing may be conducted in person, by written correspondence, or by any other manner deemed appropriate by the contracting professional. Pre-award debriefings usually include information concerning the result of the evaluation of significant elements contained in the offeror's proposal. It usually includes a summary of the reasons that the offeror's proposal was eliminated from the competition. Reasonable responses to pertinent questions are also usually given concerning the degree to which source selection procedures defined in the solicitation were actually followed.

It is important to note that information in the pre-award debriefing is restricted to conversations related only to the offeror's proposal and how it was evaluated. (*See* FAR 15.505.)

Post-Award Debriefing

Post-award debriefings are requested by unsuccessful offerors in much the same manner as pre-award debriefings. However, the permissible content of post-award debriefings is somewhat more extensive. The debriefing may be conducted in person, by written correspondence, or by any other manner deemed appropriate by the contracting professional.

Post-award debriefings usually include information concerning the evaluation of significant weaknesses or deficiencies in the offeror's proposal, the price and technical ratings of the successful offeror (as well as that of the unsuccessful offeror), and the overall ranking of all offerors if a ranking process was used. The debriefing also usually includes a summary of the rationale used to select the successful offeror and reasonable responses to pertinent questions concerning the degree to which source selection procedures defined in the solicitation were actually followed.

It is important to emphasize that the purpose of a debriefing is to provide useful information to an unsuccessful offeror so that it is aware of how it might improve its chances for selection in future acquisitions. Debriefings are not intended to provide an unsuccessful offeror with the opportunity to perform a complete and detailed analysis of the relative strengths and weaknesses of all aspects of its proposal as compared to the successful offeror

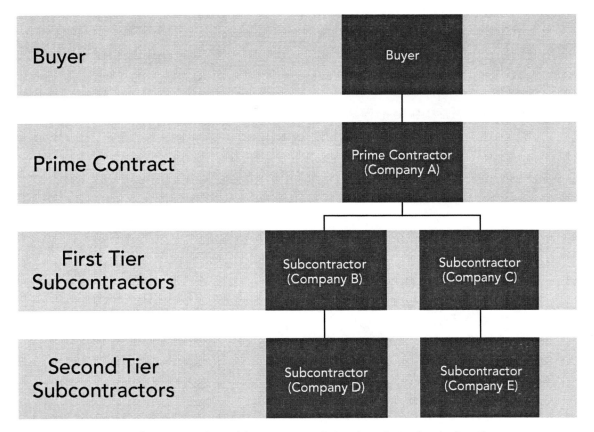

FIGURE 3-3-1. Privity of Contract (*derived from* Margaret G. Rumbaugh, *Understanding Government Contract Source Selection* (Management Concepts, Inc., 2010)

or to other unsuccessful offerors. The contracting professional should also be aware of the need to protect proprietary information, trade secrets, financial data, and other sensitive information of all offerors in the same manner as done in the notification process. (*See* FAR 15.506.)

2.7 Protests

Federal government contract awards are subject to protest if an unsuccessful offeror thinks that the contract award was done improperly in violation of statute or regulation. Though they can also surface in the pre-award phase, protests are usually raised immediately after the contract award decision is announced. This section will not deal with the detailed and rigorous processes and venues used to resolve protests; instead, it will briefly discuss some of the more common reasons for protests. Contract managers should be aware of common types of protest-related issues when writing solicitations to hopefully avoid ambiguities and prevent or reduce the frequency of such issues arising after contract award.

Protests are formal challenges to some aspect or aspects of the acquisition process and can be filed in either the pre-award or post-award phase. Federal government contractors have 10 calendar days from the date of learning the reason for protest to file a protest. For example, they cannot protest a defect in the RFP after contract award because they should have known about the defect well in advance of submitting the proposal.

Though the specific grounds for a protest can vary widely and will depend on the particular circumstances of an acquisition and the contractor's perceptions, protests generally relate to some of the following issues. The federal government's protest process has three methods:

- The contracting officer,
- The level above the contracting officer, and
- The Government Accountability Office.

2.7.1 Pre-Award Protest Issues

- *Restrictive requirements*—The protestor may claim that the requirements or specifications are unnecessarily restrictive and thereby prohibit or limit meaningful competition.

- *Inappropriate sole-source requirement*—A protestor may claim that a requirement advertised as a sole-source procurement is not, in fact, a valid use of sole-source authority and that the possibility for competition exists.

- *Ambiguous or erroneous evaluation criteria*—A protestor may claim that the criteria to be used to evaluate proposals is flawed, inaccurate, or ambiguous in some material way so as to negatively impact the protestor's ability to fairly compete.

- *Ambiguous or incomplete requirements*—The protestor may claim that the statement of work is so incomplete or ambiguous so as to preclude a clear understanding of the full nature and scope of the requirement to be performed.

- *Exclusion from the competitive range*—A protestor may claim that their exclusion from the competitive range was inappropriate or the agency did not clearly identify in the solicitation that it would establish a competitive range.

- *Unfair evaluation criteria*—The protestor may assert that one or more of the criteria used to evaluate proposals was unreasonable, unfair, or otherwise inappropriate.

2.7.2 Post-Award Protest Issues

- *Failure to evaluate as advertised*—The protestor may claim that the method used to actually evaluate proposals was significantly different than the evaluation criteria specified in the solicitation.

- *Unreasonable best value analysis*—A protestor may indicate that, in a best value procurement, the cost/technical tradeoff analysis used to justify an award to other than the highest-rated or lowest-price proposal was flawed, inaccurate, or otherwise unreasonable in some material way.

- *Unequal treatment*—A protestor may claim that other offerors received some form of special treatment or that all offerors were not treated equally, thereby adversely impacting the protestor's ability to compete effectively.

- *Failure to conduct meaningful discussions*—A protestor may claim that they were not the recipient of meaningful discussions during pre-award negotiations, which unfairly prevented them from having the opportunity to submit a more competitive, revised proposal.

Regardless of the specific nature of a pre-award or post-award protest, the underlying issue usually relates to some real or perceived flaw, error, or shortcoming in some facet of the pre-award process. A thorough and comprehensive acquisition-planning effort and the logical implementation of the acquisition plan in the solicitation phase can result in a better procurement and fewer post-award issues to resolve. Once a protest is received, the contracting professional should take all reasonable and appropriate steps necessary to resolve the issue at the lowest possible level.

3.0 Post-Award Competencies

The previous *CMBOK* sections cover the most visible and time-consuming aspects of contract management, such as acquisition strategy and pre-award competencies. In many organizations, the bulk of the professional contracting resources are devoted to "awarding the contract," or "winning the contract." After a contract is awarded, however, there are many significant and important activities required that often determine the success of the contract. Post-award contract administration competencies are equally critical to successful performance.

Contract performance begins after contract award and these tasks are usually referred to as "contract administration." The range and extent of contract administration activities required will vary greatly, depending primarily on the type of contract, complexity of the requirement, dollar value, and importance of the contract to the organization.

Effective contract administration is a shared responsibility of both the buyer and seller. The contract specifies the duties and obligations for which both parties are responsible and the benefits or consideration to which each party is entitled. Contract administration is the process that provides the oversight required to ensure that both parties follow the contract requirements.

Contract administration can be tailored based on the complexity of the requirement and size of the organization. The challenge and complexity of effective contract administration increases with the size and complexity of the buyer's and seller's organizations and the number of contracts to manage. Contracting professionals in large, complex organizations frequently find themselves simultaneously responsible for administration activities on multiple contracts, and usually require technical assistance and communication with internal professional resources, management, and other stakeholders.

In this set of competencies, the following post-award competencies will be discussed:

- Contract management (3.1),

- Quality assurance (3.2),

- Subcontract management (3.3),

- Contract changes and modifications (3.4),

- Transportation (3.5),

- Contract interpretation and disputes (3.6),

- Contract closeout (3.7), and

- Contract termination and excusable delay (3.8).

These competencies are outlined in **FIGURE 3-1** on page 84.

3.1 Contract Management

Contract management begins with reading the contract to understand the terms and conditions of the contract. The contract manager should be thoroughly familiar with the contract requirements to facilitate effective communication between the buyer and seller. Timely, effective communication between the buyer and seller is critical to program success and must be coincident with contract award.

The following sections describe important elements of post-award contract management.

- Using effective communication (3.1.1),

- Attending a post-award kick-off meeting (3.1.2),

- Conducting periodic status review meetings (3.1.3),

- Preparing written status reports (3.1.4),

- Observing and monitoring performance (3.1.5), and

- Documenting performance (3.1.6).

3.1.1 Using Effective Communication

An essential element of successful contract administration is establishing and maintaining effective communications between the buyer and seller, and within the buyer's and seller's organizations. Maintaining a productive, two-way professional dialogue between buyer and seller during the period of contract performance is a critical aspect of contract administration. Inadequate oversight can cause cost, schedule, technical, or other compliance problems that may result in failure of the program and poor customer relations.

3.1.2 Attending a Post-Award Kick-Off Meeting

A post-award meeting held promptly after award can help mitigate the potential for issues and problems during contract performance. In addition to the benefits of conducting a post-award conference, a more comprehensive post-award, pre-performance meeting can set the foundation for good communication and expectations between the buyer and seller. When conducted, this meeting should be chaired by contracting professionals from the buyer and seller and include appropriate managers and staff personnel from the buyer's organization and appropriate managers and staff personnel from the seller's organization.

A post-award meeting includes a detailed review of the contract, including all work to be performed, the performance schedule, terms and conditions for payment, and other related terms and conditions. The intent of this review is to achieve a clear, mutual understanding of what needs to be done and who will do the work. It could include the development of a procedure for continuing written and verbal communications. This procedure should clearly specify, for both the buyer and seller:

- Who is authorized to communicate,

- The subject matter appropriate for communication, and

- The form and format such communication should take.

Since many of the players on both sides will not be contracting professionals, this agreement can be of significant value in reducing or eliminating issues related to constructive changes, apparent authority, etc. At the post-award meeting, there is usually discussion and agreement on progress reporting requirements to include the frequency, format, and content of required reports; procedures for reporting unusual or urgent issues; and similar subjects. There is also discussion and agreement on methods and processes to be used to resolve minor disagreements or questions about contract interpretation, with provisions for escalation when appropriate. The subjects discussed and agreements reached during these meetings should be thoroughly documented, approved by both the buyer and seller, and distributed throughout both organizations.

3.1.3 Conducting Periodic Status Review Meetings

Status review meetings should be specified in the contract and conducted on a regularly scheduled basis (monthly, quarterly, etc., or upon completion of specified milestones such as delivery of a product or service). The contract should specify when these status review meetings occur in the statement of work or as a formal deliverable including the frequency, content, and required attendees. Updated information on status, issues, and concerns should be shared between the buyer and seller during these meetings. Each meeting should have a written agenda. These meetings should augment any written reports required and help serve as a means to continue an open and honest dialogue for issues related to contract performance.

3.1.4 Preparing Written Status Reports

When specified in the contract, the contractor should provide written status reports as a deliverable to keep the buyer's organization and customers aware of progress and issues. These reports can be narrative, statistical, or a combination of the two (consistent with contractual requirements). All reporting requirements should directly relate to some aspect of required performance, create the smallest administrative burden possible, and only be required when the information they contain will actually be used for some legitimate contract management purpose. Submitting performance status is effective only if the buyer actually reads the reports provided. Simply filing reports without reading them is not effective contract management.

3.1.5 Observing and Monitoring Performance

In addition to the information provided by a contractor in various meetings and reports, the buyer will also observe contract performance to ensure performance is in accordance with contract requirements and to validate information received from other sources such as technical representatives or inspectors. Indirect observation may be conducted by various types of reports from the contractor or reviews or audits performed by either the buyer's management staff or by internal or external auditors. Various forms of pre- and post-production testing and sampling and a variety of other methods can also provide important information.

Any kind of observation can provide valuable information regarding issues such as cost, schedule, and quality that can keep contract performance on track. If the work effort is primarily physical in nature, indirect observation is often augmented by direct observation. "Direct observation" occurs when the buyer's personnel are physical present on site to visually check on progress or compare actual work completed to planned work completed.

3.1.6 Documenting Performance

Documenting contract performance (including both positive and negative aspects of performance) is an important part of contract administration. The documentation should record contract compliance including cost, schedule, and performance issues. The documentation can take many forms: formal correspondence, memoranda for the record, telephone logs, e-mails, personal notes, journal entries, performance reporting, etc. The documentation serves as a written record of all meetings, discussions, issues, problems, solutions, and agreements. The record can be used as a ready reference source to reflect the intent of the parties over time as a means to guide future actions based on agreements reached in the past or as evidence in the event of claims, disputes, or any subsequent litigation.

3.2 Quality Assurance

Quality assurance requires the seller to ensure that the products and services delivered to the buyer conform to the contract's requirements. Quality assurance may be done on a formal or informal basis. A formal quality assurance system typically involves a separate department such as quality control or quality assurance. These organizations perform formal inspection and testing and provide written documentation of the results. Informal quality assurance, on the other hand, could be as simple as a walk-through observation of the work site to ensure contract compliance.

FAR Part 46 provides policies and procedures to ensure that supplies and services acquired under a government contract conform to the contract's quality and quantity requirements. Included are inspection, acceptance, warranty, and other measures associated with quality requirements. The contracting officer shall include in the solicitation and contract the appropriate quality requirements. The type and extent of contract quality requirements needed depends on the particular acquisition and may range from inspection at time of acceptance to a requirement for the contractor's implementation of a comprehensive program for controlling quality. Federal government contracts generally make contractors responsible for performing inspection before tendering supplies to the government.

3.2.1 Quality Assurance Tools

There are several different methods available for organizations to establish a quality assurance program, including, but not limited to, the following:

- "Total quality management" (TQM) is a continuous process improvement tool focused on customer satisfaction.

- "Six Sigma" is a quality assurance process that developed from TQM that focuses on controlling processes to +/- six sigma standard of deviation.

- The International Standards Organization (ISO) consolidates different quality standards. The ISO 9000 series of quality assurance standards establishes a framework for a quality management system. (See Fred Sollish and John Semanik, *The Procurement and Supply Manager's Desk Reference* (Hoboken, New Jersey: John Wiley & Sons, 2007).)

The ISO certification states to your customers that you have certain key quality assurance systems in place and you are following these systems. The ISO 9001 standard does not determine the seller's quality goals because it is not a measurement tool. The ISO 9001 quality management system has several key elements, including having a quality manual, requiring effective document control, establishing a quality records control system, and providing measurement analysis and improvement.

The ISO 9001 standard is based on a number of quality management principles, including a strong customer focus, the motivation and implication of top management, the process approach, and continual improvement. An organization must perform internal audits to check how its quality management system is working. An organization may decide to invite an independent certification body to verify that it is in conformity to the standard, but there is no requirement for this. Alternatively, it might invite its clients to audit the quality system for themselves. (See www.iso.org for more information.)

The ISO 9001 standard is based on eight principals:

- Customer focus,

- Leadership,

- Involvement of people,

- Process approach,

- System approach to management,

- Continual improvement,

- Factual approach to decision-making, and

- Mutually beneficial supplier relationships.

Quality assurance can be objective or subjective. Objective quality assurance is typically documented mathematically such as miles per hour, mean time between failure, or lines of code. Subjective criteria could be stated in vague terms in the contract such as "best efforts," "acceptable practices," or "as required." When establishing quality assurance measurements, the contract should state:

- What will be measured,

- How the data will be collected, and

- When the measurement will be conducted.

The quality assurance team should know what the targeted goal (acceptance criteria) is and who is responsible for gathering the data.

3.2.2 Acceptance Testing

The contract's inspection and acceptance requirements should be clearly stated detailing the location, method, and manner of inspection and/or testing along with the milestone dates when this will occur. Federal government contract quality assurance is governed by FAR Part 46.

Acceptance testing is an important part of quality assurance. Acceptance testing is a way to determine if a deliverable meets the requirements. When a

FIGURE 3-7-1. Contract Closeout

product meets the requirements and passes testing, a formal written acknowledgement is typically required to document acceptance. Some contracts may require first article testing before the contractor begins production of an entire lot.

The contract should also state the process and procedure for what happens if the product does not pass the inspection. Contracts may require rework, repair, or revision of defective products. The contract should also clearly state how the cost of such rework, repair, or revision should be handled. There should be a corrective action plan to ensure that the rework and re-inspection are documented.

3.2.3 Contract Manager's Role

While contract managers do not typically inspect products and services, they play an important role in the quality assurance process by documenting the results of the inspection/acceptance process and ensuring that invoices are sent and paid in a timely manner. Contract managers for both buyer and seller are responsible for making sure that the contractor's performance is in accordance with the contract.

Clear and concise documentation is a critical element for contract managers to support quality assurance. In many contracts, documenting inspection and acceptance is necessary for invoicing and payment.

Contract managers actively engaged in the quality assurance process help ensure a successful contract outcome where the buyer receives the goods and services as stated in the contract and the seller receives timely payment and a good past performance assessment.

3.3 Subcontract Management

Many programs rely on the combined talent of a team of contractors. When the contract includes one prime contractor, the subcontractors may be referred to as subcontractors or suppliers. Suppliers or vendors typically provide a commodity on a fixed-price basis that requires no design or engineering, although the deliverable may require specific test and acceptance by the prime contractor. Supplier products often include commercial items or raw materials. Suppliers are often the lowest tiers of the subcontract hierarchy as suppliers may supply material routinely to many prime contractors but lack insight to the ultimate product.

Some organizations make a distinction between suppliers/vendors and subcontractors. A vendor is an individual, partnership, corporation, or other entity from which items are acquired in the performance of a contract. A subcontract, on the other hand, is a contract or contractual action entered into by a prime contractor or subcontractor for the purpose of obtaining supplies, materials, equipment, or services of any kind under a prime contract. The FAR defines subcontract as any contract as defined in FAR Subpart 2.1 entered into by a subcontractor to furnish supplies or services for performance of a prime contract or subcontract. It includes, but is not limited to, purchase orders and changes and modifications to purchase orders.

Subcontract administrators ensure supplier deliveries meet the specifications, delivery schedule, and cost to meet program commitments and inventory supplies if required.

Subcontracts are negotiated agreements between the prime contractor and the subcontractor. Depending on the complexity of the deliverable, subcontractors may further subcontract, creating a hierarchy, or tiers of subcontractors. When the contract includes different levels of subcontractors, the buying organization needs to exercise a degree of caution during contract performance. For this reason, it is important to understand the concept of privity of contract, which is illustrated in **FIGURE 3-3-1** on page 85.

The buyer should therefore exercise care regarding communication with subcontractors. The prime contractor is the conduit through which information from both the buyer and the subcontractor is relayed to the other party. The prime contractor is responsible for the performance of its subcontractors and is being paid to effectively manage the program. The buyer should, by word and deed, clearly communicate to the subcontractor that the buyer's contractual relationship with the seller forms the framework for the relationship, and should not normally meet with the subcontractor without the seller's representatives present. The buyer should ensure the seller manages the subcontract in accordance with its management plan proposed for the contract.

In many cases, the ability of a prime contractor to successfully meet contractual obligations to the

buyer is critically dependent upon the ability of its subcontractors to meet contractual obligations to the prime contractor. While the contractual relationship between the buyer and the seller (i.e., the prime contract) is an important aspect of contract administration, the buyer also needs to fully understand the dependencies on the subcontractor's performance and closely monitor the prime contractor's management of its subcontractors.

In some cases, the subcontractor is simply a supplier (vendor) of goods or raw materials to the prime contractor for use in production or fabrication. In other cases, the subcontractor may provide specialized services or perform highly technical work for the prime contractor seller in direct support of their contract with the buyer. Though in both cases the prime contractor's ability to perform successfully is dependent upon the subcontractor's performance, the buyer's contracting professionals' focus should increase when the subcontractor's performance plays a direct and significant role in the overall contract performance. For example, subcontracts on the critical path should have more oversight then subcontracts that are not on the critical path.

In some cases, particularly in certain types of government contracting, the government's contracting officer should require the prime contractor to receive the government's consent to subcontract in advance of subcontract performance. FAR Part 44 provides detailed consent and advance notification requirements. The intent of these requirements is to:

- Ensure the scope of the subcontract is clearly documented and well understood by both parties;

- The subcontract meets the objectives described by the prime in terms of technical performance, delivery, and cost; and

- The subcontract includes all flow-down requirements from the prime contract and/or other legal requirements.

The primary intent of the oversight is to ensure that the government has insight into the terms and conditions of the subcontract and to ensure funds provided to the prime are used appropriately to meet contract requirements in accordance with applicable law and regulation.

FAR Part 44, "Consent to Subcontract," includes unique concepts in government subcontract management, including:

- Flow-down clauses,

- Consent to subcontract,

- Subcontracting preferences, and

- Privity (subcontractors may not seek remedies directly from the federal government). (*See U.S. v. Johnson Controls*, 713 F.2d 1541, Appeal No. 65-82, U.S. Court of Appeals, Federal Circuit (August 2, 1983).)

The government contract administrator should also ensure the government obtains appropriate data rights to any research or development performed by the subcontractor on behalf of the prime to which it would otherwise be entitled.

The government may also require that the seller's purchasing system be periodically reviewed by government personnel. The Defense Contract Management Agency reviews contractor purchasing systems against strict standards defined in *Defense FAR Supplement* 252.244-7001, "Contractor Purchasing System Administration." Noncompliance with these standards may result in contract payment withholding.

In nearly all cases, it is prudent subcontract management for a buyer to be aware of the prime and subcontractor's performance and relationships. When the subcontractor's performance will have a significant impact on the prime contractor's performance, the buyer may consider including subcontractors in some or all of the communications mentioned previously, particularly the face-to-face meetings. This request should be sent through the prime contractor.

Including the subcontractor in meetings and reviews can:

- Provide both the buyer and seller with a more complete understanding of all actions required for cost, schedule, and technical performance;

- Allow the buyer and seller to proactively address issues and potential subcontractor problems that may occur;

- Encourage the prime contractor to maintain effective management of its subcontractors;

- Provide the subcontractor with valuable insight regarding the nature of the relationship between the prime contractor and the buyer;

- Assist the subcontractor in understanding how its performance affects the prime contractor's

ability to successfully complete contract performance on time and within budget; and

- Enhance direct feedback from the buyer to the subcontractor regarding its performance.

Prime contractor disputes with a subcontractor are resolved using state law from the state where the subcontract was made, where the work was performed, or in which the dominant party is incorporated. Federal law may be incorporated by reference through flow-down clauses.

3.4 Contract Changes and Modifications

After contract award, buyers and sellers frequently find that a contract change is necessary. A contract change is necessary when the existing contract does not reflect what needs to be accomplished. Such contract changes may be necessary due to changed or unforeseen circumstances, conduct of the parties, and/or changes in buyer requirements, including funding limitations.

This section discusses contract modifications under both the UCC and the *FAR* and addresses the following competencies:

- Bilateral and unilateral changes (3.4.1),

- UCC contract modifications (3.4.2), and

- *FAR* contract modifications (3.4.3).

3.4.1 Bilateral and Unilateral Changes

Contract changes may be bilateral or unilateral. A bilateral change is a contract modification that is signed by the contractor and the contracting officer. Bilateral modifications are used to:

- Make negotiated equitable adjustments resulting from the issuance of a change order,

- Definitize letter contracts, and

- Reflect other agreements of the parties modifying the terms of contracts.

(*See Federal Acquisition Regulation* 43.103.)

A unilateral change, on the other hand, is one that the buyer makes without the concurrence of the contractor. For example, a unilateral modification would be a change to a contract that the procuring contracting officer signs but the contractor does not.

Unilateral modifications are used for the following:

- Making administrative changes;

- Issuing change orders;

- Making changes authorized by clauses other than the changes clause (e.g., options clause, property clause, etc.); and

- Issuing termination notices.

(*Ibid.*)

An administrative change is a unilateral contract change, in writing, that does not affect the substantive rights of the parties, such as a change in the paying office or the appropriation data. (*Ibid.*)

3.4.2 Uniform Commercial Code (UCC) Contract Modifications

The general principles of contract formation still apply when changing a contract. For example, did both parties agree to the modification? This is called "mutual assent." It is important to remember that there is a duty of good faith performance on both parties to a contract and neither should act in bad faith to influence a contract change. (*See* Claude D. Rohwer and Anthony M. Skrocki, *Contracts in a Nutshell*, seventh ed. (St. Paul, Minnesota: West Publishing, 2010): 324.)

In commercial contracts there are three types of modifications:

- Explicit,

- Mutual assent, and

- Conduct of the parties.

An example of an explicit change is where the buyer accepts late delivery, thereby modifying the contract's delivery date. Mutual assent changes are bilateral, meaning both parties agree to the change. (These are typically done in advance of the change occurring.) Finally, the conduct of the parties may unintentionally result in a contract change. (*See* James J. White and Robert S. Summers, *Principles of Sales Law* (St. Paul, Minnesota: West Publishing, 2009): 90.)

Some contracts may specifically require that contract changes be in writing; others may be silent on the issue. Some states may require that all written contracts to only be changed in writing. (*See* James J. White and Robert S. Summers, *Principles of Sales*

Law (St. Paul, Minnesota: West Publishing, 2009): 334.) Although not required, it is a good contract management practice to document all changes.

The UCC does not require consideration in order for the modification to be valid, but it must comply with the statute of frauds. (UCC 2-209.) The UCC states: "An agreement modifying a contract within this article needs no consideration to be binding."

3.4.3 *Federal Acquisition Regulation (FAR) Contract Modifications*

Federal government contract changes are governed by FAR Part 43. The "changes" clause describes what types of changes the contracting officer can make and the procedures for ordering the changes. Government contract changes can be unilateral (signed by one party—typically the buyer) or bilateral (signed by both parties). Unilateral modifications may be used to make administrative changes, make changes authorized by other contract clauses, and issue termination notices.

Bilateral changes, on the other hand, are modifications signed by both parties. This type of modification may also be called a "supplemental agreement." Bilateral modifications can be used to make negotiated equitable adjustments to the contract resulting from issuing a change order. They are also used to definitize letter contracts and reflect other agreements changing the terms of the contract.

Federal government contracts also identify if the change provides for an "equitable adjustment" to the contract amount or period of performance if there is a resultant change in cost or schedule. This equitable adjustment is the consideration for the contract change. An equitable adjustment is the compensation or price adjustment to which a contractor is entitled upon the occurrence of a contract change.

Only contracting officers acting within the scope of their authority may change a government contract. Other government personnel may not act in a way to make the contractor believe they have the authority to bind the government and may not even encourage the contractor to perform work that should be the subject of a contract modification. (*See* FAR 43.102.)

Like commercial contracts, there are also three types of changes:

- Directed changes,
- Constructive changes, and
- Cardinal changes.

Most contracts contain a "changes" clause that gives the buyer the right to direct changes during contract performance. The clause describes what type of changes the buyer can direct, the procedure for ordering the change, and a provision for equitable adjustment to the contract amount or period of performance if there is a resultant change in cost or schedule. A directed change usually must be within the original scope of the contract.

Federal government contracts require that a "directed change" must be within the scope of the original contract. Changes are subject to an equitable adjustment, but may be directed in:

- Drawings, designs, or specifications;
- Methods of shipping or packing; or
- Place of delivery.

If both parties want to change the contract by mutual consent, they may only do so in the areas previously noted. Changes beyond the scope of the original contract are not permitted in federal government contracts. (*See* the discussion on "cardinal changes" later in this section.)

A "constructive change" is a change resulting from the government's actions or directives that impacts the cost or schedule for performance that is construed to have the same effect as a formal change order. A constructive change generally occurs when a government employee other than the contracting officer implies or expressly orders the contractor to perform work that is not in the contract. In government contracting, equitable adjustment is granted for constructive changes only if the change caused the contractor injury or liability.

"Cardinal changes" are changes that are beyond the scope of the contract and materially alter the nature of the contract that the parties entered into. A cardinal change could be considered as a breach of contract and may be the subject of a dispute.

3.5 Transportation

When contracting for goods, the costs associated with transportation are sometimes little more than a minor afterthought for many contracting professionals. However, transportation issues can sometimes represent a significant expense, particularly when the buyer purchases a large quantity of goods or when the goods are extremely heavy, cumbersome, fragile, subject to spoilage, or otherwise difficult to transport. Transportation is another technical sub-specialty and many organizations have experts in their transportation, logistics, or shipping and receiving departments whom the contracting professional can consult to help evaluate the cost considerations of various transportation options.

Contracting professionals and transportation professionals often serve in two distinct decision-making processes. Buyers determine what orders to place, while transportation personnel determine how to route the shipments. Buyers strive to avoid stock-outs while keeping inventories low. Transportation personnel work to avoid service failures while minimizing freight costs. To achieve efficiencies in transportation, contracting professionals and transportation professionals must collaborate on a routine basis in order to create and maintain an optimized decision-making process.

Some of the more common transportation considerations include the following:

- *Required receipt dates*—The date and place that the buyer requires the items to be received sometimes determines transportation costs. The contracting professional should be aware of the potential for increased transportation costs that may be a result of a specific receipt date, particularly when the delivery schedule is aggressive or when the delivery schedule is accelerated by modification due to a change in plans or to overcome some issue or problem in production.

- *Mode of transportation*—The mode of transportation (i.e., rail, motor freight, air, etc.) is sometimes dictated by the nature of the goods being purchased and is always a factor in determining appropriate transportation methods. Consistent with other contract requirements and industry standards, the mode of transportation selected should reflect a thoughtful balance between speed, reliability, need, and cost.

- *Transportation-related services*—Additional transportation considerations sometime result from the need for transportation-related services, which may include storing, packing, marking, loading, unloading, etc.

- *Responsibility for transportation charges*— Costs associated with the transportation of goods can be the responsibility of either the buyer or the seller. The responsibility is defined by the applicable clause in the contract. If the contract stipulates "free-on-board destination," the seller is responsible for payment of transportation costs associated with delivering the contract. Such costs are normally included in the seller's price. An advantage to the buyer is that the title to the goods does not pass from the seller to the buyer until the goods have been received, thereby insulating the buyer from in-transit loss or damage issues. If the contract stipulates "free-on-board origin," the buyer is responsible for payment of transportation costs associated with delivering the goods from the seller's facility to the place or places specified by the buyer in the contract. This option may be advantageous to the buyer when the buyer can obtain the transportation at lower costs than the seller could, or when the buyer has its own transportation capability. Title to the goods transfers from the seller to the buyer when the goods leave the seller's facility.

3.6 Contract Interpretation and Disputes

Despite the planning and preparation conducted before awarding a contract, issues sometimes arise during performance that are difficult to resolve. As a general rule, contracting professionals should always seek to resolve differences in the least formal and most collaborative manner possible.

It is important for contract managers to understand contract interpretation principles in order to avoid and/or settle disputes. Judicial and administrative bodies interpret the contract language to determine the outcome of any dispute if it cannot be settled at a lower level.

Topics covered in this section include:

- Contract interpretation (3.6.1),
- Commercial contracts (3.6.2),
- Government contracts (3.6.3), and
- Alternative dispute resolution (3.6.4).

3.6.1 Contract Interpretation

The main point of contract interpretation is to determine a single interpretation of the contract that reflects the parties' intent. Dispute resolution typically involves contract interpretation and contract managers should have a good understanding of contract interpretation rules. If the dispute rises to involve the courts, then the parties should seek legal counsel. (This section does not purport to provide legal advice, but to describe the rules of contract interpretation.)

Read the contract as a whole. The contract is more than just the statement of work and delivery schedule. Both parties should read the entire document before signing to make sure that all separate parts work together and that there is no ambiguity. The courts give preference to interpreting the contract in ways where all terms work together and leave no clause meaningless.

Sometimes one section of the contract may conflict with another. If that occurs, the parties should use an "order of precedence" clause to determine which section takes priority. The *FAR* specifies the order of precedence. According to the *FAR*, any inconsistency shall be resolved by giving precedence in the following order:

- The schedule (excluding the specification);
- Representations and other instructions;
- Contract clauses;
- Other documents, exhibits, and attachments; and
- The specifications. (*Derived from FAR 52.214-29 and 52.215-8.*)

The parties must also understand key terms and their definitions. If a key term is not defined in the contract, then technical terms are given their technical meaning in that field. Negotiated terms take precedence over standard terms. These standard terms are sometimes called "boiler plate" terms that may be pre-printed on a form. In addition, specific terms take precedence over general terms. If a term has several different meanings, it is interpreted against the party who wrote the ambiguous term. (*See* Michael Cole, "Interpretation of Contracts," *Inside Supply Management* (December 2002): 29.)

Another important element of contract interpretation is extrinsic evidence. Extrinsic evidence consists of:

- Discussions and concurrent actions,

- Prior course of dealing between the parties, and

- Custom and trade usage.

For example, discussions, meetings, teleconferences, e-mails, or conduct submitting bids, quotes, or proposals may establish the intent of the parties about the disputed terms. In addition, the parties' behavior after contract award, but before the controversy, may also provide insight how to interpret the disputed terms. A prior course of dealing can establish precedence based on past actions; thus, it can be used to establish the intent of the parties. (*See* Gregory A. Garrett, "Contract Administration, Part 3: Contract Interpretation Guidelines and Best Practices," *Contract Management* Magazine (April 2010): 58.)

3.6.2 Commercial Contracts

In the case of commercial contracts, questions involving the legality or interpretation of a contract are generally governed by the law of the state where the contract was made. Questions related to contract performance are generally governed by the law of the state where such performance occurs.

The Uniform Commercial Code provides several remedies that may result after a dispute (these remedies typically occur for breach of contract):

- *Expectation damages*—Monetary damages to place the aggrieved party in the same place as if the contract had been performed.

- *Reliance damages*—Monetary damages that place the aggrieved party in the same position it was in before signing the contract, such as compensation for expenses or losses.

- *Restitution*—The defendant must pay the monetary value that received from the aggrieved party for partial contract performance.

- *Stipulated damages*—This is a fixed sum or formula that the contract provides as a remedy for breach of contract. Stipulated damages are also called "liquidated damages."

- *Interest*—May be calculated in addition to any damages awarded.

- *Punitive damages*—These are designed to punish the guilty party and are applicable only if the defendant is guilty of fraud, malice, or oppression. Punitive damages may not be applicable in breach of contract cases.

- *Specific enforcement*—Also called "specific performance," the court requires the party that breached the contract to complete contract performance.

3.6.3 Government Contracts

The disputes process in federal government contracts is governed by the Contract Disputes Act and is set forth in FAR Part 33.2, "Disputes and Appeals." A contract dispute is a post-award disagreement when it is first recognized that the government and a contractor have conflicting points of view. A dispute becomes a claim when a written demand is made, as a matter of right, to pay a specific amount of money or other relief. An appeal occurs when the contractor files for consideration with a court or board of contract appeals after the contracting officer denies its claim.

In order to be valid, a claim must:

- Be in writing,

- Be addressed to the contracting officer,

- Specify a specific sum of money if a monetary compensation is demanded, and

- Be certified (if the claim is over a certain dollar threshold).

A voucher, invoice, or other routine request for payment that is not in dispute when submitted is not a claim.

Government contracting allows the filing of claims and appeals to the boards and courts when less formal methods do not produce satisfactory results. A contractor may submit a claim with the government contracting officer who issued the contract. There are a number of procedural and time-sensitive requirements imposed on both the contractor and the government contracting officer when a claim is submitted. The government contracting officer is required to formally accept or reject the claim, in writing, within a specified period of time. When a government contracting officer denies a claim, the contractor may appeal that decision to the appropriate agency board of contract appeals or to the U.S. Court of Federal Claims.

Depending on the type of agreement and facts of the case, there are a variety of remedies available to a party who prevails in a lawsuit for breach of contract. Government contracts also have remedies for defective performance, such as:

- Stopping contract performance temporarily through a stop work order;
- Issuing preliminary notices before default actions, such as cure or show-cause notices;
- Rejecting work and demanding rework;
- Accepting work with minor defects for a reduced contract price or other consideration;
- *Seeking post-acceptance relief from:*
  - o Latent defects,
  - o Fraud, or
  - o Gross mistakes.

3.6.4 Alternative Dispute Resolution (ADR)

ADR is a procedure or combination of procedures voluntarily used to resolve "issues in controversy" without the need to resort to litigation. Government agencies are encouraged to use ADR to the maximum extent practicable when the dispute cannot be resolved by mutual agreement at the contract officer level. ADR encompasses practices for managing and quickly resolving disputes at modest cost and with minimal adverse impact on the relationship between the contracting parties.

Some examples of ADR techniques include:

- Interest-based negotiation,
- Mediation,
- Mini-trial,
- Nonbinding arbitration, and
- Binding arbitration.

These processes significantly broaden dispute resolution options beyond litigation or traditional unassisted negotiation. Some ADR procedures, such as binding arbitration and private judging, are similar to expedited litigation in that they involve a third-party decision-maker with authority to impose a resolution if the parties so desire. Other procedures, such as mediation and the mini-trial, are collaborative, with a neutral third party helping a group of individuals or entities with divergent views to reach a goal or complete a task to their mutual satisfaction.

When the parties cannot resolve or accommodate disagreements about the meaning of terms of an agreement, a court may be required to decide what the contract requires. Both commercial and government contracting allows resolution utilizing available legal means.

Regardless of whether the contracting professional is operating in the government or commercial arena, the prompt and efficient resolution of all disputes, at the lowest organizational level possible, should always be the goal.

Formal legal proceedings often require many months or years to achieve a resolution. Preparing for and participating in legal proceedings can require spending substantial amounts of funds, which can sometimes have a negative impact on other aspects of the organization's business. Few, if any, organizations will pursue legal action if they do not believe they will prevail. In most actions, however, there are winners and losers, and parties to litigation often find themselves the recipient of unpleasant surprises. Since legal proceedings are, by nature, adversarial, they can have a permanently negative effect on the relationship between the litigants. This negative effect can prevent the parties from engaging in mutually beneficial business relationships in the future.

3.7 Contract Closeout

Contract closeout is the process of declaring that the obligations under a contract have been satisfied and that a procurement file is both physically and administratively complete. A closeout can occur when the contractor's supplies or services have been accepted and paid for and all documentation on the procurement is finalized and properly assembled.

The closeout process should begin as soon as possible after the contract is physically completed, which means that the seller has delivered the required supplies and the buyer has inspected and accepted them—or the seller has performed and the buyer has accepted all services required by the contract—and the base period and any option periods exercised have expired.

"Contract closeout" consists of completing a number of procedural and administrative tasks to change the status of a contract from "active" to "complete," as listed in **FIGURE 3-7-1** on page 90. These required tasks normally include:

- Verifying that all required goods or services have been received and accepted;
- Verifying that all contractor invoices have been received and paid;

- Returning or disposing any buyer furnished property;

- Closing subcontracts by the seller;

- Agreeing that no claims, issues, or unresolved matters exist;

- Obtaining a final report of patents and royalties;

- Signing a formal notice of contract completion; and

- De-obligating excess funds remaining on the contract (federal contracting) by the buyer.

FAR 4.804-5, "Procedures for Closing Out Contract Files," documents the responsibility of the contract administrator when closing government contracts. Often, the pacing item to close government contracts that require an audit of the contractor's direct and/or indirect rates is the audit itself. Qualifying contractors may expedite this process through the use of quick closeout procedures described in FAR 42.708.

Government contract administrators should also ensure documentation of contractor performance—often called "past performance"—is completed on a timely basis and in accordance with agency procedures.

Upon completion of all required closeout actions, completed contract files should be retained for the appropriate period of time required by law, regulation, or corporate policy.

3.8 Contract Termination and Excusable Delay

In some cases, it becomes necessary to end performance on a contract before the contractual period of performance ends. Contract termination is an action taken pursuant to a contract clause in which the contracting officer unilaterally ends all or part of the work. This can be a "termination for convenience," in which the ending of work is in the best interest of the government, or a "termination for default or for cause," in which the contractor has not performed according to the terms of the contract. The most typical reason for contract termination is when one party does not perform a contract requirement, also called "termination for default" or "termination for cause."

A contract termination liability cost may be included in the contract. This is the maximum liability the buyer would incur in the event of contract termi-

nation for convenience. The contract administrator should closely monitor this estimate during performance to ensure it accurately reflects cost and is funded appropriately.

Contract termination topics that will be discussed in this section include:

- Termination for default (3.8.1),

- Commercial contract termination (3.8.2),

- Government contract termination (3.8.3),

- Excusable delay/*force majeure* (3.8.4), and

- Contract cancellation (3.8.5).

3.8.1 Termination for Default

"Termination for default," also referred to as "termination for cause," is normally a right of law as well as a right vested as the result of including appropriate terms and conditions in the contract. Termination for default can result from one party's failure to perform one or more actions required by the contract. Typical reasons to terminate for default include the following:

- *Failure to perform*—The seller's failure to provide the goods or services contracted for is a valid reason to terminate for default.

- *Failure to adhere to schedule*—If a seller fails to completely perform during the specified period of performance, that failure may be justification for a termination for default. The buyer should exercise good business judgment in this situation to determine if the failure is significant enough to justify the termination.

- *Failure to comply with other terms and conditions*—The seller's failure to comply with other significant terms and conditions contained in the contract can justify termination for default. This is another area in which the buyer should exercise sound business judgment and good faith in determining if the seller's failures are damaging enough to warrant termination.

- *Repudiation*—A contract may be terminated for default if either the buyer or seller clearly indicates to the other party, by word or deed, that it cannot or will not perform.

3.8.2 Commercial Contract Termination

Section 2-309 of the Uniform Commercial Code states the following rules for contract termination.

Where the contract provides for successive performances but is indefinite in duration, it is valid for a reasonable time but unless otherwise agreed may be terminated at any time by either party. Termination of a contract by one party, except on the happening of an agreed event, requires that reasonable notification be received by the other party and an agreement dispensing with notification is invalid if its operation would be unconscionable. (UCC 2-309, "Notice of Termination.")

As in other areas, contract termination also requires an obligation of good faith of the parties. The terminating party must give notice in a reasonable time and ensure that the other party actually received it. For example, the requirement for termination notice exists unless the party has the right to cancel for breach of contract, the contract states a specific event that will cause termination, or both parties agreed that the notice is not required. (See James J. White and Robert S. Summers, *Principles of Sales Law* (St. Paul, Minnesota: West Publishing, 2009): 184–187.)

Termination by mutual consent is a bilateral agreement indicating that the parties no longer wish to be bound by the contract, and terminating both parties' respective rights and obligations. Termination by mutual consent clauses are sometimes included in the basic contract, though they can also be negotiated and executed during the period of performance.

3.8.3 Government Contract Termination

FAR Part 49, "Termination of Contracts," describes the government's procedures for all types of government terminations, except commercial items subject to FAR Part 12. The two principal approaches to government are 1) termination for convenience and 2) termination for default.

3.8.3.1 Termination for Convenience

In government contracting, the government always has the unilateral right to terminate a contract for its convenience when the contract no longer serves the best interests of the government. Terminations for convenience often result from a change in government priorities, program termination or downsizing, or other significant events that were not anticipated at the time of contract formation. When the government pursues a termination for convenience, a termination settlement is negotiated with the seller. The goal of the buyer and seller should be to minimize cost and settle the contract as quickly as possible upon notice of termination.

3.8.3.2 Termination for Default

The general rule is that a contractor in default is not entitled to any prior notice and the contract may be terminated immediately unless there is a contract provision requiring such notice. However, there are notice requirements for other situations.

A "cure notice," for example, is used if the contractor fails to make progress, or fails to perform any other provision of the contract. It is sent by the contracting officer stating that the contractor will be subject to a default termination unless it corrects a specific contract noncompliance or makes necessary progress to meet the delivery schedule.

In contrast to a cure notice, a "show-cause notice" asks for explanation, not for action. If the contractor fails to deliver the supplies or perform the services within the time specified in the contract, or any extension, the contracting officer should send a show cause notice asking the contractor to show why the contract should not be terminated for default. A show-cause notice is a written delinquency notice informing a contractor of failure to perform within the specified terms of the contract, and advising that the government is considering termination for default. It affords the contractor the opportunity to show cause why it should not be terminated. (See FAR 49.402-3, "Procedure for Default.")

3.8.3.3 No-Cost Termination

If the requirement for supplies and services no longer exists and the contractor is not liable to the government for damages, then the contracting officer may execute a "no-cost termination settlement." (See FAR 49.402-4, "Procedure in Lieu of Termination for Default.")

3.8.4 Excusable Delay/Force Majeure

An excusable delay is a contractual provision designed to protect the contractor from sanctions for late performance. To the extent that it has been excusably delayed, the contractor is protected from default termination, liquidated damages, or excess costs of reprocurement or completion. Excusable delays also may lead to recovery of additional compensation if the government constructively accelerates performance.

An excusable delay protects contractors from penalties for delays that are beyond their control. Examples of excusable delay include:

- Acts of God or the public enemy,

- Acts of the government in either its sovereign or contractual capacity,

- Fire,

- Flood,

- Quarantines,

- Strikes,

- Epidemics,

- Unusually severe weather, and

- Freight embargoes.

A similar clause commonly used in commercial contracts is a force majeure clause. It identifies excusable conditions for nonperformance; e.g., strikes, acts of God, etc., are contained in this clause. It is a French term that refers to an unexpected or uncontrollable event that upsets the plan or releases one from obligation; literally, it means "superior force."

3.8.5 Contract Cancellation

A no-cost cancellation is a type of quasi-termination that usually occurs shortly after contract execution, often because the seller realizes that it will be unable to perform. If both parties agree, no debts or obligations are due, and if the buyer can obtain performance from other sources, a no-cost cancellation can be a quick and efficient way to sever a contractual relationship.

4.0 Specialized Knowledge Area Competencies

Specialized knowledge areas require additional contract management skills that are over and above those presented in the pre-award, acquisition planning and strategy, and post-award competencies. These additional professional skills are necessary for contract managers to 1) perform efficiently and effectively in a specific industry or work environment, or 2) interact productively with other specialized professionals.

Certain types of contracting actions require highly specialized experience and knowledge to perform effectively. This section presents a brief overview of various contracting specialty areas. Some of the areas relate exclusively to government contracting, others relate exclusively to commercial contracting, and some have a degree of application to both the government and commercial sectors. This set of competencies will examine the following specialized knowledge area competencies:

- Research and development (4.1),

- Architect-engineer services and construction (4.2),

- Information technology (4.3),

- Major systems (4.4),

- Service contracts (4.5),

- International contracting (4.6),

- State and local government (4.7),

- Supply chain management (4.8),

- Government property (4.9), and

- Other specialized areas (4.10).

4.1 Research and Development (R&D)

An R&D contract is defined as a contract for the following:

- Basic research (directed toward increasing knowledge);

- Applied research (directed toward improving or expanding new scientific discoveries, technologies, materials, processes, or techniques); or

- Development (directed production of, or improvements in, useful products to meet specific performance requirements through the systematic application of scientific knowledge).

(*See Federal Acquisition Regulation 35.001.*)

When an organization buys R&D services, it is difficult to define the requirement other than to describe the problem. This situation creates a departure from the general guidelines used when contracting for other types of products or services because the contract specialist cannot clearly define the requirement, define specific acceptance criteria, and negotiate a price based on the market. R&D contracting necessitates a different philosophy than is used for other types of procurement.

Basic research refers to study and research on pure science that is meant to increase our scientific knowledge base. This type of research is often purely theoretical with the intent of increasing our understanding of certain phenomena or behavior, but does not seek to solve or treat these problems.

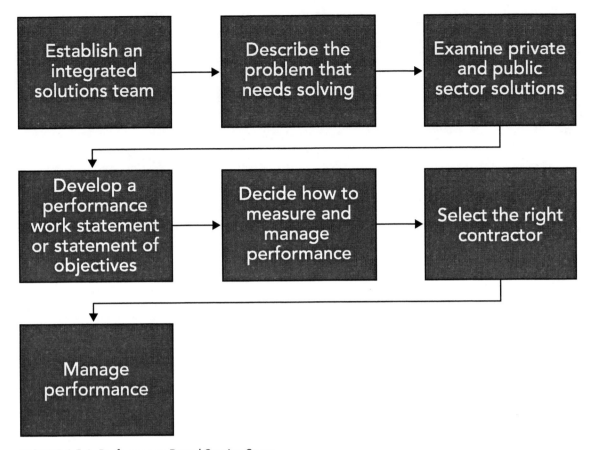

FIGURE 4-5-1. Performance-Based Service Steps

Applied research is the effort that:

- Normally follows basic research, but may not be severable from the related basic research;

- Attempts to determine and exploit the potential of scientific discoveries or improvements in technology, materials, processes, methods, devices, or techniques; and

- Attempts to advance the state of the art.

When used by contractors that must comply with cost principles, this term does not include efforts whose principal aim is the design, development, or testing of specific items or services to be considered for sale; these efforts are within the definition of "development," as defined in the next paragraph.

Development is the systematic use of scientific and technical knowledge in the design, development, testing, or evaluation of a potential new product or service (or of an improvement in an existing product or service) to meet specific performance requirements or objectives. It includes the functions of design engineering, prototyping, and engineering testing and excludes subcontracted technical effort that is for the sole purpose of developing an additional source for an existing product.

4.1.1 Commercial Research and Development

Commercial R&D has a different meaning from the government's meaning of R&D. Commercial R&D typically refers to future-oriented, long-term activities in science and technology. Profits are not realized until after a successful discovery, development, and application of a new technology, which only occurs after diligent and systematic research. The purpose is to position future products in the market place that lead to the type of cash flow that will recoup R&D investments quickly, provide for future R&D, and to obtain a market position that ensures a competitive advantage for the firm.

Firms need significant capital to fund R&D activities during the lengthy product development phase. Most companies prefer to perform R&D internally so they own the resultant technology. To share the investment costs, a company may work with another company. Alternatively, a company may choose to provide R&D services to the government for research in their areas of interest.

If a company contracts for R&D services from another firm, the important issues become acceptable clauses for control of intellectual data, data rights, ownership of inventions, license-to-use, and patents. These clauses are also important when a commercial company enters a contract to provide these services to the government.

4.1.2 Government Research and Development

The primary purpose of federal government R&D contracts and programs is to advance scientific and technical knowledge and to apply that knowledge to achieve agency and national goals. Unlike most other types of contracts, R&D contracts are intended to achieve objectives for which the work or methods cannot be precisely defined in advance. It is difficult to estimate the effort required for various R&D technical approaches, particularly when some of the approaches may offer little or no early indications or assurances that they will be successful. Due to this level of uncertainty, contracting professionals should use R&D contracting in a manner that will encourage the best scientific and industrial sources to participate and the contracts should be structured so that they provide an environment in which the work can be pursued with reasonable flexibility and minimum administrative burden.

4.1.2.1 Contract Method and Type

The fundamental nature of R&D contracting usually precludes using the sealed-bid acquisition method, and typically makes fixed-price contracts inappropriate. Due to the absence of precise specifications and the difficulties in estimating costs, R&D contracts are often cost-reimbursement contracts, sometimes with appropriate incentives. Contracting professionals should consult extensively with internal technical experts regarding the appropriate contract type.

4.1.2.2 Publicizing Requirements

R&D requirements should be publicized as widely as possible. Since a primary issue in R&D contracting is obtaining the best scientific and industrial sources, contracting professionals involved in research and development requirements should conduct market research for potential additional sources that are capable of competent performance. In addition, they should encourage potential sources to exchange information with internal technical experts.

4.1.2.3 Statement of Work

A statement of work (SOW) detailing the area of exploration for basic research or the end objectives for development and applied research is essential. The SOW should provide contractors with the freedom required to exercise innovation and creativity, while adhering to the overall objectives of the R&D effort. SOWs for R&D contracts will be different than many SOWs you may find for services and products. The emphasis will be on obtaining broader objectives rather than strict adherence to specifications and performance standards.

R&D SOWs often include some or all of the following elements:

- The R&D objectives, including a statement of the area of exploration and tasks to be performed;

- The background information necessary to help the contractor understand the requirement;

- The factors that might constrain the results of the effort, including personnel, environment, or interface issues;

- The items that the contractor will be required to furnish as the work progresses, such as reports;

- The type of contract anticipated and an estimate of the professional and technical effort required for level-of-effort requirements; and

- Any other considerations that relate to the work to be performed.

4.1.2.4 Solicitations

R&D solicitations should generally be distributed only to sources that have been identified as "technically qualified." Responses to publicized requirements, internal evaluations, or other means can be used to determine competence. Such evaluations of technical competence usually include factors such as present and past performance of similar work, professional stature and reputation, relative position in a particular field of endeavor, ability to acquire and retain the technical capability required to perform the work, and other relevant factors. The evaluation factors used to determine the most technically competent usually include the offeror's:

- Understanding of the scope of the work;

- Likelihood of accomplishing the scientific and technical objectives of the contract or the merit of the ideas and concepts proposed;

- Proposing experienced and competent technical personnel who are available to work on the contract;
- Proposing novel ideas in the specific branch of science and technology involved; and
- Having access to necessary research, test, laboratory, or shop facilities from any source

4.1.2.5 Evaluation

Generally speaking, R&D contracts are awarded to the offeror that proposes the best ideas or concepts and has the highest competence in the specific field. However, the buyer should use caution and not obtain technical capabilities that clearly exceed those required by the solicitation. It is also customary to evaluate the offeror's proposed cost or price as a means to verify that the offeror has a clear understanding of the scope of the project, perception of risks involved, and the ability to organize and perform the work.

4.1.2.6 Independent Research and Development (IR&D)

- *Federal*—The contractor effort that is neither sponsored by a grant nor required in performing a contract and that falls within any of the following four areas:
  - o Basic research,
  - o Applied research,
  - o Development, and
  - o Systems and other concept formulation studies.
- *Commercial*—This is the effort that is neither sponsored by a grant nor required in performing a contract and which falls within any of the following four areas:
  - o Basic research,
  - o Applied research,
  - o Development, and
  - o Systems and other concept formulation studies that are pursued independently by an organization to further a specific business purpose.

4.2 Architect-Engineer Services and Construction

Contracts for architect, engineering, and construction services are unique and are often awarded by contracting professionals with specialized knowledge and skills experience in engineering and construction contracts.

Terminology associated with this type of contracting includes:

- *Design*—The process that defines a construction requirement, including the functional relationships and technical systems to be used, producing the technical specifications and drawings, and preparing the construction cost estimate.
- *Design-bid-build*—The traditional construction delivery method where design and construction are sequential and contracted for separately with two contracts and two contractors.
- *Design-build*—A method of construction contracting that combines the architectural, engineering and construction services required for a project into a single agreement.
- *Two-phase design-build*—A construction term for a selection procedure that selects a number of offerors, based on qualifications in the first phase to submit detailed proposals for evaluation and award in the second phase.

4.2.1 Architect-Engineer (A-E) Services

Architect-engineer (A-E) services include professional services of an architectural or engineering nature that are required to be performed or approved by a person licensed, registered, or certified to provide such services or are associated with research, planning, development, design, construction, alteration, or repair of real property or other related professional services, such as studies and surveys.

When acquiring A-E services, the government normally publicizes the requirements for such services and negotiates contracts based on demonstrated competence and qualifications to perform the services at fair and reasonable prices. A-E services are generally defined to include:

- Professional services of an architectural or engineering nature, as defined by applicable state law, which the state law requires to be performed by a registered architect or engineer;
- Professional architectural or engineering services associated with the design or construction of real property;

- Other professional architectural or engineering services related to studies, investigations, surveying, mapping, soils engineering, construction phase conceptual design, and similar tasks that require performance by a registered architect, engineer, or their employees; and

- Professional surveying and mapping services when the mapping services are associated with the construction or alteration of real property.

4.2.1.1 Qualification-Based Selection

Federal government A-E services are procured using "qualification-based selection" pursuant to the Brooks Act. According to the American Council of Engineering Companies, and based upon the requirements of the Brooks Act (*Pub. L.* 95-582), there are seven basic steps involved in pursuing federal design work under qualification-based selection:

- Public solicitation for A-E services,

- Submission of an annual statement of qualifications and supplemental statements of ability to design specific projects for which public announcements were made,

- Evaluation of both the annual and project-specific statements,

- Development of a short list of at least three submitting firms in order to conduct an interview with them,

- Interviews with the firms,

- Ranking of at least three of the most-qualified firms, and

- Negotiation with the top ranked firm.

(*Derived from* American Council of Engineering Companies, "The Brooks Act: How to Use Qualifications-Based Selection" (Originally produced by the Texas Society of Architects), *available at* **www.acec. org/advocacy/committees/brooks2.cfm**.)

4.2.1.2 Evaluation and Selection

Normal evaluation and selection criteria for A-E services usually include having:

- The professional qualifications necessary for satisfactory performance of the required services.

- The specialized experience and technical competence in the type of work required.

- The capacity to accomplish the work in the required time.

- The past performance in both the government and commercial sectors in terms of cost control, quality of work, and compliance with performance schedules.

- The proximity to the general geographical area of the project and knowledge of the local conditions.

The selection process usually results in the preparing of a selection report that ranks competent contractors in order of preference. The contracting professional then begins specific negotiations with the contractor(s) to agree upon terms and conditions and award a contract.

4.2.1.3 Architect and Design Services

Architect and design services are professional services of an architectural or engineering nature that are required to be performed or approved by a person licensed, registered, or certified to provide such services or are associated with research, planning, development, design, construction, alteration, or repair of real property, or other related professional services, such as studies and surveys.

4.2.1.4 Construction Services

The term *construction* means alteration of the landscape, assembly and fitting out of structures, installation of furnishings and fixtures, decoration, or repair of real property. The term construction services is defined as construction, alteration, or repair (including dredging, excavating, and painting) of buildings, structures, or other real property. Construction does not include the manufacture, production, furnishing, construction, alteration, repair, processing, or assembling of vessels, or other kinds of personal property. Construction contracting traditionally uses the phases of design, bid, and build for construction projects.

In commercial construction contracting, there are both formal and informal policies and procedures used in acquiring construction services. Construction contracts are subject to many outside restraints that have an impact on the successful contract performance, such as inspections, permits, and licenses. Careful planning is necessary to ensure adequate coordination of the acquisition.

In government construction contracting, sealed-bid procedures may be used for construction contracts. The following steps are commonly used by the government as part of a construction contracting process:

- *Pre-solicitation notice*—A pre-solicitation notice is issued containing sufficient detail to identify the nature, volume, location, and schedule for the requirement. These notices are usually issued well in advance of the invitation for bids in order to stimulate the interest of the greatest number of prospective bidders.

- *Invitation for bids*—This is the solicitation instrument used in the sealed-bidding method of procurement. It should allow sufficient time for bidders to perform the many tasks and issues associated with the bid process, including:
    o Site inspection,
    o Obtaining required subcontracting bids,
    o Examining plans and specifications, and
    o Preparing the required estimates.

- *Pre-bid conferences*—These conferences are often held to ensure that all prospective bidders have a clear and complete understanding of all aspects of the requirement.

- *Notice of award*—This is done in writing or electronically and contains the following information:
    o Identifies the invitation for bids,
    o Identifies the contractor's bid,
    o States the award price,
    o Advises the contractor that any required payment and performance bonds must be promptly executed and returned to the contracting officer, and
    o Specifies the date of commencement of work, or advises that a notice to proceed will be issued.

- *Pre-construction orientation*—A pre-construction conference is often held with the successful offeror before the construction effort begins to again ensure that there is a complete understanding of all issues related to the effort.

4.3 Information Technology

IT is any equipment or interconnected system or subsystem of equipment that is used in the automatic acquisition, storage, manipulation, management, movement, control, display, switching, interchange, transmission, or reception of data or information by the executive agency. IT includes:

- Computers,
- Ancillary equipment,
- Software,
- Firmware and similar procedures,
- Services (including support services), and
- Related resources, including national security systems.

It does not include any equipment that is acquired by a federal contractor incidental to a federal contract.

IT contracting concerns the acquisition and collection of technologies that deal specifically with processing, storing, and communicating information, and includes all types of computer and communication systems. It involves special policies and procedures applicable to the acquisition and use of computers, telecommunications, and related resources.

IT requirements often present a unique set of challenges for the contracting professional. The rapid pace of technological advancements often makes it difficult to acquire state-of-the-art IT items without exposing the buying organization to a significant amount of inherent risk. Contracting professionals must be cognizant of the stage of the life cycle in which procurement is taking place:

- *Information life cycle*—The stages through which information passes, typically characterized as creation or collection, processing, dissemination, use, storage, and disposition.

- *Information systems life cycle*—The phases through which an information system passes, typically characterized as initiation, development, operation, and termination.

"Information management" is the planning, budgeting, manipulating, and controlling of information throughout its life cycle.

Common risk elements include:

- Schedule risk,
- Risk of technical obsolescence,
- Cost risk,

- Technical feasibility,

- Dependencies between new projects and existing projects or systems,

- The number of simultaneous high-risk projects to be monitored,

- Funding availability, and

- Program management risk.

Typical techniques to manage and mitigate risks associated with IT acquisitions include:

- Prudent project management,

- Thorough acquisition planning related to budget planning,

- Continuous collection and evaluation of risk-based assessment data,

- Prototyping systems prior to implementation,

- Post-implementation reviews to determine actual costs and benefits,

- Using quantifiable measures to assess risks and returns, and

- The use of modular contracting.

"Modular contracting" is a contracting approach under which the need for a system is satisfied in successive acquisitions of interoperable increments. Each increment complies with common or commercially acceptable standards applicable to IT so that the increments are compatible with the other increments of the IT comprising the system.

The benefits of modular contracting include:

- Smaller increments are easier to manage than would be possible in one comprehensive acquisition;

- Complex IT objectives are addressed incrementally, enhancing the likelihood of achieving workable solutions for each of the objectives;

- Each increment can be tested and implemented, resulting in a functional system or solution that is not dependent upon any subsequent increment in order to perform its principal functions;

- Subsequent increments can take advantage of evolutionary enhancements in technology or changes in needs that occur during the implementation and use of preceding increments; and

- Potential adverse consequences can be isolated, mitigated, or resolved without potentially affecting the entire project.

4.4 Major Systems

"Major system" means that combination of elements that will function together to produce the capabilities required to fulfill a mission need. The elements may include, for example, hardware, equipment, software, construction or other improvements, or real property. Major system acquisition programs are those programs that:

- Are directed at and critical to fulfilling an agency mission,

- Entail the allocation of relatively large resources, and

- Warrant special management attention.

Additional criteria and relative dollar thresholds for the determination of agency programs to be considered major systems under the purview of Office of Management and Budget Circular A-109 may be established at the discretion of the agency head.

Major systems acquisition policies are designed to ensure that agencies acquire major systems in the most effective, economical, and timely manner. The policies require agencies to promote innovation and full and open competition in the development of major system concepts by:

- Expressing agency needs and program objectives in terms of the agency's mission and not in terms of specified systems to satisfy needs,

- Focusing agency resources and special management attention on activities conducted in the initial stage of major programs, and

- Sustaining effective competition between alternative system concepts and sources for as long as it is beneficial.

Major systems acquisition requires the direct involvement of senior agency management, including the agency head, in the planning, execution, and continuing evaluation of the status of the program. Contracting professionals in major systems acquisition must be aware of conditions and processes such as:

- Design to cost;

- Effective competition;

- Acquisition life cycles;

- Exploration, demonstration, full production, and full-scale development contracts;

- Program management;

- Quality assurance;

- Reliability;

- Scheduling;

- Validation; and

- Work breakdown structures.

4.5 Service Contracts

Government service contracts account for more than half of all federal contracts and have increased 44 percent over the past five years. Thus, it is important for contract managers to be aware of service contract concepts. This section explains basic concepts of government service contracts, including:

- The Service Contract Act (4.5.1),

- Office of Management and Budget Circular A-76 (4.5.2), and

- Performance-based acquisition (4.5.3).

The government's service contract policy includes the following:

- Performance-based acquisition is the preferred method for obtaining services,

- Government agencies shall generally rely on the private sector for commercial services,

- Agencies shall not award a contract for the performance of inherently governmental functions,

- Program officials are responsible for accurately describing the service contracting requirement in a manner that ensures full understanding and performance by contractors, and

- Services should be obtained in the most cost-effective manner, without barriers to full and open competition, and free of any potential conflicts of interest.

A *service contract* is defined as 1) a contract for the time and services of individuals for organizations in support of a government objective; or 2) a contract that directly engages the time and effort of a contractor whose primary purpose is to perform an identifiable task rather than furnish an end item of supply. Service contracts can be personal or nonpersonal; professional or nonprofessional:

- *Personal services contract*—A contract under which the personnel providing the services are subject, either by the contract's terms or the manner in which it is administered, to the supervision and control usually prevailing in relationships between employers and employees.

- *Nonpersonal services contract*—A contract under which the personnel providing the services are not subject, either by the contract's terms or the manner in which it is administered, to the supervision and control usually prevailing in relationships between employers and employees.

Personal services contracts in government contracting are of particular concern to contracting professionals. A personal services contract is characterized by the employer-employee relationship it creates between the government agency and the contractor's personnel. The government is normally required to obtain its employees under direct hire under competitive appointment or other procedures required by civil service law. Obtaining personal services by contract, rather than by direct hire, can circumvent those laws. Accordingly, agencies are prohibited from awarding personal service contracts, except when specifically authorized by statute to do so. Also, a nonpersonal services contract can, in effect, become a personal services contract based on the manner in which the contract is administered after award. This can occur when contractor personnel are subject to the relatively continuous supervision and control of a government manager or employee.

4.5.1 The Service Contract Act (SCA)

The SCA requires contractors and subcontractors performing services on covered federal or District of Columbia contracts in excess of $2,500 to pay service employees in various classes no less than the monetary wage rates and to furnish fringe benefits found prevailing in the locality or in a collective bargaining agreement. *Service employee* means any person engaged in the performance of a contract other than any person employed in a bona fide executive, administrative, or professional capacity, as these terms are defined in Part 541 of Title 29, *Code of Federal Regulations*, as revised.

The compensation requirements of the SCA are enforced by the Employment Standards Administration's Wage and Hour Division within the U.S. Department of Labor. The SCA safety and health requirements are enforced by the Occupational Safety and Health Administration within the Department of Labor.

Contracting professionals need to be aware of the potential impact of this law on prospective service contracts, such as the need to incorporate SCA wage determinations in contractual documents. Each contractor and subcontractor performing work subject to the SCA shall maintain certain records for each employee performing work on the covered contract.

The SCA does not apply to the following:

- Contracts for construction, alteration, and/or repair, including painting and decorating of public buildings or public works;

- Work covered by the Walsh-Healey Public Contracts Act;

- Contracts for the carriage of freight or personnel by vessel, airplane, bus, truck, railway line, or oil or gas pipeline where published tariff rates are in effect;

- Contracts for the furnishing of services by radio, telephone, telegraph, or cable companies subject to the Communications Act of 1934;

- Contracts for public utility services, including electric light and power, water, steam, and gas;

- Contracts for direct services to a federal agency by an individual or individuals;

- Contracts for the operation of postal contract stations; and

- Services performed outside of the geographical scope.

4.5.2 OMB Circular A-76

The Office of Management and Budget (OMB) Circular A-76, "Performance of Commercial Activities," provides guidance to define "inherently governmental" and "commercial functions." There is no precise method to determine what constitutes an inherently governmental function and what constitutes a commercial function; their determination is often based on the facts of each situation. OMB Circular A-76 states:

An inherently governmental activity is one that is so intimately related to the public interest as to mandate performance by government personnel. These activities require the exercise of substantial discretion in applying government authority and/or in making decisions for the government. Inherently governmental activities normally fall into two categories: the exercise of sovereign government authority or the establishment of procedures and processes related to the oversight of monetary transactions or entitlements. An inherently governmental activity involves:

(1) Binding the United States to take or not to take some action by contract, policy, regulation, authorization, order, or otherwise;

(2) Determining, protecting, and advancing economic, political, territorial, property, or other interests by military or diplomatic action, civil or criminal judicial proceedings, contract management, or otherwise;

(3) Significantly affecting the life, liberty, or property of private persons; or

(4) Exerting ultimate control over the acquisition, use, or disposition of United States property (real or personal, tangible or intangible), including establishing policies or procedures for the collection, control, or disbursement of appropriated and other federal funds.

Inherently governmental functions, by definition, necessarily involve the exercise of (substantial) discretion, although not every exercise of discretion means that a function is inherently governmental. The discretion must commit the government to a course of action when two or more alternatives exist.

4.5.2.1 Advisory and Assistance Services

The acquisition of advisory and assistance services is sometimes used to help government managers achieve maximum effectiveness or economy in their operations. Advisory and assistance service contracts can be used to:

- Obtain outside points of view to avoid limited judgment on critical issues;

- Obtain advice regarding developments in industry, university, or foundation research;

- Obtain the opinions, special knowledge, or skills of noted experts;

- Enhance the understanding of, and develop alternative solutions to, complex issues;

- Support and improve the operation of organizations; and

- Ensure the more efficient or effective operation of managerial or hardware systems.

(*See Federal Acquisition Regulation 37.203.*)

Advisory and assistance service contracts may not be used to:

- Perform work of a policy, decision-making, or managerial nature, which is the direct responsibility of agency officials;

- Bypass or undermine personnel ceilings, pay limitations, or competitive employment procedures;

- Contract for, on a preferential basis, former federal employees;

- Specifically aid in influencing or enacting legislation; or

- Obtain professional or other technical advice, which is readily available within the agency or another federal agency.

(*Ibid.*)

FAR Part 37.2 provides additional information about advisory and assistance services.

4.5.3 Performance-Based Acquisition

Performance-based acquisition is intended to ensure that required outcome quality levels are achieved and that total payment is related to the degree that outcomes achieved meet contract standards. Performance-based contracts should:

- Describe the requirements in terms of results required, rather than the methods of performing the work;

- Use measurable performance standards and quality assurance plans;

- Specify procedures for reductions of fees or for reductions to the price of fixed-price contracts when services are not performed or do not meet certain specified requirements;

- Include performance incentives, where appropriate; and

- Use quality assurance surveillance plans to determine that the services conform to contract requirements.

There are seven steps to conducting performance-based service acquisition, as illustrated in **FIGURE 4-5-1** on page 101.

Performance-based service acquisition has many benefits that include:
- An increased likelihood of meeting mission needs;

- A focus on intended results, not process;

- Better value and enhanced performance;

- Less performance risk;

- No detailed specification or process description is needed;

- The contractor has flexibility in proposing solutions;

- Better competition is present—not just contractors, but solutions;

- Contractor buy-in and shared interests;

- Shared incentives permit innovation and cost effectiveness;

- There is less likelihood of a successful protest;

- Surveillance is less frequent, but more meaningful;

- The results are documented for Government Performance and Results Act reporting as a byproduct of acquisition; and

- There are a variety of solutions from which to choose.

(*Derived from* "Benefits of Performance-Based Acquisition," *available at* **www.acquisition.gov/ sevensteps/introduction.html**.)

FAR Part 37.6 provides additional information about performance-based acquisition.

4.6 International Contracting

International contracting is comprised of the policies and procedures that govern the acquisition and sale of goods and services with foreign nationals and governments. International contracting can have many unique aspects depending on the country and the individual, organization, or government entity with which one contracts. Whether functioning as a buyer or seller, contracting professionals who operate in the international market require an enhanced set of skills and knowledge to be effective. International contracting can sometimes result in lower costs and improved quality for buyers, and increased sales and profitability for sellers. However, there are many significant differences between operating in the domestic market and the international market. Some of those differences include the following:

- *Currency differences*—Currency differences, and the constantly changing exchange rates, can have impacts on the business relationship and feasibility of doing business in certain countries.

- *Different meanings of common business terms*—Common business terms, such as "bi-monthly" or "relationship," often have different meanings in different countries and can be the source of unintended issues.

- *Different processes*—Some companies in less-developed countries may be less sophisticated and knowledgeable in various production, quality control, or management processes, and may be unable or reluctant to modify their systems and procedures to conform to one's expectations.

- *Export issues*—"Export" is defined as the transfer of commodities, technical data, articles, or services from the United States to a foreign person, corporation, or other entity. The company may be required to obtain export permission from the Bureau of Industry and Security within the Department of Commerce or the Office of Defense Trade Controls within the U.S. Department of State.

- *Import issues*—Bringing goods, services, or information into a foreign country is often subject to that country's laws, taxes, and duties, as well as restrictions on use of the goods and services.

- *Language*—There are obvious potential issues when multiple languages are introduced into the contracting process. Some international firms have personnel who are multilingual. In other cases, the use of third-party interpreters may be appropriate. Regardless, the contracting professional needs to ensure that the sometimes subtle context and nuances inherent in one language are accurately reflected in the translation to a different language.

- *Legal processes*—Legal terms and processes may differ significantly in various countries and can inject additional risk in the contracting process. Local laws vary widely from country to country in the areas of employment, labor, and severance. In the cases where contract perfor-

mance will be done in-country, this can impose substantial financial burdens on a company.

- *Location*—Dealing with organizations located abroad can present a number of challenges related to time differences and distance. Buyers and sellers may need to adjust their work hours to be able to converse directly with international firms, or they may have to accept the fact that most communication will be indirect; e.g., electronic.

- *Political climate*—The political and social climate in many countries is sometimes subject to abrupt and significant change. Contracting professionals must have a thorough understanding of past, present, and future trends that may influence the degree to which business in a foreign country may be affected by changes in the political and social climate.

- *Social customs*—Business, cultural, and social customs and norms, to the degree that they are different from one's experience and expectations, can present significant obstacles to the successful completion of business agreements.

- *Tax implications*—The tax-cost implications of doing business in foreign countries can be tremendous; for example, the foreign country may have a right to assess its own income or value-added tax on the company's global earnings that have a connection to that country. There may be personal tax implications for company employees who are temporarily transferred to the country for contract performance.

- *Third-party involvement*—Buying and selling internationally often requires the use of various third-party entities, such as trading companies, local representatives, foreign banks, freight forwarders, customs brokers, etc. Some foreign countries require an in-country firm on the company team.

- *Entry into a foreign country by expatriates*— Many countries have restrictions on the number of expatriates that can be in that country for a particular purpose. Entry into a foreign country is generally controlled by a visa process.

Contracting professionals should ensure they have a complete understanding of this dynamic environment, and use appropriate caution to avoid mistakes.

4.6.1 Agreements and Restrictions

Agreements exist among the United States and its trading partners regarding international procurement. These include the General Agreement on Tariffs and Trade (GATT), the GATT Government Procurement Code, the North American Free Trade Agreement (NAFTA), as well as bilateral agreements that have been negotiated between the United States and other countries (such as the U.S.-Canada Free Trade Agreement). Congress has routinely included in appropriation acts restrictions on the procurement of certain foreign items, usually to protect domestic industries.

Contracting professionals conducting international contracting transactions must be aware of the relevant agreements and restrictions associated with this discipline. The following are some of the agreements and restrictions of which contracting professionals should be familiar with:

- *Free trade agreement*—A treaty between two or more countries that do not impose tariffs for commerce conducted across their borders. This does not mean capital and labor moves freely between them, and tariffs are still imposed upon nonmember countries. The intent is to open markets and to provide opportunities for businesses to compete globally.

- Export Administration Regulation (EAR)—Regulations administered by the Department of Commerce/Bureau of Industry and Security that, among other things, provide specific instructions on the use and types of export licenses required for certain commodities, software, and technology.

- *International Commercial Terms (Incoterms)*—The Incoterms rules are an internationally recognized standard and are used worldwide in international and domestic contracts for the sale of goods. First published in 1936, Incoterms rules provide internationally accepted definitions and rules of interpretation for most common commercial terms.

- International Traffic in Arms Regulation (ITAR)—U.S. Department of State regulations that govern the export of restricted defense technology and services maintained on the U.S. Munitions List to foreign states.

4.7 State and Local Government

When viewed as a single entity, the purchasing power of state and local governments represents a huge, and often untapped, source of business for commercial contracting professionals. However, the unfortunate reality is that state and local govern-

ment is not a homogenous market segment, but rather a somewhat artificial category that, in fact, is comprised of literally thousands of buying entities, often with their own unique processes, procedures, and challenges.

"Cooperative purchasing" is a process whereby two or more communities, counties, or other governmental jurisdictions voluntarily agree to coordinate their purchases of one or more commodities to obtain the best unit price through volume buying.

"Intergovernmental relations" is a range of cooperative activities among governments, including:

- Various forms of intergovernmental cooperative purchasing,

- Joint or shared use of facilities and supplies, and

- Procurements made by one government from another.

Advantages in pursuing business in the state and local government sector include the following:

- State and local governments tend to be more commercially oriented than their federal counterparts. Many potentially new customers already exist for firms that deal in commercial goods and services.

- The local government can benefit from the close proximity of a company that can provide high-quality goods and services at competitive prices and that can be available for consultation and advice.

- The success of local businesses generates additional tax revenue for the state and local governments, which can be used to help provide additional government services and also to reinvest in the local business community and infrastructure to create more businesses and economic growth.

- Dealing locally tends to help both the buyer and the seller by developing personal, long-term relationships based on mutual need and mutual benefit.

Disadvantages in dealing with the state and local government segment include the following:

- A lack of standardized processes, procedures, and regulatory guidance. Many state and local government entities have unique requirements, forms, and local ordinances that may increase the cost to the seller of doing business with multiple entities simultaneously.

- Many local governments seek out the best value, which may make some local businesses, particularly smaller ones, less competitive.

- Local and regional politics often influence purchasing decisions. Vendors should be aware that sometimes buying decisions are made based on facts or perceptions that have little or nothing to do with price, quality, or service.

4.7.1 Differing Definitions of Basic Contracting Terms

Though basic contracting terms may appear to be familiar, those who conduct business in federal, state, or local government contracts should be aware that the definitions may not always align. For instance, a federal contracting officer may be the equivalent of a state procurement officer. Also, the federal contracting officer's representative could be the equivalent of a state contract manager.

4.8 Supply Chain Management

Supply chain management is the sum total of all functions, operations, and facilities that are involved in the procurement and delivery of goods to a customer. It includes manufacturers, warehouses, transportation, distribution centers, retail outlets, and inventory at stages from raw materials to finished packages that flow between and among facilities.

The concept of supply chain management as a natural, evolutionary managerial advancement over the traditional purchasing function has become more prevalent and commonly accepted in recent years. Traditional supply chain management theory holds that an organization can reduce procurement costs, reduce procurement cycle time, and add value to the procurement process by taking actions such as the following:

- Reducing the number of suppliers used. Many organizations have found that maintaining large numbers of suppliers for the same or similar products or services and attempting to manage that supplier base was more expensive than the savings potentially realized from extensive competition among the suppliers for orders. Having many suppliers also introduced quality and consistent performance issues that were more difficult to manage.

- Negotiating long-term contracts with the few preferred suppliers. Cost savings can be realized by making significant commitments to a few suppliers as opposed to making only short-term commitments to many suppliers.

- Conducting more rigorous and detailed timeliness and quality tracking of the preferred supplier base. The significant purchase commitments made to a few suppliers are coupled with increased requirements for quality and performance.

- Analyzing and seeking to improve every action and link in the supply chain, from the end customer to the lowest-level supplier, with involvement, input, and cooperation from all stakeholders.

Supply chain management concepts recognize the acquisition function does not operate in a reactive vacuum, but rather is a component in a larger management system that provides value and profitability by merging customer needs and supplier capabilities with the value-added processes of the organization. Supply chain management also recognizes the interdependencies and interrelationships between and among all members of the supply chain and seeks to maximize the power and competitiveness of the entire supply chain through collaboration, cooperation, continuous improvement, and the maintenance of long-term relationships that benefit all members of the chain.

Contracting proficiency can be built through mastery of the following elements of supply chain management:

- *Constructive acceleration*—This describes a requirement (based on the reasonable interpretation of the buyer's words, acts, or inaction) that a contractor complete its work by a date earlier than one that would reflect the time extensions to which it is entitled because of excusable delays.

- *Economies of scale*—The most efficient operating level. This is the point where it costs less per unit to produce.

- *Forward buying*—This is the practice of buying materials in a quantity exceeding specified current requirements, but not beyond the actual foreseeable requirements.

- *Quantity Discount*—A price reduction given to a buyer for purchasing increasingly larger quantities of materials. A quantity discount is normally offered for:

o Purchasing a specific quantity of items at one time,

o Purchasing a specified dollar total at one time, or

o Purchasing a specified dollar total over an agreed-upon time period (also known as a "cumulative discount").

4.8.1 Logistics Management

According to the Council of Supply Chain Management Professionals (CSCMP), *logistics management* is defined as follows:

> Logistics management is that part of supply chain management that plans, implements, and controls the efficient, effective forward and reverse flow and storage of goods, services, and related information between the point of origin and the point of consumption in order to meet customers' requirements.

(Council of Supply Chain Management Professionals (CSCMP), "CSCMP's Definition of Logistics Management," *available at* http://cscmp.org/about-us/supply-chain-management-definitions.)

Logistics management includes a varied list of activities and functions. The CSCMP states:

> Logistics management activities typically include inbound and outbound transportation management, fleet management, warehousing, materials handling, order fulfillment, logistics network design, inventory management, supply/demand planning, and management of third-party logistics services providers. To varying degrees, the logistics function also includes sourcing and procurement, production planning and scheduling, packaging and assembly, and customer service. It is involved in all levels of planning and execution—strategic, operational, and tactical. Logistics management is an integrating function that coordinates and optimizes all logistics activities, as well as integrates logistics activities with other functions, including marketing, sales manufacturing, finance, and information technology.

(CSCMP, "Logistics Management—Boundaries and Relationships," *available at* http://cscmp.org/about-us/supply-chain/management-definitions.)

Contracting proficiency can be built through mastery of the following elements of logistics management:

- *Forecast*—An estimation of the future demand for a product. It is usually stated as a quantity (or value) over a specific time period. There are a number of inputs into a forecast, such as historical data, market trends, marketing data, and sales force feedback.

- *Forecast error*—A comparison between actual demand and forecasted demand. It is usually stated as a percentage.

- *Horizontal integration*—This describes a firm that owns several plants, each of which does the same thing. For example, a company buying two retail stores in a mall is an example of horizontal integration.

- *"Hub and spoke"*—A distribution model where stock is held at the "hub" location and then sent out to the "spoke" locations (distribution centers) when needed. This model usually allows for reduced overall inventory because the safety stock is mostly held at the hub rather than at the numerous spokes.

- *Reorder point*—A predetermined number usually calculated based on a number of factors. Once the inventory drops below the reorder point, a replenishment order is created.

- *Vertical integration*—This describes firms that own several plants, each of which owns a different stage in the production process. For example, a food manufacturer buying a chain of supermarkets would be vertical integration.

4.9 Government Property

Generally speaking, most contracts require total performance from the contractor. That is, under the requirements and terms and conditions contained in the contract, the contractor is usually required to provide all the resources necessary for successful performance. In some cases, however, the buyer can provide various forms of property to a contractor or subcontractor. The fundamental reason for the buyer to provide property to the seller is cost savings. It may be less expensive for a buyer to provide property to a contractor for use during performance than it would be for the contractor to purchase the property, particularly when the property can be reused for future contracts. Reutilization of government property promotes cost savings and efficiency for the government. The federal government also has a responsibility to protect the public trust, and serves as the guardian of the property with public funds.

Contracting professionals should command a strong understanding of the different types of property and their ownership:

- *Government property*—All property owned by, leased to, or acquired by the U.S. government under the terms of a contract. It includes property delivered or otherwise made available to the contractor (e.g., government-furnished property) and property provided by the contractor (i.e., property purchased by the contractor for use in performance of the contract); title in the latter case depends on the type of contract used and the specific provisions of the contract.

- *Government-furnished property*—Any property in the possession of or directly acquired by the government and subsequently made available to a contractor. The *FAR* distinguishes between government-furnished property and contractor-acquired property under contracts. A simple definition of *government-furnished property* is any property the government makes available or provides to a contractor for use in performance of a contract.

- *Contractor-acquired property*—Property that is acquired or otherwise provided by the contractor for performing a contract and to which the government has title. Under the terms of a contract, a contractor may be required to buy certain materials, equipment, or other property to perform the contract. The rights to title for such property purchased for use in performing a contract are generally placed (vested) in the government.

- *Ownership*—The collection of rights to use and enjoy property, including the right to transmit or convey these rights to others.

- *Title*—The right to control and dispose of property.

The federal government classifies government property into five categories:

1. *Material*—Property that may be consumed or expended during the performance of a contract, component parts of a higher assembly, or items that lose their individual identity through incorporation into an end-item. Material does not include equipment, special tooling, and special test equipment. The qualifiers for the definition of material are: incorporated, consumed, or expended. The descriptors include parts, assemblies, components, raw and processed materials, liquids, and other items. Examples of material are nuts, bolts, screws, washers, gasoline, oil, paint, solvents, chemicals, wire, switches, circuit boards, cable, sheet metal, bar stock, copper tubing, etc. Parts may also include more complex items such as starters, fuel injectors, radios, radar, sonar, and jet engines provided they are to be incorporated into the next higher assembly of the finished end item.

2. *Equipment*—A tangible asset that is functionally complete for its intended purpose, durable, nonexpendable, and needed for the performance of a contract. Equipment is not intended for sale, and does not ordinarily lose its identity or become a component part of another article when put into use. Equipment is a very broad classification for government property and includes items that are typically used for production, maintenance, repair, and providing services. Examples include machining centers, lathes, milling machines, presses, welders, heat treat ovens, fork trucks, cranes, tractors, cars, trucks, lawn mowers, tools (but not special tooling), test equipment (but not special test equipment), cafeteria equipment (mixers, ovens, coffee pots, dish washers, steamers, flatware, dinnerware, etc.), drills, printers, computers, cameras, projectors, etc.

3. *Real property*—Land and rights in land, ground improvements, utility distribution systems, and buildings and other structures. It does not include foundations and other work necessary for installing special tooling, special test equipment, or plant equipment. Real property includes land (real estate) as well as land rights. Land rights may include the rights to the water (riparian) on top of, running through, or below the land (rivers, streams, lakes, wells, etc.). Mineral rights may include the rights to coal, oil, silver, gold, copper, etc. that may be found within the boundaries of the land. Utility distribution systems distribute electricity, gas, water, sewage, etc. within and through the land, buildings, and structures.

4. *Special tooling*—Jigs, dies, fixtures, molds, patterns, taps, gauges, and all components of these items including foundations and similar improvements necessary for installing special test equipment, and which are of such a specialized nature that without substantial modification or alteration their use is limited to the development or production of particular

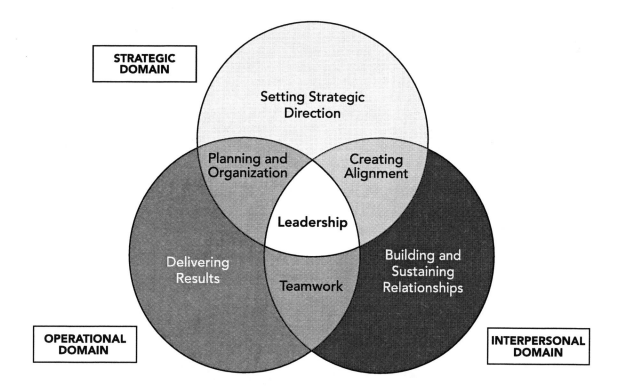

Figure 5-2-1. The Primary Colours Model of Leadership
Derived from David Pendleton and Adrian Furnham, *Leadership: All You Need to Know* (London: Palgrave Macmillan, 2012). (Copyright held by Primary Colours Consulting (**www.primarycoloursconsulting.co.uk**), used with permission.)

supplies or parts thereof or to the performance of particular services. Special tooling does not include material, special test equipment, real property, equipment, machine tools, or similar capital items. The descriptors for special tooling include jigs, dies, fixtures, molds, patterns, taps, gauges, other equipment and manufacturing aids, and all components of these items. The qualifiers for this class of government property are that they are of such a "specialized nature" and without "substantial modification their use is limited to the development or production of particular supplies or parts." An example would include the forging dies that are used to make the landing gear for the U.S. Air Force F-22. Holding fixtures are used to hold aircraft carrier hull components together during the welding process. Molds are used to make metal and plastic castings for various aircraft components (canopies, handles, cranks, dials, etc.).

5. *Special test equipment*—Either single or multipurpose integrated test units engineered, designed, fabricated, or modified to accomplish special purpose testing in performing a contract.

It consists of items or assemblies of equipment including foundations and similar improvements necessary for installing special test equipment, and standard or general purpose items or components that are interconnected and interdependent so as to become a new functional entity for special testing purposes. Special test equipment does not include material, special tooling, real property, and equipment items used for general testing purposes or property that with relatively minor expense can be made suitable for general purpose use. Special test equipment descriptors are single or multipurpose integrated test units, items or assemblies of equipment, and standard or general purpose items. The important thing to remember is that standard or general purpose items may be used to construct special test equipment. The qualifiers are "engineered, designed, fabricated, or modified to accomplish special purpose testing" and that it becomes "a new functional entity." Special test equipment excludes "property that with relatively minor expense can be made suitable for general purpose use." An example of special test equipment is the unit used to calibrate the main gun on the U.S. Army Abrams Main Battle Tank.

4.9.1 Major Phases and Key Activities

If the government plans to award a contract requiring the use of property outlined in *CMBOK* 4.9, there are formal procedures for the incorporation of such property based on some fundamental considerations. There are four major phases and key activities associated with property:

1. *Solicitation*—During the solicitation phase, property is identified and made available for inspection or used "as is." Existing government-furnished property is also identified, and a determination is made whether to include it in the procurement. If such property is included, it is made available for inspection and is offered either "as-is" or with a guarantee of suitability for use in the procurement. Contractors are allowed to inspect property in order to verify the suitability or the "as-is" condition of such for use in performance of the contract.

   o *Competitive advantage*—Particularly as it relates to government contracting, the possession of government-furnished property can provide an incumbent contractor with a competitive advantage when competing with other sellers for future contracts. Buying professionals often create a more competitive environment in which all selling professionals are assessed evenly. Typically, this is done by taking the value of the property into account when evaluating competing offers.

2. *Delivery of property*—The government is responsible for providing the property in accordance with the contract schedule, or in such time to allow the contractor to reasonably meet delivery requirements. The contractor may receive an equitable adjustment due to the late delivery or other circumstances that may jeopardize performance in accordance with the agreed-upon terms of the contract.

3. *Control, accountability, and use*—The contractor is generally responsible for having a property control system, as required by the contract and FAR Part 45. The contractor is generally required to maintain property in good condition, less normal wear and tear, while also keeping custodial records that include information regarding the location, cost, allocability to contracts, condition, and disposition of government property.

4. *Disposition*—Upon completion or termination of a contract, the contractor is generally responsible for requesting disposition instructions and disposing of any property as directed by the government.

4.9.1.1 Property Administration

The post-award administration of property is a highly specialized aspect of contract administration, normally handled by a trained sub-specialist within the buyer's contracting organization. However, there are some general concepts related to property that are important, including the following:

- *Ownership*—Usually, the buyer retains ownership of and all rights to buyer-provided property. The question of ownership of property acquired by the seller to perform the contract is sometimes more complex, and may be dependent upon the type of contract under which the seller is performing.

- *Accountability*—The buying organization usually retains internal organizational accountability for all property the buyer provides to a seller, but the seller is required to document the property receipt and record relevant facts about the property, such as its condition or if overages, shortages, or damages occurred. In addition, the seller should maintain the property in its possession. The contractor's maintenance program shall enable the identification, disclosure, and performance of normal and routine preventative maintenance and repair.

- *Property administration*—When a buyer furnishes property to a contractor, several property administration issues are normally part of the acquisition. The availability of buyer-furnished property is usually included in the solicitation, and potential offerors are normally provided an opportunity to review and inspect the property to verify its existence and condition.

The buyer is most often responsible for delivering buyer-furnished property to the contractor. The buyer should be careful to ensure that delivery delays do not occur, since that may adversely affect contractor performance.

The contractor is usually required to have a system in place to ensure that all property provided by the buyer is accounted for, maintained as appropriate, and used as specified in the contract. Both the buyer and seller should periodically review or audit these control systems to ensure they are operating properly.

Upon completion or termination of a contract, the contractor is usually held responsible for requesting property disposition instructions from the buyer for disposing of the property as directed. (FAR Part 45 provides additional information about government property.).

4.10 Other Specialized Areas

As contracting becomes more complex, there are many more areas in which the contracting professional needs to be familiar. Contracting professionals need to have a working knowledge of the basic concepts of:

- Contingency contracting;
- Contractor system reviews;
- Environmental contracting;
- Foreign military sales;
- Government purchase cards;
- Inter-agency contracting;
- Security (industrial, physical, personal, information assurance);
- Spend analysis; and
- Undefinitized contract actions.

5.0 Business Competencies

Contract managers must understand various aspects of business, even if they are U.S. federal government employees. In order to make sound business decisions, contract managers' skill sets should go beyond knowing the contract's terms and conditions; they must also know about the marketplace in which their organization operates, including finance, economics, and accounting. They must be able to manage and lead a team and understand how to use technology to meet the organization's goals.

Over 10 years ago, one noted professional, W. Gregor Macfarlan, predicted that "[t]he success of contracting professionals will be measured by their business management skills, not how many contracts are awarded or changes processed." (W. Gregor Macfarlan, "The Buyer as a Business Manager?" *Contract Management* Magazine

(August 2000).) That prediction has come true. Today, a contract manager's job is more strategic and team-oriented, requiring technical competency and acquisition skills to meet customer needs. (*See ibid*.) Understanding and applying the business principles discussed in this *CMBOK* section are important steps toward providing valued customer service to your organization.

This set of competencies defines several key business competencies, including the following:

- Management (5.1),
- Leadership skills (5.2),
- Marketing (5.3),
- Operations management (5.4),
- Financial analysis (5.5),
- Accounting (5.6),
- Economics (5.7), and
- Information science/technology (5.8).

5.1 Management

The ability to manage is essential for a contracts professional because it consists of the functions used to accomplish an organization's goals. The four commonly accepted key functions of management include:

- Planning,
- Organizing,
- Directing/leading, and
- Controlling.

5.1.1 The Four Key Functions of Management

"Planning" involves preparing your organization for the future, which includes different levels, such as:

- *Strategic planning*—looks at long-term (e.g., five-year) goals and objectives. A strategic plan is typically based on the organization's mission statement.
- *Tactical planning*—focuses on short-term (e.g., one- to two-year) goals and involves evaluating economic and environmental issues such as competition (for sellers) and requirements planning (for buyers) to meet the strategic plan's goals.
- *Operational planning*—looks at the near-term (e.g., from the next few months up to one year)

goals and typically identifies how the organization will meet its tactical goals.

- *Contingency planning*—involves "what if?" analysis to look at various situations in the event that certain environmental or economic conditions change.

"Organizing" consists of allocating resources to meet goals identified during the planning process. Such resources typically include the personnel, financial assets, and property necessary to meet the organization's mission. Organizing also requires that managers understand the work that needs to be done and how to sort (organize) that effort into tasks or departments and assign personnel to accomplish those tasks.

"Directing" or "leading" requires a manager to influence others to complete the required tasks and achieve personal and organizational goals. There are many different leadership styles that managers can use to motivate others and managers should be open to learning new techniques to motivate their workforce. ("Leadership" is discussed in more detail in *CMBOK* 5.2.)

"Controlling" involves monitoring and evaluating how well the tasks are completed. It uses performance measurement to evaluate how well a person or department is meeting goals. (*See* D.L. Kurtz and L.E. Boone, *Contemporary Business* (Fort Worth, Texas: Harcourt College Publishers, 2002).)

Organizations use different measurements to evaluate contract management. One survey suggested that contract professionals be evaluated using the following five factors:

- Knowing the rules of the game,
- Exercising sound business judgment,
- Understanding strategy and tactics,
- Knowing the marketplace, and
- Functioning as a team member.

(Contract Management Institute, *Metrics for the Contract Management Discipline* (Vienna, Virginia, NCMA, 2002).)

For buyers and sellers, measuring performance typically involves contract award and cost/profit considerations. For example, buyers might be measured on

the final contract price negotiated within the budget estimate and sellers might be evaluated on the contract's profitability. Other contract management metrics might include timeliness, responsiveness, and/or customer satisfaction. Providing customer service typically involves the following five elements:

- *Reliability*—Provide the service consistently and accurately,
- *Responsiveness*—Anticipate and take action to meet (and exceed) the customer's needs,
- *Value*—Make the customer feel valuable,
- *Empathy*—Let the customer know that you share their concerns, and
- *Competency*—Have technical knowledge of contracting laws and regulations.

(*Derived from* J.F. Newhart, "Service With a Smile," *Contract Management* Magazine (December 2003).)

The size of an organization and the complexity of its mission normally dictate the contract management staff composition. A small business may have only one person in charge of all contract management activities. A large corporation or government agency, on the other hand, may have hundreds or even thousands of managers, each responsible for some segment of the organization's contract activities. Regardless of the entity's size and purpose, the four key functions of management previously noted are essential.

In addition to the four key functions of management, contract managers should also have the following skills to be effective.

5.1.2 Additional Management Skills

5.1.2.1 Technical Skills

Contract managers need to be technically competent in the laws and regulations that impact their organization. This means having at least a foundational understanding of contract principles and the ability to do the work they ask staff to do. In some cases, managers might be less proficient than their staff in actually performing the day-to-day work, but the managers' technical knowledge impacts their ability to manage staff.

5.1.2.2 Communication Skills

The ability to communicate verbally and in writing is an essential skill for managers. Effective communication is a two-way street and has multiple facets, including:

Balance Sheet

[Date]
(all numbers in $000)

ASSETS		LIABILITIES	
Current Assets		**Current Liabilities**	
Cash		Accounts payable	
Accounts receivable		Short-term notes	
(less doubtful accounts)		Current portion of long-term notes	
Inventory		Interest payable	
Temporary investment		Taxes payable	
Prepaid expenses		Accrued payroll	
Total Current Assets		**Total Current Liabilities**	
Fixed Assets		**Long-term Liabilities**	
Long-term investments		Mortgage	
Land		Other long-term liabilities	
Buildings		**Total Long-Term Liabilities**	
(less accumulated depreciation)			
Plant and equipment			
(less accumulated depreciation)		**Shareholders' Equity**	
Furniture and fixtures		Capital stock	
(less accumulated depreciation)		Retained earnings	
Total Net Fixed Assets		**Total Shareholders' Equity**	
TOTAL ASSETS		**TOTAL LIABILITIES & EQUITY**	

Figure 5-5-1. Balance Sheet
Derived from Microsoft, "Microsoft Templates," *available at* **http://office.microsoft.com/en-us/templates/word-templates-FX102825522.aspx.**

- The ability to speak clearly and concisely to individuals, small groups, and large groups;

- The ability to listen and understand others, at all levels within an organization;

- The ability to plan, conduct, and control formal and informal meetings; and

- The ability to convey information in written form in a format and at a level appropriate to the intended recipient.

5.1.2.3 Human Relations Skills

Effective managers must be able to work with a wide variety of other individuals and groups with differing social, educational, and experience backgrounds and with varying capabilities to ensure that the organization's goals are accomplished. These human relations skills, often more art than science, are of increasing importance as the workforces of most organizations continue to become more and more diverse.

5.1.2.4 Time Management Skills

Contract managers need to be able to juggle multiple tasks and prioritize those tasks so that the most important ones get done in a timely manner. The ability to know what is important now and what can be deferred, to organize and plan one's day, and to know when to modify the plans are all vital to a manager's ability to succeed.

5.2 Leadership Skills

People are an organization's most important asset and the organization will struggle to survive without motivated employees. Leaders can make the difference between having great employees who are motivated to do whatever it takes to get the job done, or they can have employees who just sit in a room and go through the motions of actually working. Leadership is about motivating people to work together and do great things.

A leader needs to have a clear vision that inspires their employees. This vision should be defined and communicated in such a way to provide a clear path that people can follow with integrity. The vision must be articulated in such a way to generate enthusiasm so employees are eager to participate and meet the organization's goals. (*See* Jeff Wolf, "Leadership in

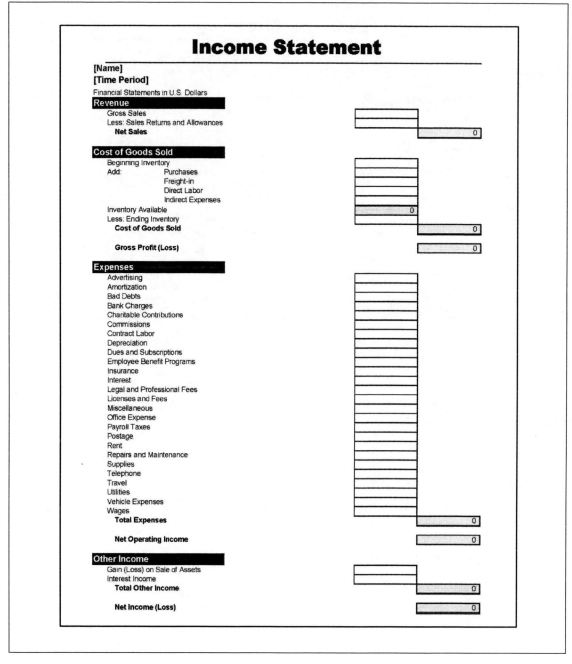

Figure 5-5-2. Income Statement
Derived from Microsoft, "Microsoft Templates," *available at* **http://office.microsoft.com/en-us/templates/word-templates-FX102825522.aspx.**

Crisis: Take 8 Steps to Avoid Pitfalls," *available at* **www.wolfmotivation.com/articles/leadership-in-crisis-take-8-steps-to-avoid-pitfalls**.)

Dr. David Pendleton, a psychologist specializing in leadership, suggests that leadership has three domains to it that overlap like a Venn diagram (see **FIGURE 5-2-1** *on page 115). These three domains are:*

- *The Strategic Domain*—This domain looks at tomorrow and its possibilities. It's not really interested in what is practical, but what is possible. Leaders should ask: "Where can we take our organization? What could it look like three or five years from now?" Leaders are encouraged to imagine the possibilities. (*Derived from* "The Primary Colors of Leadership,"

Statement of Cash Flows [Name] [Time Period]

Cash flows from operating activities	
Cash received from customers	
Cash paid for merchandise	
Cash paid for wages and other operating expenses	
Cash paid for interest	
Cash paid for taxes	
Other	
Net cash provided (used) by operating activities	
Cash flows from investing activities	
Cash received from sale of capital assets (plant and equipment, etc.)	
Cash received from disposition of business segments	
Cash received from collection of notes receivable	
Cash paid for purchase of capital assets	
Cash paid to acquire businesses	
Other	
Net cash provided (used) by investing activities	
Cash flows from financing activities	
Cash received from issuing stock	
Cash received from long term borrowings	
Cash paid to repurchase stock	
Cash paid to retire long-term debt	
Cash paid for dividends	
Other	
Net cash provided (used) in financing activities	
Increase (decrease) in cash during the period	
Cash balance at the beginning of the period	
Cash balance at the end of the period	

Figure 5-5-5. Cash Flow Statement
Derived from Microsoft, "Microsoft Templates," *available at* **http://office.microsoft.com/en-us/templates/word-templates-FX102825522.aspx.**

interview with Dr. David Pendleton, *Contract Management* Magazine (June 2013).)

- *The Operational Domain*—This domain is concerned with the present and the practicalities of getting the job done. Leaders can ask: "What does it take to get the job done? What resources do we need?" (*Ibid.*)

- *The Interpersonal Domain*—This domain is about emotional intelligence and getting along with each other. (*Ibid.*)

Within the domains, there are seven tasks that leaders need to accomplish, which include:

- Setting strategic direction,
- Delivering results,
- Building and sustaining relationships,
- Planning and organizing,
- Teamwork,
- Creating alignment, and

- Leadership.

Note that "leadership" is the competency that is the central element and is created when all three domains and all seven tasks come together. However, it is very difficult for one person to do all seven tasks within all three domains well. A leader needs to identify which people have the right skills in each domain in order to accomplish a well-rounded team or group. This requires a diverse leadership team with a variety of skills and abilities. (*Ibid.*)

5.3 Marketing

Successful marketing requires timely and relevant information about the marketplace. The "marketplace" can mean different things to buyers and sellers. Buyers consider the sources from which they choose as the marketplace. A seller might have multiple products and services and each one might be considered a separate "line of business" or marketplace.

Many sellers develop a marketing strategy to identify potential customers and retain existing customers. A marketing strategy identifies customers or potential customers a business can serve. Businesses should tailor their marketing strategy as well as the products and services they offer toward the specific customer's needs. In order to do this, a company would consider prices charged, distribution methods, and promotion avenues. A successful marketing strategy addresses a customer's needs that will also make a profit.

An important element of any marketing strategy is to identify a "target market," which is a way to divide or segment the total market to the ones that the company can best serve. For example, there are two ways to segment a market:

- *Geographic*—Specializing in serving the needs of customers in a particular location or area, such as a state or region; and

- *Customer*—Identifying the customers most likely to need your product or service and targeting those groups, such as a government agency or prime contractor.

In addition to segmenting the target market, sellers also need to identify the four essential elements of any marketing program, which consist of the following:

- *Products/services*—Identifying the right products and services to meet the needs of your target market.

- *Price*—Offering products and services at the right price is important in order to make your business successful. Understanding the marketplace, such as supply, demand, and competition, will help in determining the right price. (More information about supply and demand is discussed in CMBOK 5.7.)

- *Promotion*—Promotion strategies identify ways to advertise and sell products and services. Many businesses use the Internet to promote their products and/or services. It is one way businesses let their target market know what they offer for sale.

- *Place*—This aspect of the marketing program refers to how businesses get products and services to their target market. If the business sells products, will they have a storefront presence or an online presence (or both)?

To summarize, marketing involves the following steps:

1. Define a target market.

2. Discover what products or services the customers in your target market need.

3. Set a price for the products/services.

4. Advertise the products/services to potential customers.

5. Make the product/services available to customers.

(*Derived from* Small Business Administration, "Marketing" (2013), *available at* **www.sba.gov/category/ navigation-structure/starting-managing-business/ managing-business/running-business/marketing**.)

5.4 Operations Management

Operations management is a type of management activity that is mostly concerned with the directing and controlling of management functions. It includes all the activities necessary to manufacture a product or provide a service. Operations management looks for ways to improve the activities or add value to a product or service. Operations management uses customer feedback to improve processes and productivity. The formula for measuring productivity is: productivity = output/input. Input is usually labor hours used to produce the output. Typical outputs include sales made, products delivered, or customers serviced, and can be measured in either units or dollars. When an organization is more productive, it can expand its ability to provide goods and services. (*See* Roberta S. Russell and Bernard W. Taylor, *Operations Management: Creating Value Along the Supply Chain* (Hoboken, New Jersey: John Wiley & Sons, Inc., 2009).) For example, a customer might say that the procurement department is slow in awarding contracts. Operations management would find a way to improve the procurement department's productivity. Some organizations use "administrative lead time" to measure how long it takes to award a contract. The start date is when a procurement request is received in the contracts/procurement department and ends when the contract is awarded. Improving productivity might involve getting complete procurement requests the first time. Operations management would identify that the requesting department did not always provide accurate information, which would cause the delays in contract award.

Competition	Buyers	Sellers	Market Entry	Pricing Power
Perfect	Many independent	Many independent	Relatively easy	Pricing balance between buyers and sellers
Monopoly	Many independent	One	Restrictions	Considerable pricing power to sellers
Oligopoly	Many independent	Few independent	Restrictions	Relatively great pricing advantage to sellers
Monopsony	One	Many independent	Relatively easy	Considerable pricing power to buyers

Figure 5-7-2. Competition's Impact on Pricing
Derived from Deputy Director of Defense Procurement and Acquisition Policy (Cost, Pricing, and Finance), *Contract Pricing Reference Guide*, volume 4 (Washington, DC: Department of Defense, 2012).

Operations management confirms that:

- The organization has the required inputs, such as materials, labor, etc., required to perform the necessary tasks;

- The way inputs become what the organization needs (e.g., an accounting report) is effective and efficient;

- The outputs are what the organization needs and that they follow to the quality and quantity requested; and

- The management/employee exchange feedback, including ways to:

  o Seek clarification, discuss improvements, and share ideas;

  o Point out mistakes and make improvements;

  o Praise employees for a job well done or for exceeding standards; and

  o Promote continued improvements.

In order to improve processes and productivity, it is important for managers to understand the organization's core competencies. The core competency is what the organization does better than others and is typically based on experience and knowledge. Operations management uses several tools to measure how well an organization meets its core competency, including:

- *Quality control*—evaluates how the product/service meets the customer's needs.

- *Statistical process control*—looks at identifying and preventing quality problems.

- *Project management*—typically uses a work breakdown structure (WBS) to organize the work done on a project. A WBS breaks down each task in a hierarchical fashion into components and subcomponents.

- *Supply chain management*—involves integrating goods, services, and information to meet the customer's needs. A "supply chain" includes all the tasks associated with taking raw materials and transforming them into the final product to deliver to the customer. Supply chain management involves managing the activities to produce and deliver a product or service from suppliers (and their vendors) to the end-user customer. Successful supply chain management involves information, communication, and cooperation. Suppliers and customers need to share information about customer requirements, quality, and delivery issues.

(*See* Russell and Taylor, *ibid.*)

5.5 Financial Analysis

Contract managers use financial analysis to determine if a company is stable enough to receive a contract award. That is why it is important for contracting professionals to have a basic understanding of how finance interrelates to both contract management and business competencies. The tools used to conduct financial analysis are various financial statements that identify how a company gets money, where the money goes, and where it is now.

The three primary financial statements used in financial analysis are:

- *Balance sheet*—documents what a company currently owns and what it owes at a specific point in time.

- *Income statement*—shows how much money a company made or spent over a period of time.

- *Cash flow statement*—shows the exchange of money between a company and the outside world over time.

(*Derived from* Securities and Exchange Commission, "Beginner's Guide to Financial Statements" (August 5, 2013), *available at* **www.sec.gov/investor/pubs/ begfinstmtguide.htm.**)

Each of these is discussed in the following sections.

5.5.1 Balance Sheet

A "balance sheet" provides detailed information about a company's assets, liabilities, and shareholders' equity. A company's assets have to equal, or "balance," the sum of its liabilities and shareholders' equity. (*Derived from* Securities and Exchange Commission, "Beginner's Guide to Financial Statements" (August 5, 2013), *available at* **www.sec.gov/investor/pubs/ begfinstmtguide.htm.**) (*See* **FIGURE 5-5-1** on page 119.)

5.5.1.1 Assets

"Assets" are things that a company owns that have value. This typically means they can either be sold or used by the company to make products or provide services that can be sold. Assets include physical property, such as buildings, equipment, and inventory. It also includes things that can't be physically touched, but still have value, such as trademarks and patents. Finally, cash itself is also an asset. A company's assets are calculated using this formula: assets = liabilities + shareholders' equity. (*Ibid.*)

5.5.1.2 Liabilities

"Liabilities" are amounts of money that a company owes to others. This can include different kinds of obligations such as money borrowed from a bank to launch a new product, rent to use a building, money owed to suppliers for materials, payroll a company owes to its employees, environmental cleanup costs, or taxes owed to the government. (*Ibid.*)

5.5.1.3 Shareholders' Equity

"Shareholders' equity" is sometimes called "capital" or "net worth." It is the money that would be left if a company sold all of its assets and paid off all of its liabilities. This leftover money belongs to the shareholders (i.e., the owners) of the company. Shareholders' equity is typically expressed in this formula: shareholders' equity = total assets – total liabilities. (*Ibid.*)

5.5.2 Income Statements

An "income statement" is a report that shows how much revenue a company earned over a specific period of time. An income statement also shows the costs and expenses associated with earning that revenue. The literal "bottom line" of the statement usually shows the company's net earnings or losses. This identifies how much the company earned or lost over the period. (*Derived from* Securities and Exchange Commission, "Beginner's Guide to Financial Statements" (August 5, 2013), *available at* **www. sec.gov/investor/pubs/begfinstmtguide.htm.**)

To understand income statements, start at the top with the total revenue made during the accounting period. The next line is money the company doesn't expect to collect on certain sales, such as returns and discounts. When the returns and discounts are subtracted from the gross revenues, it shows the company's net revenues. (*Ibid.*)

The next major section identifies the costs of goods sold. This part deducts costs or other operating expenses associated with earning the revenue. The subtotal is called "gross profit." The amount is considered "gross" because certain expenses have not been deducted from it yet. (*Ibid.*)
The income statement also identifies expenses. These are operating expenses that a company pays to conduct its business. After deducting the operating expenses from gross profit, the next subtotal is called "net operating income." (*Ibid.*)

The last section identifies other income, such as interest. The net income, or "bottom line," is how much the company actually earned or lost during the accounting period. Some income statements also account for income tax deduction to arrive at the net profit or net loss. (*Ibid.*) **FIGURE 5-5-2** on page 120 illustrates an income statement.

To conduct a financial analysis, contract managers must also understand the relationship between assets, liabilities, and shareholders' equity. The first step is to understand the different types of assets.

5.5.3 Types of Assets

Assets can be "tangible" and "intangible," and can be classified as "current" or "long-term."

5.5.3.1 Tangible Assets

Most assets are "tangible" because their value comes from their physical substance. Examples include land, buildings, and equipment. (David Marshall, Wayne McManus, and Daniel Viele; *Accounting: What the Numbers Mean, 9/e* (McGraw Hill, 2011).)

5.5.3.2 Intangible Assets

Other assets are "intangible" because their value comes from a legal claim or additional earning power from a business transaction such as goodwill, patents, or trademarks. (Louis E. Boone and David L. Kurtz, *Contemporary Business*, thirteenth ed. (John Wiley and Sons, Inc. 2009).)

5.5.3.3 Current Assets

"Current assets" are assets that can be converted into cash within one year. They include the following:

- *Cash*—represents money in the bank or on hand. This term only applies to cash that is readily available to withdraw to meet company liabilities.

- *Marketable securities*—temporary cash investments to earn interest such as securities listed for trade through a licensed brokerage firm. They may include U.S. government obligations, state and municipal obligations, corporate securities, and money market instruments.

- *Accounts receivable*—amounts due from customers from sales made and billed to customers on credit terms. Only customer accounts receivable from the company's sales can be classified as a current asset.

- *Inventory*—merchandise that a company has but hasn't sold. For example, manufacturers typically show three different classes of inventory:

   o Raw materials,

   o Work-in-process, and

   o Finished goods.

(David Marshall, Wayne McManus, and Daniel Viele; *Accounting: What the Numbers Mean, 9/e* (McGraw Hill, 2011).)

5.5.3.4 Long-Term Assets

"Long-term assets" are items that the business will use for more than 12 months. Examples of long-term assets include land, buildings, furniture, and equipment. When accounting for land, the purchase price is used. Similarly, the purchase price is also used when accounting for buildings. The difference between the two is that a building's value depreciates over time and is annotated in "accumulated depreciation." The land's value, on the other hand, does not depreciate. Furniture and equipment is also accounted for based on the purchase price and is depreciated over the item's useful life. (Lita Epstein and Susan Myers, *Small Business Accounting*, John Wiley and Sons, Inc., 2009).)

5.5.4 Types of Liabilities

Most liabilities require paying a specific sum of money to a particular party at a specified time in the future. Some liabilities, however, may be indefinite because the debt may be settled other than paying money, the creditor may not be known, or the due date may be uncertain. Liabilities may be classified as "current" or "long-term."

5.5.4.1 Current Liabilities

"Current liabilities" are liabilities that are likely to be paid within a year. Generally, they are obligations that are due by a specific date (usually within 30 to 90 days). However, trade practices may permit excluding certain accounts, such as customer's deposits and deferred income, provided the company's records include an appropriate explanation. Current liabilities include the following:

- *Notes payable*—these include notes payable to banks, notes payable to officers or stockholders of affiliated companies, notes payable to the trade, and notes payable to others.

- *Accounts payable*—An amount payable to another entity typically for purchasing supplies or services on credit.

- *Accrued liabilities*—Amounts owed by an organization on the date the balance sheet was prepared and may include a reserve for amounts due.

(David Marshall, Wayne McManus, and Daniel Viele; *Accounting: What the Numbers Mean, 9/e* (McGraw Hill, 2011).)

5.5.4.2 Long-Term Liabilities

"Long-term liabilities" are debts due more than one year from the balance sheet date. Long-term liabilities include mortgages, loans, and post-employment benefit obligations. When a company has a five-year car loan, for example, one fifth would be a current liability in the first year and the remaining four years of the loan amount is a long-term liability.

5.5.5 Cash Flow Statements

"Cash flow statements" report a company's inflow and outflow of cash. This is important because a company needs to have enough cash on hand to pay its expenses and buy additional assets if needed. A cash flow statement identifies if the company generated cash during its business operations. A cash flow statement shows changes over time, not absolute dollar amounts at a specific point in time. (*Derived from* Securities and Exchange Commission, "Beginner's Guide to Financial Statements" (August 5, 2013), *available at* **www.sec.gov/investor/pubs/ begfinstmtguide.htm**.)

The bottom line of a cash flow statement illustrates the net increase or decrease in cash for the stated time period. Cash flow statements are typically divided into three sections:

- *Operating activities*—This part identifies a company's cash flow from net income or losses.

- *Investing activities*—The next part states the cash flow from all investing activities that include purchases or sales of long-term assets.

- *Financing activities*—The last section identifies cash flow from all financing activities.

(*Ibid.*)

A typical cash flow statement is illustrated in **FIGURE 5-5-5** on page 121.

Now that we have reviewed the tools of financial analysis, we will now discuss how the analysis is conducted.

5.5.6 Financial Indicator Ratios

Most financial analysis involves using ratios. Managers interpret actual performance and compare it to what was forecast. There are different ratios that managers can calculate to support financial analysis. Contract managers should determine which ratios will provide the type of information needed to support the analysis they are conducting. These ratios include the following:

- *Liquidity ratio*—measures a company's ability to meet its short-term obligations. Two frequently used liquidity ratios are "acid test" and "current ratio."

- *Acid test ratio*—determines how well the company can meet its debt payments on short notice. Acid test ratio = (cash + accounts receivable + short-term investments)/current liabilities.

- *Current ratio*—the ratio of current assets to current liabilities. Current ratio = current assets/ current liabilities.

- *Debt to equity ratio*—compares a company's total debt to shareholders' equity. Debt to equity ratio = total liabilities/shareholders' equity. (*Derived from* Louis E. Boone and David L. Kurtz, *Contemporary Business*, thirteenth ed. (John Wiley and Sons, Inc. 2009) and Securities and Exchange Commission, "Beginner's Guide to Financial Statements" (August 5, 2013), *available at* **http://www.sec.gov/investor/pubs/ begfinstmtguide.htm**.)

The Securities Act and the Securities Exchange Act both prescribe the form and content to prepare financial statements required under those Acts.

A company's financial statements form the core of its required Securities and Exchange Commission (SEC) filings. According to Robert K. Herdman, chief accountant, SEC, "it is critical that all public companies provide transparent disclosures that result in an understandable, comprehensive, and reliable portrayal of their financial condition and performance." (Robert K. Herdman, "The Roles of the SEC and the FASB in Establishing GAAP," Testimony Before the House Subcommittee on Capital Markets, Insurance, and Government-Sponsored Enterprises, Committee on Financial Services (May 14, 2012).)

Since a financial statement only provides some information about a company within a certain window of time, the company's management may provide a narrative explanation in a section of their annual report called "Management's Discussion and Analysis of Financial Condition and Results of Operations." This section gives management an opportunity to explain more about the financial statements, including any trends or risks that shaped the past or are likely to influence the company's future. (*See* Securities and Exchange Commission, "Beginner's Guide to Financial Statements" (August 5, 2013), *available at* **http://www.sec.gov/investor/pubs/ begfinstmtguide.htm**.)

5.6 Accounting

Accounting is the way an organization collects, organizes, and records financial information for making management decisions. It is also the way to report a company's transactions and to maintain accountability for its assets and liabilities. The accounting system should be designed to provide reliable data and prevent mistakes that would otherwise occur. To avoid mistakes, organizations follow established principles to guide their accounting system.

5.6.1 Accounting Standards

"Generally Accepted Accounting Principles" (GAAP) are general rules used by businesses that are non-regulatory guidance developed and used by certified public accountants. The Financial Accounting Standards Board (FASB) establishes accounting standards to be used by public companies. The FASB's standards are designated as the primary level of GAAP, which is the framework for accounting. These standards establish accounting principles that are used in preparing financial statements. Financial statements, and the GAAP standards that underlie them, play a fundamental role in making the marketplace efficient and resilient. (Robert K. Herdman, "The Roles of the SEC and the FASB in Establishing GAAP," Testimony Before the House Subcommittee on Capital Markets, Insurance, and Government-Sponsored Enterprises, Committee on Financial Services (May 14, 2011).)

Federal agencies also have accounting standards to follow. The Federal Accounting Standards Advisory Board (FASAB) is the body designated by the American Institute of Certified Public Accountants as the source of GAAP for federal entities. The FASAB's mission is to improve federal financial reporting by issuing federal financial accounting standards and providing guidance.

The *FASAB Handbook of Federal Accounting Standards and Other Pronouncements* explains the accounting concepts and standards for the U.S. government. The standards, interpretations, and technical bulletins in the *FASAB Handbook* are issued in accordance with policies and procedures approved by the Department of the Treasury, the Office of Management and Budget, and the Government Accountability Office. (*See* FASAB, *FASAB Handbook of Federal Accounting Standards and Other Pronouncements* (Norwalk: FASAB, 2012).)

An organization's accounting system is the primary source for an effective cost estimating system and it should integrate applicable information from a variety of company management systems. Since both buyers and sellers use cost estimates in contract management, contract managers should be familiar with basic cost accounting concepts.

5.6.2 Cost Accounting

"Cost accounting" is the process of collecting, measuring, analyzing, and reporting cost information for internal and external group use. Cost accounting is how an organization uses, accounts for, safeguards, and controls its financial resources to meet its objectives.

Cost accounting produces information for management use that typically uses budgetary and financial accounting data. Cost information is used for many different purposes, such as the following:

- Measuring performance;
- Reducing and controlling cost;
- Determining prices and fees;
- Authorizing, modifying, and stopping programs; and
- Determining production methods.

(*Derived from* Federal Accounting Standards Advisory Board (FASAB), *FASAB Handbook of Federal Accounting Standards and Other Pronouncements* (Norwalk: FASAB, 2012).)

There are three methods that are primarily used for cost accounting:

- Job-order,
- Process, and
- Activity based.

5.6.2.1 Job-Order Cost System

Under a "job-order cost system," the company accounts for output by identifying specific physical units. The costs for each job or contract are accumulated under separate job orders.

Since the physical units of production under a job-order cost system are identified with specific job orders (or contracts), the labor distribution and accumulation method identifies the direct labor cost associated with the units produced. Supporting data in a job-order cost system will typically identify the following:

- The labor hours expended to produce the items,

- The employees and their pay rates, and

- The total labor cost with subtotals and breakdowns by types of labor.

(*Ibid.*)

5.6.2.2 Process Cost System

Under a "process cost system," direct costs are charged to a process for more than one contract that are run through the process at the same time, even though the end-items may not be identical. At the end of the accounting period, the costs incurred for that process are assigned to the units completed during the period and to the incomplete units still in process. Process cost systems are typically used by companies that continuously manufacture a specific end-item—like vehicles or chemicals—that requires identical or very similar production processes. A process is just one element of a comprehensive set of activities that an item must complete during its production. (*Ibid.*)

5.6.2.3 Activity Based Costing Systems

"Activity based costing" is focused on a production cycle and is based on the principles that an output needs activities to produce it and those activities use certain resources. Activity based costing systems assign costs through cost drivers that the activities use to create the outputs. The activity based costing method uses a two-step process: The first step assigns the resource costs of each activity and the second step assigns activity costs to the output. (Federal Accounting Standards Advisory Board (FASAB), *FASAB Handbook of Federal Accounting Standards and Other Pronouncements* (Norwalk: FASAB, 2012).)

5.7 Economics

Economics is concerned with making decisions with scarce resources such as labor, capital, goods, and natural resources. Economics influences what gets produced and how much gets produced. Supply and demand are important components in economic production and pricing decisions.

5.7.1 Supply and Demand

"Demand" describes how buyers behave in the marketplace. The quantity a buyer demands is what a buyer is willing to buy at a particular price. Typically, demand is represented with a downward sloping curve that indicates the quantity demanded drops when the price increases. As prices go up, fewer buyers are willing to pay the higher price. Excess demand means there is more demand than the marketplace can supply. (*See* M. Mandel, *Economics: The Basics* (New York: McGraw-Hill, 2012).)

"Supply" indicates how sellers behave in the marketplace. Supply is represented by an upward-sloping curve that indicates quantity supplied increases as the price increases. Higher prices may increase the quantity supplied because if a business can get more for its products and services, it has an incentive to increase supply. On the other hand, too much supply in a market means there is more quantity than what buyers demand. (*Ibid.*)

There are four essential laws of supply and demand, assuming that all other factors remain equal:

- If demand increases and supply doesn't change, then the price will increase;

- If demand decreases and the supply doesn't change, then the price will decrease;

- If supply increases and demand doesn't change, then the price will decrease; and

- If supply decreases and demand doesn't change, then the price will increase.

(*Ibid.*)

Various factors influence supply and demand, such as technology, interest rates, government regulations, and changes in raw material prices.

In addition to supply and demand, contract managers should also understand how the different types of competition impact the marketplace.

5.7.2 Types of Competition

Competition is the central principle of the American economy. When competition does not exist, the forces of supply and demand may not work effectively. The buyer and seller may have an advantage in the pricing decision process.

The different types of competition are used to describe the structure of a market. (Refer to **FIGURE 5-7-2** on page 123.) The market is used to inform buyers and sellers of a particular product or service. The market structure is influenced by how many buyers and sellers exist, the type of products and services involved, and what barriers to entry exist. Barriers to entry include regulatory, procedural, or technological factors that reduce the number of firms that can participate. Technological factors may be barriers to entry for some companies to compete for contracts in certain industries. (CMBOK 5.8 describes how information science/technology is applied in the contract management field.)

5.7.2.1 Perfect Competition

"Perfect competition" exists when many small companies produce identical goods/services and no one company can influence the market. There are no barriers to entry with perfect competition. (S.M. Flynn, *Eyeing the Four Basic Market Structures* (New York: John Wiley & Sons, 2013).)

5.7.2.2 Monopoly

A "monopoly" exists when there is only one company in the marketplace and it has no competitors. In a monopoly, the company can reduce output or supply to drive up prices and increase profits. There are typically significant barriers to entry for other companies to consider entering the marketplace. (*Ibid.*)

5.7.2.3 Oligopoly

An "oligopoly" exists when there are only a few companies in an industry with slight differences in products/services. There are some barriers to entry in an oligopoly. (*Ibid.*)

5.7.2.4 Monopsony

A "monopsony" happens when there is only one buyer, such as when only one entity can purchase certain supplies or services. For example, the U.S. federal government is the only buyer for nuclear submarines. (*Ibid.*)

5.8 Information Science/Technology

The field of information science is concerned with collecting, organizing, storing, and retrieving recorded data. Contract managers frequently use these information science tools and technology in their organizations. Many organizations use e-contract, e-procurement, and other online tools to manage suppliers, solicitations, and contracts.

Electronic business uses electronic methods such as e-mail, electronic funds transfer, the Internet, and other media to conduct business transactions. Some of the benefits of electronic business include the following:

- The realization of cost savings from lower transaction costs,

- The shortening of transaction times for ordering and delivering,

- The increase of visibility, and

- Providing more choices and information for customers.

(*Derived from* Roberta S. Russell and Bernard W. Taylor, *Operations Management: Creating Value Along the Supply Chain* (Hoboken, New Jersey: John Wiley & Sons, Inc., 2009).)

5.8.1 Government

The E-Government Act (*Pub. L.* 107-347) defines "electronic government" (e-government) as the use by the government of the Internet and other information technologies, together with the processes and people needed to implement them, to enhance the delivery of information and services to the public and others to make improvements in government operations. The basic goals of the act are to use e-government to improve the effectiveness, efficiency, and quality of government service.

The major purposes of the E-Government Act are to promote the use of the Internet and emerging technologies to provide citizens with government information and services, improving decision-making by policy-makers, and making the government more transparent and accountable. Toward these ends, the act established the Office of Electronic Government within the Office of Management and Budget to oversee the implementation of its provisions and mandated specific actions for federal agencies to take, such as improving public access to agency information and allowing for electronic access to rulemaking proceedings. (*See* Government Accountability Office, "Electronic Government Act: Agencies Have Implemented Most Provisions, But Key Areas of Attention Remain" (2012).) FedBizOpps (**www.fbo.gov**) is a Web-based portal that allows vendors to review federal business opportunities. Using secured accounts that are password protected, vendors can maintain account profiles in the system. Buyers also use secured accounts that are password protected to establish a buyer profile to create, modify/amend, or cancel an opportunity notice and create an award. (*Derived from* Symplicity Corporation, "FedBizOpps Vendor Guide" (Washington, DC: FedBizOpps, 2012).)

5.8.2 Commercial

Private industry also uses electronic commerce tools. For example, Microsoft uses a suite of online tools for its e-procurement process. (Microsoft, "E-Procurement" (2013), *available at* **www.microsoft. com/about/companyinformation/procurement/ process/en/us/online.aspx**.) These tools help employees find suppliers, create purchase orders, and track order fulfillment. They can also establish remote access accounts for suppliers electronically. For suppliers, the system automates project start-up and creates purchase orders so suppliers don't have to wait for paper forms. (*Ibid.*) Suppliers submit invoices online and they can track payment progress online as well. (*Ibid.*) Microsoft deposits payments directly into the supplier's bank account within 24 to 48 hours. (*Ibid.*)

Many businesses offer an online account for individuals, small businesses, and government customers. Online accounts provide easy ordering and payment via credit card. Delivery options from overnight to less costly methods are also available.

5.8.3 Contract Management Software

In addition to the technology used for buying and selling discussed in 5.8.2, many organizations are using automated contract management software to manage solicitations, bids/proposals, and contracts. There are many different kinds of contract management software available. Typically, they help an organization automate and manage contracts, agreements, and licenses. These software programs standardize contract writing, including terms and conditions. They can also generate post-award reports to help with change management, cost control, and timely delivery.

The federal government uses the System for Award Management (SAM) to create an integrated acquisition environment. This system consolidates the previously-used Central Contractor Registration (CCR), Federal Agency Registry (FedReg), Online Representations and Certifications Application (ORCA), and the Excluded Parties List System (EPLS). SAM allows government agencies and contractors to search the SAM database to find companies based on their capability, size, location, experience, ownership, and more.

The continuing advancements in information technology and communications technology provide significant opportunities for contract managers to be more effective. It is important that all managers become familiar with and have the necessary skills to use the available technology to provide value to their organization.

Terms and Definitions

Acronyms

ACAT
acquisition category

ACO
Administrative contracting officer

ADR
alternative dispute resolution

A-E
architect-engineer

AP
acquisition plan

APB
acquisition program baseline

APL
approved parts list

APPN
appropriation

BAA
broad agency announcement

BAC
budget at completion

BAFO
best and final offer

BCWP
budgeted cost for work performed (also called "earned value")

BCWS
budgeted cost for work scheduled (also called "planned value" (PV) or "performance measurement baseline" (PMB))

B&P
bid and proposal

BOA
basic ordering agreement

BOE
basis of estimate

BOM
Bill of materials

BPA
blanket purchase agreement

CAS
Cost accounting standards

CBL
commercial bill of lading

CCP
contract change proposal

CCR
Central Contractor Registration

CDR
critical design review

CDRL
contract data requirements list

CER
cost estimating relationship

CFE
contractor-furnished equipment

CFSR
contract funds status report

CICA
Competition in Contracting Act

CID
commercial item description

CLIN
contract line item number

CO
contracting officer; change order

COC
certificate of competency

COI
conflict of interest

COR
contracting officer's representative

COTS
commercially available off-the-shelf

CPAF
cost-plus-award-fee

CPAR
contractor performance assessment report

CPARS
Contractor Performance Assessment Reporting System

CPFF
cost-plus-fixed-fee

CPIF
cost-plus-incentive-fee

CPPC
cost-plus-percentage-of-cost

CPSR
contractor purchasing system review

CR
clarification request; continuing resolution; cost reimbursement

CS
contract specialist

CSP
commercial sales practices

CV
cost variance

C-V-P
cost-volume-profit

DARO
delivery after receipt of order

DID
data item description

D&F
determination and findings

DO
debarment official; delivery order

DRFP
draft request for proposal

DTC
design-to-cost

EA
environmental assessment; evolutionary acquisition

EAC
estimate at completion

EAR
Export Administration Regulations

ECP
engineering change proposal

ECRC
electronic commerce resource center

EO
executive order

EOQ
economic order quantity

EPA
economic price adjustment

EPLS
Excluded Parties List System

EPP
environmentally preferable purchasing

ESI
early supplier involvement

ETC
estimate to complete

EVM
earned value management

EVMS
earned value management system

FAR
Federal Acquisition Regulation

FAT
first article testing

FDO
fee-determining official

FFP
firm-fixed-price

FFP-LOE
firm-fixed-price, level-of-effort

FMS
foreign military sales

FPAF
fixed-price award fee

FPEPA
fixed-price with economic price adjustment

FPI
fixed price incentive

FPIF
fixed price incentive (firm target)

FPIS
fixed price incentive (successive target)

FPLOE
fixed-price level of effort

FPR
fixed-price redeterminable;
final proposal revision

FPRA
forward pricing rate agreement

FSD
full-scale development

FSS
Federal Supply Schedule

FTA
free trade agreement

FTE
full-time equivalent

FY
fiscal year

GFE
government-furnished equipment

GFI
government-furnished information

GFM
government-furnished material

GFP
government-furnished property

G&A
general and administrative

GPE
governmentwide point of entry

GPLR
government purpose license rights

GWAC
governmentwide acquisition contract

ICE
independent cost estimate

IDIQ
indefinite delivery/indefinite quantity

IDWA
interdivision work authorization

IDWO
interdivision work order

IFB
invitation for bids

IFSS
International Federal Supply Schedule

IGCE
independent government cost estimate

ILS
integrated logistics support

incoterms
international commercial terms

IR&D
independent research and development

IV&V
independent verification and validation

IWO
inter-division work order

J&A
justification and approval

KO
contracting officer

KR/Kr/KTR/Ktr
contractor

LCC
life cycle cost

LCCE
life cycle cost estimate

LLT
long-lead-time (material and/or funding)

LOC
limitation of cost

LOE
level of effort

LOF
limitation of funds

LOI
letter of intent

LRE
latest revised estimate

LTOP
lease-to-ownership program

LWOP
lease with option to purchase

MAC
multi-agency contract

MAS
Multiple Award Schedule

MDA
milestone decision authority

MDAP
major defense acquisition program

MEO
[U.S. government's] most efficient organization

MILSPEC
military specification

MILSTRIP
Military Standard Requisitioning and
Issue Procedures

MIPR
military interdepartmental purchase request

MMAS
material management and accounting system

MOA
memorandum of agreement

MOL
maximum ordering limitation

MOU
memorandum of understanding

MPC
model procurement code

MRP
material requirements planning;
manufacturing resource planning

MYP
multiyear procurement

NDA
nondisclosure agreement

NDI
nondevelopmental item

NSN
National Stock Number

NTE
Not-to-exceed

OBS
organizational breakdown structure

OCI
organizational conflict of interest (also "OCOI")

ODC
other direct cost

OEM
original equipment manufacturer

OFPP
Office of Federal Procurement Policy

O&M
operation and maintenance

OT
other transaction

OTA
other transaction authority

PALT
procurement administrative lead time

PBA
performance-based acquisition

PBC
performance-based costing

PBL
performance-based logistics

PBWS
performance-based work statement

PCA
physical configuration audit

PCI
personal conflict of interest (also "PCOI")

PCO
procuring contracting officer

PEA
price evaluation adjustment

PIID
procurement instrument identifier

PM
program manager

P&L
profit and loss

PNM
price negotiation memorandum

PO
purchase order

POC
point of contact

POE
program office estimate

POS
point of sale

PR
procurement request; purchase request; purchase requisition

PRR
production readiness review

PRS
performance requirements summary

PWBS
program work breakdown structure

PWS
performance work statement

QA
quality assurance

QAR
quality assurance representative

QASP
quality assurance surveillance plan

QBL
qualified bidders list

QBS
qualifications-based selection

QML
qualified manufacturers list

QPL
qualified products list

RDA
research, development, and acquisition

RDT&E
research, development, test, and evaluation

REA
request for equitable adjustment

RFI
request for information

RFP
request for proposals

RFQ
request for quotations

SAS
Single Award Schedule

SAT
simplified acquisition threshold

SCDRL
subcontract data requirements list

SDO
suspension and debarment official

SDRL
subcontractor's data requirements list

SF
standard form

SLA
service level agreement

SOO
statement of objectives

SOW
statement of work

SSA
source selection authority

SSAC
source selection advisory council

SSEB
source selection evaluation board

SSP
source selection plan

T4C
termination for convenience

T4D
termination for default

TCO
termination contracting officer

TIA
technology investment agreements

T&M
time and materials

TO
task order

T's and C's
terms and conditions

UCF
uniform contract format

UPS
uniform procurement system

VE
value engineering

VECP
value engineering change proposal

WBS
work breakdown structure

WGM
weighted guidelines method

WP
work package

ZBB
zero-based budgeting

The CMBOK Lexicon

abstract of bids

A list of the bidders for a particular sealed-bid procurement showing the significant portions of their bids.

accelerated delivery

The advancing, in whole or in part, of the scheduled delivery of material in order to meet emergency requirements.

acceleration

Direction to complete performance on time, despite the existence of an excusable delay.

acceptance

1. The act of an authorized representative of the buyer by which the buyer assents to ownership of existing and identified supplies, or approves specific services rendered, as partial or complete performance of a contract.

2. An offeree's manifestation of assent to the terms of an offer made to him or her by an offeror. The acceptance is the act, the verbal or written assent, or, in certain instances, the silence that creates contractual liabilities for both the offeror and the offeree.

3. The taking and receiving of anything in good part and as if it were a tacit agreement to a preceding act that might have been defeated or avoided if such acceptance had not been made.

4. Agreement to the terms offered in a contract. An acceptance must be communicated, and (in common law) it must be the mirror image of the offer.

acceptance period

The number of calendar days available to the buyer to award a contract from the date specified in the solicitation.

acceptance sampling

1. Evaluating a portion of a lot for the purpose of accepting or rejecting the entire lot as either conforming or not conforming to a quality specification.

2. A statistical quality control technique used to evaluate the overall condition of a given lot by inspecting only a portion or sample of the lot.

accord and satisfaction

1. A method of discharging a claim whereby the parties agree to give and accept something in settlement of the claim and perform the agreement. The accord is execution or performance.

2. Two persons agree that one of them has a right of action against the other, but they accept a substitute or different act or value as performance.

accounting period

The accounting process recognizes the necessity of providing financial information over specified time periods. This facilitates a comparison of the entity's performance between time periods and provides relevant financial information on a timely basis to be used in managerial decisions.

accounting system

A formal communications network that supplies relevant information for planning, control, decision-making, and evaluation.

accrual accounting

The accrual basis of accounting recognizes important concepts, such as receivables due from customers, payables due to vendors, interest due from investments, and other "matching" concepts as a means of providing an accurate picture of a company's financial (economic) position.

accumulating costs

Collecting cost data in an organized manner, such as through a system of accounts.

acknowledgement

1. A form used to inform the buyer that the supplier has accepted the purchase order. As a result of this acknowledgment, a bilateral agreement is consummated, as long as the terms of the acknowledgment are not substantively different from those of the purchase order.

2. The government's Standard Form 30 (SF30) requires bidders/offerors to acknowledge amendments. Failure to acknowledge amendments may cause the offer to be rejected.

acquisition

1. A process that begins with establishment of needs and includes the description of requirements, solicitations and source selection, contract award, contract financing, contract performance, contract administration, and all

technical and management functions directly related to the process of fulfilling an organization's needs by contract.

2. The process of obtaining supplies, services, or systems by contract with appropriated funds, whether the supplies, services, or systems exist or must be created.

3. The acquiring by contract with appropriated funds or supplies or services (including construction) by and for the use of the federal government through purchase or lease, whether the supplies or services are already in existence or must be created, developed, demonstrated, and evaluated. Acquisition begins at the point when agency needs are established and includes the description of requirements to satisfy agency needs, solicitation, selection of sources, award of contracts, contract financing, contract performance, contract administration, and those technical and management functions directly related to the process of fulfilling agency needs by contract.

acquisition cost
1. In the context of economic order quantity analysis, the acquisition cost includes all costs associated with generating and processing an order and its related paperwork.

2. In a broader management sense, the acquisition cost is the sum of the ordering, transporting, handling, and all inventory holding costs associated with the acquisition of a material.

3. The money invested up front to bring in new customers.

acquisition methodology
A means of requesting or inviting offerors to submit offers, generally by issuing a solicitation. Solicitations basically consist of a draft contact, provisions for preparing and submitting offers, and evaluation factors.

acquisition plan (AP)
A plan for an acquisition that serves as the basis for initiating the individual contracting actions necessary to acquire a system or support a program. The acquisition plan should identify the milestones at which decisions should be made and address all the technical, business, management, and other significant considerations that will control the acquisition.

acquisition planning
The process by which efforts of all personnel responsible for an acquisition are coordinated and integrated through a comprehensive plan for fulfilling the agency need in a timely manner at a reasonable cost. It includes developing the overall strategy for managing the acquisition.

acquisition risk
The chance that some element of an acquisition program produces an unintended result with an adverse effect on system effectiveness, suitability cost, or availability for deployment.

acquisition strategy
1. The conceptual framework for conducting systems acquisition. It encompasses the broad concepts and objectives that direct and control the overall development, production, and deployment of a system. An acquisition strategy is required by OMB Circular A-109 and government department directives for virtually all programs.

2. A business and technical management approach designed to achieve program objectives within the resource constraints imposed. It is the framework for planning, directing, contracting for, and managing a program. It provides a master schedule for research, development, test, production, fielding, modification, post-production management, and other activities essential for success.

acquisition streamlining
Any effort that results in more efficient and effective use of resources to design, develop, or produce quality systems. This includes ensuring that only necessary and cost-effective requirements are included, at the most appropriate time in the acquisition cycle, in solicitations and resulting contracts for the design, development, and production of new systems, or for modifications to existing systems that involve redesign of systems or subsystems.

acquisition team
The acquisition team consists of all participants in government acquisition including not only representatives of the technical, supply, and procurement communities, but also the customers they serve and the contractors who provide the products and services. The role of each member of the acquisition team is to exercise personal initiative and sound business judgment in providing the best-value

product or service to meet the customer's needs. In exercising initiative, government members of the acquisition team may assume if a specific strategy, practice, policy, or procedure is in the best interests of the government and is not addressed in the *Federal Acquisition Regulation*, nor prohibited by law (statute or case law), executive order, or other regulation, that the strategy, practice, policy, or procedure is a permissible exercise of authority.

act of God

An inevitable, accidental, or extraordinary event that cannot be foreseen and guarded against, such as lightning, tornadoes, or earthquakes.

actual cost

A cost sustained in fact, on the basis of costs incurred, as distinguished from forecasted or estimated costs. Amounts are determined on the basis of costs incurred, as distinguished from forecasted costs. Actual costs include standard costs properly adjusted for applicable variances.

actual cost basis

A means of pricing equitable adjustments that relies on direct costing, whereby the contractor (seller) tracks all the actual direct costs that are incurred as a result of the change. This method requires that the pricing action occur after the work has been completed (retrospectively), and that the contractor (seller) segregates the actual costs. It is rare that both these factors will be met completely.

adequate price competition

A price is based on adequate price competition if:

- Two or more responsible offerors, competing independently, submit priced offers that satisfy the government's expressed requirement and if—

  o Award will be made to the offeror whose proposal represents the best value where price is a substantial factor in source selection, and

  o There is no finding that the price of the otherwise successful offeror is unreasonable. (Any finding that the price is unreasonable must be supported by a statement of the facts and approved at a level above the contracting officer.);

- There was a reasonable expectation, based on market research or other assessment, that two or more responsible offerors, competing independently, would submit priced offers in response to the solicitation's expressed requirement, even though only one offer is received from a responsible offeror and if—

  o Based on the offer received, the contracting officer can reasonably conclude that the offer was submitted with the expectation of competition; e.g., circumstances indicate that—

- The offeror believed that at least one other offeror was capable of submitting a meaningful offer, and

- The offeror had no reason to believe that other potential offerors did not intend to submit an offer; and

  o The determination that the proposed price is based on adequate price competition and is reasonable has been approved at a level above the contracting officer; and

- Price analysis clearly demonstrates that the proposed price is reasonable in comparison with current or recent prices for the same or similar items, adjusted to reflect changes in market conditions, economic conditions, quantities, or terms and conditions under contracts that resulted from adequate price competition.

administrative change

A unilateral contract change, in writing, that does not affect the substantive rights of the parties, such as a change in the paying office or the appropriation data.

administrative contracting officer (ACO)

The government contracting officer, often at an installation other than the one making the contract, who is authorized to perform post-award contract administration duties, monitor the contractor's performance, and perform post-award contractual functions delegated by the purchasing office.

administrative costs

General overhead expenses incident to the issue, sale, and transfer of material.

administrative lead time

The time interval between initiating a procurement and awarding the contract or placing an order. Administrative lead time begins with the identification of a material requirement and continues until a contract is awarded for the creation of the material. (Also called "procurement administrative lead time" (PALT).)

advance agreement

An agreement between the seller and the buyer regarding the treatment of specified costs negotiated either before or during contract performance but preferably before the cost covered by the agreement is incurred.

advance buy

1. A procurement to provide for components that require a longer lead time than the system of which they are a part.

2. Also called "forward buying," it is the commitment of purchases in anticipation of future requirements beyond current lead times. Organizations may buy ahead as a matter of strategy or because of anticipated shortages, strikes, or price increases.

advance payment

An advance of money made by the buyer to a seller prior to, in anticipation of, and for the purpose of performance under a contract.

advance payment bond

This bond secures fulfillment of the contractor's obligations under an advance payment provision.

advisory and assistance services

Those services provided under contract by nongovernmental sources to support or improve organizational policy development, decision-making, management and administration, program and/or project management and administration, or research and development activities. It can also mean the furnishing of professional advice or assistance rendered to improve the effectiveness of federal management processes or procedures (including those of an engineering and technical nature). In rendering the foregoing services, outputs may take the form of information, advice, opinions, alternatives, analyses, evaluations, recommendations, training, and the day-to-day aid of support personnel needed for the successful performance of ongoing federal operations.

agency

1. A relationship whereby the principal authorizes another (the agent) to act for and on behalf of the principal and to bind the principal in contract.

2. Any executive department, military department, government corporation, government-controlled corporation, or other establishment in the executive branch of the federal government, or any independent regulatory agency. Within the Executive Office of the President, the term includes only the Office of Management and Budget and the Office of Administration.

3. A relationship that exists when there is a delegation of authority to perform all acts connected within a particular trade, business, or company. It gives authority to the agent to act in all matters relating to the business of the principal.

agent

An employee (usually a contract manager) empowered to bind his or her organization legally in contract negotiations.

agent authority

The power delegated by a principal to his or her agent; a right to exercise power. Includes the following:

- "Actual authority": Authority that the principal intentionally confers on the agent or allows the agent to believe himself or herself to possess.

- "Apparent authority": The principal knowingly permits the agent to exercise authority, though not actually granted.

- "Express authority": Authority delegated to an agent intentionally, distinctly, and plainly expressed verbally or in writing.

- "Implied authority": Authority implied from the principal's conduct; includes only such acts as are incident and necessary to the exercise of the authority expressly granted.

allocable cost

1. A cost whose relative benefits make it assignable or chargeable to one or more of the cost objectives agreed to between contractual parties.

2. A cost is allocable to a government contract if it is incurred specifically for the contract, benefits both the contract and other work and can be distributed to them in reasonable proportion to the benefits received, or is necessary to the overall operation of the business, although a direct relationship to any particular cost objective cannot be shown.

allocate

Assignment of an item of cost, or a group of items of cost, to one or more cost objectives. This term includes both direct assignment of cost and the reassignment of a share from an indirect cost pool.

allowable cost
A cost that is reasonable, allocable, within accepted standards, or otherwise conforms to generally accepted accounting principles, specific limitations or exclusions, or agreed-to terms between contractual parties.

alternate bid
One of two or more bids on the same item, submitted on different bases by the same bidder, as provided by the invitation for bids.

alternative dispute resolution (ADR)
Any type of procedure or combination of procedures voluntarily used, in lieu of litigation, to resolve issues in controversy. These procedures may include, but are not limited to, conciliation, facilitation, mediation, fact-finding, mini-trials, arbitration, and use of ombudsmen.

amendment
A change (correction, deletion, or addition) to any information contained in an invitation for bids or request for proposals (or previous amendment thereto). The amendment becomes part of the solicitation and any resulting contract.

anticipatory breach/ anticipatory repudiation
Occurs when the promisor, without justification and before he or she has committed a breach, makes a positive statement to the promisee indicating he or she will not or cannot perform his or her contractual duties.

anticipatory profit
Profits payable for work not performed. This payment is viewed as a reasonable sanction to be imposed upon defaulters in ordinary contractual relationships. Anticipatory profits are not allowed when the government terminates a contract for convenience.

antitrust violations
Anticompetitive practices such as collusive bidding, follow-the-leader pricing, rotated low bids, and collusive price estimating systems.

apparent authority
Authority that a third party reasonably believes an agent has, based on the third party's dealings with the principal.

appeal
To resort to a superior (i.e., appellate) court to review the decision of an inferior (i.e., trial) court or administrative agency.

arbitration
1. A nonjudicial method for settling matters of disputes between parties with an objective outside party acting as a fact-finder and a primary decision-maker.

2. Procedure whereby a dispute is referred to one or more impartial persons (selected by the disputing parties) for a final and binding determination.

3. To settle a dispute, an appointed arbitrator (third person) comes in to help the parties make an out-of-court decision. This saves the time and expense of litigation.

assignment
1. A transfer of rights (usually contract rights) from an assignor to an assignee.

2. A transference of a property right (such as a contact or a purchase order) or title to another party. In shipping, it is commonly used with a bill of lading, which involves transfer of rights, title, and interest for the purpose of endorsement. Such endorsement gives, to the party named, the title to the property covered by the bill of lading.

assignment of claims
The transfer or making over by the contractor to a bank, trust company, or other financing institution, as security for a loan to the contractor, of its right to be paid by the government for contract performance.

auction
Sale in which property, services, or merchandise are sold to the highest bidder.

audit
The systematic examination of records and documents and/or the securing of other evidence by confirmation, physical inspection, or otherwise, for one or more of the following purposes:

- Determining the propriety or legality of proposed or completed transactions,

- Ascertaining whether all transactions have been recorded and are reflected accurately in accounts,

- Determining the existence of recorded assets and inclusiveness of recorded liabilities,

- Determining the accuracy of financial or statistical statements or reports and the fairness of the facts they represent,

- Determining the degree of compliance with established policies and procedures in terms of financial transactions and business management, and

- Appraising an account system and making recommendations concerning it.

authorized work

That effort that has been definitized and is on contract, plus that which definitized contract costs have not been agreed to but for which written authorization has been received.

award

1. Notification to bidder or offeror that their bid/ proposal is accepted.

2. The procurement decision to buy a supply or service from a specific concern on specified terms, including dollar amount.

award fee contract

Contracts that provide for a fee consisting of a base amount fixed at inception of the contract (if applicable and at the discretion of the contracting officer) and an award amount that the contractor may earn in whole or in part during performance and that is sufficient to provide motivation for excellence in the areas of cost, schedule, and technical performance. Award fee contracts may be fixed-price or cost-reimbursement.

base fee

Used in award-fee contracting, a base fee is a base amount fixed at inception of the contract (if applicable and at the discretion of the contracting officer). Base fee is a fixed amount that the contractor earns for satisfactory contract performance awarded in addition to the award fee amount that the contractor may earn in whole or in part during performance and that is sufficient to provide motivation for excellence in the areas of cost, schedule, and technical performance.

base profit

The money a company is paid by a customer that exceeds the company's cost.

basic agreement

A basic agreement is not a contract. It is a written instrument of understanding, negotiated between an agency or contracting activity and a contractor, which contains contract clauses applying to future contracts between the parties during its term and contemplates separate future contracts that will incorporate by reference or attachment the required and applicable clauses agreed upon in the basic agreement.

basic ordering agreement (BOA)

1. An instrument of understanding (not a contract) executed between a procuring activity (buyer) and a contractor (seller) setting forth negotiated contract clauses applicable to future procurements entered into between the parties during the term of the agreement. It includes as specific as possible a description of the supplies or services and a description of the method for determination of prices.

2. A BOA contains all applicable clauses and must specify when an order actually becomes a binding contract. Depending on the circumstances, a contract could be established upon the issuance of an order, upon the contractor's failure to reject the order within a specified time, or upon actual acceptance of the order by the contractor through performance (e.g., shipping the goods) or formal acceptance.

basic research

Research directed toward increasing knowledge in science. The primary aim of basic research is a fuller knowledge or understanding of the subject under study, rather than any practical application of that knowledge.

best and final offer (BAFO)

A buyer requests a best and final offer to indicate that no further negotiation will take place. This is the seller's last opportunity to make changes to its cost and technical proposals. This term is used in commercial and state/local contracts, but not in federal government contracting since the *Federal Acquisition Regulation* Part 15 rewrite of 1997. This is when the term "final proposal revision" was adopted.

best value

1. The essential principle of best value is to obtain the best tradeoff between competing factors for a particular purchase requirement. The keys to successful best value contracting are

consideration of life cycle costs and marginal analysis (i.e., the use of quantitative as well as qualitative techniques to measure price and technical performance tradeoffs between various proposals). The best value concept applies to acquisitions where price or price-related factors are *not* the primary determinant of who receives the contract award.

2. The expected outcome of an acquisition that, in the government's estimation, provides the greatest overall benefit in response to the requirement.

3. The most advantageous trade-off between price and performance for the government. Best value is determined through a process that compares strengths, weaknesses, risk, price, and performance, in accordance with selection criteria, to select the most advantageous value to the government.

bid

(1.) An offer in response to an invitation for bids. (2.) In purchasing, a bid can be an offer to sell or an offer to buy. In public-sector purchasing, a bid is the offer in the sealed-bid process (as opposed to other than sealed-bid procurement, where the offer may be referred to as a "proposal" or a "quotation").

bid and proposal costs

Costs incurred in preparing, submitting, and supporting bids and proposals (whether or not solicited) on potential government or nongovernment contracts.

bid bond

In government contract administration, an insurance document in which a third party agrees to pay a specific amount of money if the bonded (insured) bidder fails to sign a contract as bid upon and accepted by the government.

bid guarantee

A form of security accompanying a bid or proposal as assurance that the bidder will not withdraw its bid during the specified time period, will execute a written contract, and will furnish such bonds as may be required.

bid/no-bid decision

Determination made by the seller's management whether or not to submit an offer or bid, usually in response to a customer request.

bid opening

The public announcement of all the bids submitted in response to an invitation for bids.

bid phase

The period of time a seller of goods and/or services uses to develop a bid/proposal, conduct internal bid reviews, and obtain stakeholder approval to submit a bid/proposal.

bid sample

A sample to be furnished by a bidder to show the characteristics of the product offered in the bid.

bidders' list

A list, maintained by the procurement office, of contractors and suppliers that have expressed interest in furnishing a specific supply or service to the government. (Also known as "bidders' mailing list.")

bilateral change

A change to a contract formed by the exchange of promises to perform reciprocal obligations for the other party.

bilateral contract

A contract formed by the exchange of promises in which the promise of one party is consideration supporting the promise of the other. It contrasts with a "unilateral contract," which is formed by the exchange of a promise for an act.

bilateral notice

Used when terminating a contract by mutual consent. Typically initiated when one party notifies the other that it is exercising a contractual right to terminate based on particular circumstances. Generally, both the circumstances permitting the termination and the process for termination are predetermined in the contract.

bilateral modification

A contract modification that is signed by the contractor and the contracting officer. Bilateral modifications are used to:

- Make negotiated equitable adjustments resulting from the issuance of a change order,

- Definitize letter contracts, and

- Reflect other agreements of the parties modifying the terms of contracts.

bill of sale

A written document formally transferring ownership of personal property specified in the document from the supplier to the purchaser.

billing rate

An indirect cost rate established temporarily for interim reimbursement of incurred indirect costs and adjusted as necessary pending establishment of final indirect cost rates.

blanket order

A term commitment (usually one year or more) to a supplier for certain goods or services over a predetermined period of time at predetermined prices, most-favored customer prices, or prices to be revised due to market or other conditions. This practice is aimed at reducing the number of small orders utilizing short-term releases to satisfy demand requirements.

blanket purchase agreement (BPA)

1. A method for the government to fill purchase requirements for related supplies, material, equipment, or services by establishing accounts with established sources of supply. It includes certain conditions and provisions that have been negotiated and agreed to in advance. It also allows the government to make frequent purchases or calls, verbally or in writing, and receive one monthly bill for all supplies or services purchased.

2. A BPA is not a contract; it is viewed as a type of "charge account" with certain qualified vendors. It serves as the baseline for future transactions between the parties. An individual BPA is considered complete when the amount purchased under it equals the total dollar limitation, if any, or when the stated time limitation (period of performance) expires.

3. Regulations limit the use of BPAs to small purchases of items or services needed to fill anticipated recurring needs.

board of contract appeals

A designated administrative tribunal within an executive agency that is authorized to hear, examine, and decide on written requests asking for a change (an appeal) of a contracting officer's decision, and related to a contract made by that agency.

boilerplate

The term used for printed terms and conditions that are frequently found on the back of purchase order forms in contracts, usually attached as "general provisions."

bond

A written instrument executed by a bidder or contractor (the "principal") and a second party (the "surety" or "sureties") to assure fulfillment of the principal's obligations to a third party (the "obligee" or "government") identified in the bond. If the principal's obligations are not met, the bond assures payment, to the extent stipulated, of any loss sustained by the obligee.

breach of contract

The failure, without legal excuse, to perform any promise that forms the whole or part of a contract.

breach of warranty

Occurs when the material or product fails to meet the quality or other specification warranted by the supplier.

budget

1. A plan of operations for a fiscal period in terms of estimated costs, obligations, and expenditures; a source of funds for financing including anticipated reimbursements and other resources; and history and workload data for the projected program and activities.

2. A comprehensive financial plan for the federal government, encompassing the totality of federal receipts and outlays (expenditures). Budget documents routinely include the on-budget and off-budget amounts and combine them to derive a total of federal fiscal activity, with a focus on combined totals.

budget authority

1. Authority provided by law to enter into financial obligations that will result in immediate or future outlays involving federal government funds. The basic forms of budget authority include:

   - Appropriations,
   - Borrowing authority,
   - Contract authority, and
   - Authority to obligate and expend offsetting receipts and collections.

2. May be classified by its duration (one-year, multiple-year, or no-year) by the timing of the legislation providing the authority (current or

permanent), by the manner of determining the amount available (definite or indefinite), or by its availability for new obligations.

burden
An aspect of indirect cost. (Also called "overhead.")

business evaluation factors
Aspects used to assess performance of the offerors; e.g., relevant experience, past performance, management plan, company resources, and/or quality of product/service.

buyer
1. A professional buying specialist. Buyers typically specialize in a given group of materials or commodities and are responsible for market analysis, purchase planning, coordination with users, supplier qualification and selection, order placement, and follow-up activities.

2. The party contracting for goods and/or services with one or more sellers.

buy-in
Submitting an offer below anticipated cost, with the expectation of increasing the contract amount after award or receiving follow-on contracts at artificially high prices.

capture team
Small group of individuals within an organization who are delegated responsibility to manage a pursuit from the pursuit decision to contract award, typically including a capture manager, a technical lead, and the prospective program manager as a minimum (depending on the specific requirements of the pursuit).

cardinal change
1. A change to a contract that is made outside the scope of the contract and is, therefore, unenforceable by the government.

2. Having the effect of making the work as performed not essentially the same work as the parties bargained for when the contract was awarded, and thus constituting a breach of contract by the government.

cash flow
1. The cash generated from the property. It is different than net income; cash flow looks to the amount left after all payments are made,

whether they are tax deductible or not. Also defined as cash receipts minus disbursements from a given asset, or group of assets, for a given period.

2. The net effect of cash receipts and disbursements.

catalog price
A price included in a catalog, price list, schedule, or other form that is regularly maintained by the manufacturer or vendor, is either published or otherwise available for inspection by customers, and states prices at which sales are currently, or were last made, to a significant number of buyers constituting the general public.

categories of procurement
The major categories of procurement are as follows:

*   Supplies,

*   Construction,

*   Services, and

*   Research and development.

Within each of these major categories are numerous specialized types of procurement. The classification of the procurement is important for purposes of funding, types of contracts to be used, applicability of contract clauses, and coverage of socioeconomic provisions.

caucus
A technique used to break away from formal negotiations for the team to consider a point. When a counteroffer is made, a caucus can be used to confer with the negotiation team to consider all aspects of the counteroffer. A caucus is useful to discuss anything about the ongoing negotiation that one side doesn't want the other team to hear. It can be used when a team member wants to bring to the negotiator's attention an important fact, if a fact needs to be checked with a team member, or if management approval is necessary in order to make a concession or counteroffer.

caveat emptor
A Latin phrase that means "let the buyer beware"; i.e., the purchase is at the buyer's risk.

certificate of current cost or pricing data
1. A document submitted by the contractor attesting that the cost or pricing data provided to the government were accurate, complete,

and current as of the date negotiations were completed.

2. Prescribed certificate required to be executed by contractors that must submit certified cost or pricing data under the Truth in Negotiations Act.

certification of a claim
The requirement, under the Contract Disputes Act, that contract claims over $100,000 be accompanied by a statement that simultaneously asserts that the claim is made in good faith, supporting data is accurate and complete, and the amount requested reflects the contract adjustment believed due. (*See* FAR 33.207.)

certified cost or pricing data
Cost or pricing data that were required to be submitted in accordance with *Federal Acquisition Regulation (FAR)* 15.403-4–5 and have been certified, or are required to be certified, in accordance with FAR 15.406-2. This certification states that, to the best of the person's knowledge and belief, the cost or pricing data are accurate, complete, and current as of a date certain before contract award. Cost or pricing data are required to be certified in certain procurements (per 10 U.S.C. 2306a and 41 U.S.C. 254b).

change in scope
Change to approved program requirements or specifications after negotiation of a basic contract. It may result in an increase or decrease in cost or time for performance.

change-of-name agreement
A legal instrument executed by the contractor and the government that recognizes the legal change of name of the contractor without disturbing the original contractual rights and obligations of the parties.

change order (CO)
A written order signed by the contracting officer or buyer that is authorized by contract clause to modify contractual requirements within the scope of the contract.

changes clause
A standard clause in government contracts. There are several versions corresponding to the specific type of contract, but all have certain common characteristics. The clause, mandatory for most government contracts, provides a contractual grant of authority to the government by its supplier. It gives the government the right to alter unilaterally specific matters affecting the performance of the contract.

Christian Doctrine
Based on a court case (*G.L. Christian & Assoc. v. United States*, 312 F.2d at 424, 427), it is a principle stating that if a contract clause is required either by a statute, regulation, or executive order, the required clause is automatically incorporated by operation of law into an existing contract.

claim
1. A written demand or written assertion by one of the contracting parties seeking, as a matter of right, the payment of money in a sum certain, the adjustment or interpretation of the contract terms, or other relief arising under or relating to the contract. A claim arising under a contract, unlike a claim relating to that contract, is a claim that can be resolved under a contract clause that provides for the relief sought by the claimant. A voucher, invoice, or other routine request for payment that is not in dispute when submitted is not a claim. The submission is not a claim; however, the submission may be converted to a claim by written notice to the contracting officer.

2. A demand by one party to contract for something from another party, usually but not necessarily for more money or more time. Claims are usually based on an argument that the party making the demand is entitled to an adjustment by virtue of the contract terms or some violation of those terms by the other party. The word does not imply any disagreement between the parties, although claims often lead to disagreements.

clarification
1. A communication in negotiations for the sole purpose of eliminating minor irregularities, informalities, or apparent clerical mistakes in a proposal.

2. Limited exchanges between the government and offerors that may occur when award without discussions is contemplated. If award will be made without conducting discussions, offerors may be given the opportunity to clarify certain aspects of proposals (e.g., the relevance of an offeror's past performance information and adverse past performance information to which the offeror has not previously had an opportunity to respond) or to resolve minor or clerical errors.

clause

A term or condition used in contracts or in both solicitations and contracts, and applying after contract award or both before and after award. Clauses state the rights and obligations of the parties to a contract.

closed contract

A contract on which all contractor and government obligations and administrative actions have been completed.

closeout

The process of declaring that the obligations under a contract have been satisfied and that a procurement file is both physically and administratively complete. A closeout can occur when the contractor's supplies or services have been accepted and paid for and all documentation on the procurement is finalized and properly assembled.

closing date

The last day on which proposals or quotations will be accepted.

collusion

1. Any understanding or agreement— expressed, implied, formal, or informal— among bidders or competitors concerning bids or proposals for the sale of products or services.

2. Disclosure of a bid or proposal by a bidder to any other bidder or competitor prior to the official opening of all bids or proposals.

3. Any attempt to induce a competitor not to submit a bid or proposal.

color of money

A term used to describe the type of procurement money used for a particular item. Different kinds of appropriated funds must be used for various procurements (e.g., research, development, test, and evaluation; operations and maintenance; and foreign military sales).

commercial bill of lading (CBL)

1. A document signed by a carrier (a transporter of goods) or the carrier's representative and issued to a consignor (the shipper of goods) that evidences the receipt of goods for shipment to a specified designation and person.

2. Represents the receipt of goods, the contract of carriage, and is documentary evidence of title to goods. It must contain a description of the articles comprising the shipment.

CBLs are subject to the terms and conditions set forth for a government bill of lading and any other applicable contract or agreement of the transportation service provider for the transportation of shipments for the United States on U.S. government bills of lading.

commercial item

1. Any item, other than real property, that is of a type customarily used for nongovernmental purposes and that:

   - Has been sold, leased, or licensed to the general public; or

   - Has been offered for sale, lease, or license to the general public.

2. Any item that evolved from an item described in (1.) of this definition through advances in technology or performance and that is not yet available in the commercial marketplace, but will be available in the commercial marketplace in time to satisfy the delivery requirements under a government solicitation.

3. Any item that would satisfy a criterion expressed in (1.) or (2.) of this definition, but for:

   - Modifications of a type customarily available in the commercial marketplace; or

   - Minor modifications of a type not customarily available in the commercial marketplace made to meet federal government requirements. Minor modifications means modifications that do not significantly alter the nongovernmental function or essential physical characteristics of an item or component, or change the purpose of a process. Factors to be considered in determining whether a modification is minor include the value and size of the modification and the comparative value and size of the final product. Dollar values and percentages may be used as guideposts, but are not conclusive evidence that a modification is minor.

4. Any combination of items meeting the requirements of (1.), (2.), or (3.) of this definition that are of a type customarily combined and sold in combination to the general public.

commercial item description (CID)

An indexed, simplified product description that describes (by function or performance characteristic) the available, acceptable commercial products that will satisfy the government's needs. These documents are issued or controlled by the General Services

Administration (GSA) and are listed in GSA's "Index of Federal Specifications, Standards, and Commercial Item Descriptions."

commercial sale

A sale of defense articles or defense services made under a Department of State–issued license by U.S. industry directly to a foreign buyer, and which is not administered through foreign military sales procedures. (Also referred to as a "direct commercial sale.")

commercially available off-the-shelf (COTS)

Any item or supply (including construction material) that is a commercial item (i.e., any item, other than real property, that is of a type customarily used by the general public or by nongovernmental entities for purposes other than governmental purposes, and has been sold, leased, or licensed to the general public or has been offered for sale, lease, or license to the general public); sold in substantial quantities in the commercial marketplace; and offered to the government, under a contract or subcontract at any tier, without modification, in the same form in which it is sold in the commercial marketplace. COTS items do not include bulk cargo, as defined in 46 U.S.C. 40102(4), such as agricultural products and petroleum products.

communications

1. In a negotiated acquisition, communications are exchanges between the government and offerors, after receipt of proposals, which lead to establishment of the competitive range. When the contracting officer establishes competitive range, these communications are held with offerors whose past performance information is the determining factor preventing them from being placed within the competitive range. Such communications shall address adverse past performance information to which an offeror has not had a prior opportunity to respond, and may only be held with those offerors whose exclusion from, or inclusion in, the competitive range is uncertain.

2. May be conducted to enhance government understanding of the proposal, allow reasonable interpretation of the proposal, or facilitate the government's evaluation process. Such communications shall not be used to cure proposal deficiencies or material omissions, materially alter the technical or cost elements of the proposal, and/or otherwise revise the proposal. Such communications may be considered in rating proposals for the purpose of establishing the competitive range.

3. Are for the purpose of addressing issues that must be explored to determine whether a proposal should be placed in the competitive range. Such communications shall not provide an opportunity for the offeror to revise its proposal, but may address—

   - Ambiguities in the proposal or other concerns (e.g., perceived deficiencies, weaknesses, errors, omissions, or mistakes);

   - Information relating to relevant past performance; and

   - Adverse past performance information to which the offeror has not previously had an opportunity to comment.

compensable delay

1. A delay for which the government is contractually responsible that excuses the contractor's failure to perform and is compensable. "Suspension of Work" (FAR 52.242-14), "Stop Work" (FAR 52.242- 15), and "Government Delay of Work" (FAR 52.242-17) are examples of compensable delays.

2. A delay for which the buyer is contractually responsible that excuses the seller's failure to perform and is compensable.

compensatory damages

Damages that will compensate the injured party for the loss sustained and nothing more. They are awarded by the court as the measure of actual loss and not as punishment for outrageous conduct or to deter future transgressions. Compensatory damages are often referred to as "actual damages."

competition

1. Part of an acquisition strategy whereby more than one company is asked to submit an offer (quote, bid, or proposal) to deliver supplies or perform services. The winner is selected on the basis of criteria established in the solicitation (request for quotations, invitation for bids, or request for proposals).

2. The effort or action of two or more commercial companies to obtain the same business from a third party.

competitive bidding

A common method of source selection; the offer of prices and specified elements of performance by firms competing for a contract. Major public-sector purchases are commonly requested to be on a sealed-bid basis, with the law requiring that the award be made to the lowest responsive and responsible bidder. In industrial purchasing, preliminary bids are sometimes solicited with the stated intention of selecting those firms with whom negotiations subsequently will be conducted to arrive at a final sourcing decision.

competitive negotiation

A procurement involving:

- A request for proposals that states the government's requirements and criteria for evaluation,

- The submission of timely proposals by a maximum number of offerors,

- Discussions with those offerors found to be within the competitive range, and

- Award of a contract to the offeror whose offer, price, and other evaluation factors are most advantageous to the government.

competitive proposal

A competitive procurement practice in government purchasing that:

- Is initiated by a request for proposal,

- Contemplates the submission of timely proposals by the maximum number of possible suppliers,

- Permits discussions with those suppliers found to be within the competitive range, and

- Concludes with the award of a contract to the one supplier whose proposal is most advantageous to the government (considering price and the other factors included in the solicitation).

competitive range

A range of acceptable standards determined by the contracting officer on the basis of price, cost, or technical factors. The contracting officer must conduct written or verbal discussions with all responsible offerors that submit proposals within this range. The competitive range is comprised of all of the most highly rated proposals, unless the range is further reduced for purposes of efficiency.

compliance matrix

A common technique used to identify gaps in the seller's ability to meet the customer's needs as defined in the request for proposals. It lists all the solicitation references and functional requirements, along with indicators of the level of compliance (i.e., full, partial, or none).

condition precedent

1. A condition that activates a term in a contract.

2. An event that must occur before a party must perform.

condition subsequent

1. A condition that suspends a term in a contract.

2. An event that terminates the duty of a party to perform.

conflict of interest (COI)

Term used in connection with public officials and fiduciaries and their relationship to matters of private interest or gain to them. Ethical problems connected therewith are covered by statutes in most jurisdictions and by federal statutes on the federal level. A conflict of interest arises when an employee's personal or financial interest conflicts or appears to conflict with his or her official responsibility.

consent to subcontract

Some government contracts require the government to consent to a prime contractor's subcontract. Consent is required when subcontract work is complex, the dollar value is substantial, or the government's interest is not adequately protected by competition and the type of prime or subcontract.

consequential damages

Those costs that result from a particular cause. For example, a product failure may mean that the purchaser has incurred not only the added cost necessary to replace the product, but has also lost income that would have resulted had the product not failed. The lost income would be a consequential damage. The extent to which consequential damages may be recovered depends on the language contained in the contract and the law in a particular jurisdiction.

consideration

1. Anything of value that changes hands between the parties to a contract.

2. The thing of value (amount of money or acts to be done or not done) that must change hands

between the parties to a contract.

3. The inducement to a contract—the cause, motive, price, or impelling influence that induces a contracting party to enter a contract.

constructive acceleration

A requirement (based on the reasonable interpretation of the words, acts, or inaction of authorized government employees) that a contractor complete its work by a date earlier than one that would reflect the time extensions to which it is entitled because of excusable delays.

constructive change

A verbal or written act or omission by an authorized government official that is of such a nature that it is construed to have the same effect as a written change order.

contingency contracting

Contracting in an emergency involving military forces, caused by natural disasters, terrorists, subversives, or required military operations. Due to the uncertainty of the situation, contingencies require plans, rapid response, and special procedures to ensure the safety and readiness of personnel, installations, and equipment.

contingent contract

A contract that provides for the possibility of its termination when a specified occurrence takes place or does not take place.

contingent fee

Any commission, percentage, brokerage, or other fee that is contingent upon the success that a person or concern has in securing a government contract.

continued portion of the contract

The portion of a contract that the contractor must continue to perform following a partial termination.

continuing resolution (CR)

1. If the appropriations bill has not been signed by the beginning of the fiscal year, this legislation allows an agency to continue operating at the previous year's spending level. The resolution has a set expiration date.

2. Legislation enacted by Congress to provide budget authority for specific ongoing activities in cases where the regular fiscal year appropriation has not been enacted by the beginning of the fiscal year. A continuing resolution usually specifies a designated period and maximum

rate at which the agency may incur obligations, based on the rate of the prior year, the president's budget request, or an appropriation bill passed by either or both Houses of the Congress. Normally, new programs cannot be started under a continuing resolution.

contra proferentem

Means "against the one bringing forth." Used in connection with the preparing of written documents to the effect that an ambiguous provision is construed most strongly against the party who selected the language.

contract

1. An agreement, enforceable by law, between two or more competent parties to do or not do something not prohibited by law, for legal consideration. Involves both an offer and an acceptance.

2. A mutually binding legal relationship obligating the seller to furnish the supplies or services (including construction) and the buyer to pay for them. It includes all types of commitments that obligate the government to an expenditure of appropriated funds and that, except as otherwise authorized, are in writing. In addition to bilateral instruments, contracts include (but are not limited to):

   • Awards and notices of awards;

   • Job orders or task letters issued under basic ordering agreements;

   • Letter contracts;

   • Orders, such as purchase orders, under which the contract becomes effective by written acceptance or performance; and

   • Bilateral contract modifications.

Contracts do not include grants and cooperative agreements.

3. A relationship between two parties—such as a buyer and seller—that is defined by an agreement about their respective rights and responsibilities.

4. A document that describes such an agreement.

contract administration

1. The oversight of a contractor's (supplier's) performance pursuant to the fulfillment of the terms, conditions, and specifications of a contract.

2. Includes those inherently governmental activities performed by warranted contracting officers, the

contracting officer's technical representatives, and related payment evaluation staff. Contract administration is not to be confused with contract quality control, performance evaluation, or inspection, which are defined as "commercial activities" by OFPP Policy Letter 92-1.

3. The process of ensuring compliance with contractual terms and conditions during contract performance up to contract closeout or termination.

contract audit

The evaluation of the accuracy and propriety of contractors' cost representations and claims by the review and analysis of contractors' and subcontractors' policies, systems, and controls. Includes examination of books, accounts, basic records, and operations.

contract award

Takes place when a contracting officer (buyer) has signed and distributed the contract to the contractor (seller).

contract bond

A guarantee—backed by cash or other security—of the faithful performance and fulfillment of the undertakings, covenants, terms, and conditions contained in a contract.

contract bundling

1. Involves consolidating two or more procurement requirements for goods or services previously provided or performed under separate, smaller contracts into a solicitation of offers for a single contract that is unlikely to be suitable for award to a small business concern.

2. The practice of combining requirements into one "umbrella" solicitation, with the result that the offeror must be able to perform increasingly larger contracts covering multiple and diverse elements of performance.

contract claim

Any request for relief, adjustment, or consideration by a party to the contract for an act which, in the opinion of the claimant, is not within the scope or intent of the original contract.

contract cost

The aggregate dollar amount paid to the contractor (supplier).

contract data requirements list (CDRL)

1. Document used to order (buy) and require delivery of data. It tells the contractor what data to deliver, when and how such data will be accepted, and where to look for instructions.

2. The standard format for identifying potential data requirements in a solicitation, and deliverable data requirements in a contract. The purpose of the CDRL is to provide a standardized method of clearly and unambiguously delineating the government's minimum essential data needs. The CDRL groups all of the data requirements in a single place rather than having them scattered throughout the solicitation or contract.

contract financing (commercial)

Financing in commercial contracting may include obtaining loans and lines of credit from financial institutions, obtaining advance funding of accounts receivable or funding of purchase orders from private firms, or obtaining funds from venture capitalists. It may also include negotiating favorable payment clauses such as a sizable down payment or milestone payments as the work progresses. Commercial contract financing could also include such methods as commercial advance payments made before performance has begun, commercial interim payments made after some work has been done, and delivery payments made after receiving and accepting a portion of the total work to be performed.

contract financing (government)

In some cases, successfully completing a government contract may require the government's assistance with some form of contract financing. For example, contract financing might be appropriate in a multimillion-dollar contract for goods that require the contractor to make substantial initial investments in labor, materials, and production costs. In cases where the government determines that some type of contract financing is appropriate, it usually takes one of two forms, private or government. When a contractor requests financing, the government contracting officer is to consider the following order of preference for methods of contract financing:

- Private financing,

- Customary contract financing other than loan guarantees,

- Loan guarantees,

- Unusual contract financing, and

- Advance payments.

contract formation
The elements of offer, acceptance, mutuality of consideration, competent parties, legal subject matter, and mutuality of agreement.

contract fulfillment
The joint buyer/seller actions taken to successfully perform and administer a contractual agreement and meet or exceed all contractual obligations, including effective changes management and timely contract closeout.

contract interpretation
The entire process of determining what the parties agreed to in their bargain. The basic objective of contract interpretation is to determine the intent of the parties. Rules calling for interpretation of the document against the drafter (contra proferentem, and imposing a duty to seek clarification on the contractor) allocate risks of contractual ambiguities by resolving disputes in favor of the party least responsible for the ambiguity.

contract line item number (CLIN)
The supplies or services to be delivered under the contract as set forth in Section B of the solicitation are categorized into CLINs. The CLIN structure and description can have significant impact on both the government and the contractor. CLINs are based on the work breakdown structure. To effectively determine exactly what the government requires and to create a means to monitor the contractor's work progress, analyze the work breakdown structure, and then design the CLINs to match this structure.

contract management
The art and science of managing a contractual agreement throughout the contracting process.

contract manager
A buyer or seller who administers and oversees the organization's contracts. During the pre-award phase, he or she may participate in acquisition strategy and negotiate pricing and terms while procuring or selling products or services. During the award phase, he or she may develop the contract. During the post-award phase, he or she may participate in modifications and work to ensure the right product is delivered to the right place at the right time. A strong teamwork ethic is a desired trait for the successful contract manager.

contract modification
1. Any written alteration in the specification, delivery point, rate of delivery, contract period, price, quantity, or other provision of an existing contract, accomplished in accordance with a contract clause. May be unilateral or bilateral.

2. Any written change in the terms of a contract.

contract negotiation
The process of unifying different positions into a unanimous joint decision regarding the buying and selling of products and/or services.

contract pricing proposal
The instrument required of an offeror for the submission or identification of cost or pricing data, by which an offeror submits to the government a summary of estimated (or incurred) costs suitable for detailed review and analysis.

contract requirements
In addition to specified performance requirements, contract requirements include those defined in the statement of work; specifications, standards, and related documents; the contract data requirements list; management systems; and contract terms and conditions.

contract schedule
The complete statement of the requirement in the solicitation, including not only the statement of work and specifications, but also the terms and conditions with respect to packaging and marking, inspection and acceptance, deliveries or performance, contract administration data, and other special contract requirements. The schedule includes Sections A through H of the uniform contract format.

contract type
A specific pricing arrangement employed for the performance of work under the contract.

contracting
1. The entire spectrum of action associated with obtaining supplies or services, from initial description through solicitation and contract award and all phases of contract administration.

2. Purchasing, renting, leasing, or otherwise obtaining supplies or services from nonfederal sources. Contracting includes description (but not determination) of supplies and services required, selection and solicitation of sources, preparation and award of contracts, and all phases of contract

administration. It does not include making grants or cooperative agreements.

contracting office
An office that prepares solicitations and awards or executes a contract for supplies or services and performs post-award functions not assigned to a contract administration office.

contracting officer (CO; KO)
The only person with the authority to obligate government funds and enter into, administer, and/or terminate contracts. Also applies to any authorized representatives of the contracting officer acting within their limits of authority as delegated by the contracting officer. Not to be confused with "administrative contracting officer," which refers to a contracting officer who is administering contracts, or "termination contracting officer," which refers to a contracting officer who is settling terminated contracts. A single contracting officer may be responsible for duties in any or all of these areas.

contracting officer's representative (COR)
A qualified individual appointed by the contracting officer to assist in the technical monitoring or administration (i.e., inspection, acceptance) of a contract. CORs must be government employees (either military or civilian) and possess the necessary qualifications (training) and experience commensurate with the responsibilities delegated to them.

contracting out
The process by which a government activity contracts with private enterprise (as opposed to performing work in-house) for commercial or industrial products or services.

contractor (KR; Kr; KTR; Ktr)
A supplier, vendor, or manufacturer having a contract (commitment) to provide specific supplies or services.

contractor bid or proposal information
Any of the following information submitted to a federal agency as part of or in connection with a bid or proposal to enter into a federal agency procurement contract, if that information has not been previously made available to the public or disclosed publicly:

- Cost or pricing data (as defined by 10 U.S.C. 2306a(h) with respect to procurements subject to that section and section 304A(h) of the Fede-

ral Property and Administrative Services Act of 1949 (41 U.S.C. 254b(h)) with respect to procurements subject to that section;

- Indirect costs and direct labor rates;

- Proprietary information about manufacturing processes, operations, or techniques marked by the contractor in accordance with applicable law or regulation;

- Information marked by the contractor as "contractor bid or proposal information" in accordance with applicable law or regulation; and

- Information marked in accordance with FAR 52.215-1(e).

contractor financing
The provision of capital to a contractor through equity capital, private financing, customary progress payments, guaranteed loans, unusual progress payments, or advance payments.

contractor inventory
1. Any property acquired by and in the possession of a contractor or subcontractor under a contract for which title is vested in the government and which exceeds the amounts needed to complete full performance under the entire contract.

2. Any property that the government is obligated or has the option to take over under any type of contract (e.g., as a result either of any changes in the specifications or plans), or of the termination of the contract (or subcontract), before completion of the work, for the convenience or at the option of the government.

3. Government-furnished property that exceeds the amounts needed to complete full performance under the entire contract.

contractor performance assessment report (CPAR)
A detailed document that presents the performance and tasks a contractor has performed for an organization. The report assesses how well the contractor addresses the organization's needs, how well the budget is utilized, and the general outcome from the contractor's work in comparison to the expectations.

contractor purchasing system review (CPSR)
An evaluation of the efficiency and effectiveness with which the prime contractor spends government funds and complies with government policy when subcontracting. It is an annual government audit

of contractor management systems for contractors whose sales to the government exceed, or are anticipated to exceed, $25 million during the next 12 months. (*See* FAR 44.302.)

contractor team arrangement

1. An arrangement in which two or more companies form a partnership or joint venture to act as a potential prime contractor.

2. A potential prime contractor agrees with one or more other companies to have them act as its subcontractors under a specified government contract or acquisition program.

contractor teaming agreement

An agreement that allows two or more companies to fulfill a contract by working together, but maintain their own relationship with the government client and not assume responsibility for managing the other company.

cooperative purchasing

1. A process whereby two or more communities, counties, or other governmental jurisdictions voluntarily agree to coordinate their purchases of one or more commodities to obtain the best unit price through volume buying.

2. A purchasing approach used primarily by institutions in which a group of institutions form or utilize a centralized buying service that purchases specified types of items for all institutional members of the group. The resulting volume buying usually produces significant cost savings for group members. Educational and Institutional Cooperative Service, Inc. (E&I) is perhaps the largest and most widely known cooperative purchasing organization.

cost

1. The amount of money expended in acquiring a product or obtaining a service.

2. The total of acquisition costs plus all expenses related to operating and maintaining an item once acquired.

cost analysis

The review and evaluation of a contractor's costs or pricing data, and of the judgmental factors applied in projecting from the data to the estimated costs, for the purpose of determining the degree to which the contractor's proposed costs represent what contract performance should cost (assuming reasonable economy and efficiency).

cost comparison

The process whereby the estimated cost of government performance of a commercial activity is formally compared, in accordance with the principles and procedures of OMB Circular A-76 and supplement to the cost of performance by commercial or inter-service support agreement sources.

cost contract

A cost-reimbursement contract that provides no fee. This is the least complicated type of cost reimbursement contract.

cost estimating

1. The process of forecasting future results in terms of cost based upon information *available at* the time.

2. A judgment or opinion regarding the cost of an object, commodity, or service. A result or product of an estimating procedure that specifies the expected dollar cost required to perform a stipulated task or to acquire an item. A cost estimate may constitute a single value or a range of values.

cost estimating relationship (CER)

A type of secondary comparison used in performing price analysis. CERs are used to adjust comparisons by establishing a common denominator between different items. For example, dollars per pound, per foot, or per loaded labor hour are yardsticks to measure a relationship between offers.

cost growth

A term related to the net change of an estimated or actual amount over a base figure previously established. The base must be relatable to a program, project, or contract and be clearly identified including source, approval authority, specific items included, specific assumptions made, date, and the amount.

cost incentives

Most incentive contracts include only cost incentives, which take the form of a profit or fee adjustment formula and are intended to motivate the contractor to effectively manage costs. No incentive contract may provide for other incentives without also providing a cost incentive (or constraint). Incentive contracts typically include a target cost, a target profit or fee, and a profit or fee adjustment formula. These targets and the formula provide that (within the constraints of a price ceiling or minimum and maximum fee):

- The actual cost that meets the target will result in the target profit or fee,

- The actual cost that exceeds the target will result in downward adjustment of target profit or fee, and

- The actual cost that is below the target will result in upward adjustment of target profit or fee.

cost objective
A function, organizational subdivision, contract, or other work unit for which cost data are desired and for which provision is made to accumulate and measure the cost of processes, products, jobs, capitalized projects, etc.

cost or price evaluation
Information used to evaluate what the proposed offer will most likely cost the government. Cost/price should not be scored or rated. Examples include cost/price reasonableness, cost/price realism, life cycle cost, and cost risk. When contracting on a cost-reimbursement basis, evaluations shall include a cost realism analysis to determine what the government should realistically expect to pay for the proposed effort, the offeror's understanding of the work, and the offeror's ability to perform the contract.

cost or pricing data
1. All verifiable facts that could reasonably have a significant effect on price negotiations and are *available* at the time of agreement on price.

2. All facts that, as of the date of price agreement or, if applicable, an earlier date agreed upon between the parties that is as close as practicable to the date of agreement on price, prudent buyers and sellers would reasonably expect to affect price negotiations significantly. Cost or pricing data are factual, not judgmental, and are verifiable. While they do not indicate the accuracy of the prospective contractor's judgment about estimated future costs or projections, they do include the data forming the basis for that judgment. Cost or pricing data are more than historical accounting data; they are all the facts that can be reasonably expected to contribute to the soundness of estimates of future costs and to the validity of determinations of costs already incurred. They also include such factors as:

   - Vendor quotations,

   - Nonrecurring costs,

   - Information on changes in production methods and in production or purchasing volume,

   - Data supporting projections of business prospects and objectives and related operations costs,

   - Unit-cost trends such as those associated with labor efficiency,

   - Make-or-buy decisions, and

   - Estimated resources to attain business goals.

3. Information on management decisions that could have a significant bearing on costs.

cost overrun
1. A net change in contractual amount beyond that contemplated by a contract target price (fixed-price-incentive contract), estimated cost plus fee (any cost reimbursable contract), or redeterminable price (fixed-price-redeterminable contract) due to the contractor's actual costs being over target or anticipated contract costs.

2. The amount by which a contractor exceeds the estimated cost and/or the final limitation (ceiling) of the contract.

cost-plus-a-percentage-of-cost contract (CPPC)
An outlawed contract type that bases the contractor's fee on the amount of funds it expends. This type of contract shall not be used in federal contracting.

cost-plus-award-fee (CPAF) contract
A cost-reimbursement type contract with special incentive fee provisions used to provide motivation for excellence in contract performance in such areas as quality, timeliness, ingenuity, and cost effectiveness.

cost-plus-fixed-fee (CPFF) contract
A cost-reimbursement type contract that provides for the payment of a fixed fee to the contractor. The fee does not vary with actual costs, but may be adjusted as a result of any subsequent changes in the work or services to be performed under the contract.

cost-plus-incentive-fee (CPIF) contract
A cost-reimbursement type of contract with a provision for a fee that is adjusted by a formula in accordance with the relationship between total allowable costs and target costs.

cost principles

The regulations that establish rules and policies relating to the general treatment of costs in government contracts, particularly the allowability of costs.

cost proposal

The instrument required of an offeror for the submission or identification of cost or pricing data by which an offeror submits to the buyer a summary of estimated (or incurred) costs, suitable for detailed review and analysis.

cost realism

The costs in an offeror's proposal must:

- Be realistic for the work to be performed,

- Reflect a clear understanding of the requirements, and

- Be consistent with the various elements of the offeror's technical proposal.

cost realism analysis

The process of independently reviewing and evaluating specific elements of each offeror's proposed cost estimate to determine whether the estimated proposed cost elements are:

- Realistic for the work to be performed,

- Reflect a clear understanding of the r equirements, and

- Are consistent with the unique methods of performance and materials described in the offeror's technical proposal.

Cost realism analyses shall be performed on cost-reimbursement contracts to determine the probable cost of performance for each offeror.

cost reasonableness

A cost is reasonable in nature and amount if it does not exceed that which would be incurred by a prudent person in the conduct of competitive business.

cost-reimbursement contract

1. A form of pricing arrangement that provides for payment of allowable, allocable, and reasonable costs incurred in the performance of a contract to the extent that such costs are prescribed or permitted by the contract.

2 A family of pricing arrangements or contract types that provide for payment of allowable, allocable, and reasonable costs incurred in the performance of a contract, to the extent that such costs are prescribed or permitted by the contract. These contracts establish an estimate of total cost for the purpose of obligating funds and establishing a ceiling that the contractor may not exceed without the approval of the buyer. Types of cost-reimbursement contracts include:

- Cost without fee,

- Cost-sharing,

- Cost-plus-incentive-fee,

- Cost-plus-award-fee, and

- Cost-plus-fixed-fee.

cost risk

1. An assumption of possible monetary loss or gain in light of the job or work to be done; an element to be considered in the negotiation of a fair and reasonable price, as well as in the determination of contract type.

2. The risk that a program will not meet its acquisition strategy cost objectives that were developed using cost as an independent variable or cost objectives established by the acquisition authority.

cost savings

1. A reduction in actual expenditures below the projected level of costs to achieve a specific objective.

2. An action that will result in a smaller-than-projected level of costs to achieve a specific objective. Incentive contracts where the contractor and government share in any difference in cost below the estimated target cost incurred by the contractor to achieve the objective of the contract is a cost savings. It differs from a "cost avoidance" in that a cost target has been set from which the amount of savings can be measured. In a cost avoidance, the amount is determined as the difference between two estimated cost patterns.

cost-sharing contract

Cost sharing is an explicit arrangement under which the contractor bears some of the burden of reasonable, allocable, and allowable contract cost. A cost-sharing contract is a cost-reimbursement contract in which the contractor receives no fee and is reimbursed only for an agreed-upon portion of its allowable costs.

counteroffer

1. The non-acceptance of the government's offer to buy as presented. A counteroffer introduces a new condition, item, quantity, or quality, or it varies from the original terms in the government's offer. Counteroffers by suppliers under sealed-bid procedures are rejected. However, under negotiated procedures (including small purchases), counteroffers are permissible and may be negotiated; e.g., a purchase order is only an offer to buy and the terms of acceptance may be negotiated.

2. A counterproposal different from an offer that an offeree makes in response to the offer. In making a counteroffer, the offeree rejects the previous offer.

3. An offer made in response to an original offer that changes the terms of the original.

cure notice

A notice sent by the contracting officer stating that the contractor will be subject to a default termination unless it corrects a specific contract noncompliance or makes necessary progress to meet the delivery schedule.

damages

In a purchasing context, damages are compensation of a specific value, determined by a court, to be paid for loss or injury suffered by one party to a contract as a result of the other contractual party's breach of the contract.

debarment

Action taken by a debarring official to exclude a contractor from government contracting and subcontracting for a reasonable, specified period. The following are some causes for debarment (per FAR 9.406-2):

- Conviction of or civil judgment for any offense indicating a lack of business integrity (e.g., fraud, antitrust violations, theft, bribery, etc.);

- Violation of the terms of a government contract so serious as to justify debarment;

- Violations of the Drug-Free Workplace Act of 1988; or

- Any other cause of so serious or compelling a nature that it affects the present responsibility of a government contractor or subcontractor.

debrief(ing)

1. An explanation given by government personnel to an offeror detailing the reasons its proposal was unsuccessful.

2. At a minimum, the debriefing information shall include:

- The government's evaluation of the significant weaknesses or deficiencies in the offeror's proposal, if applicable;

- The overall evaluated cost or price (including unit prices) and technical rating, if applicable, of the successful offeror and the debriefed offeror, and past performance information on the debriefed offeror;

- The overall ranking of all offerors, when any ranking was developed by the agency during the source selection;

- A summary of the rationale for award;

- For acquisitions of commercial items, the make and model of the item to be delivered by the successful offeror; and

- Reasonable responses to relevant questions about whether source selection procedures contained in the solicitation, applicable regulations, and other applicable authorities were followed.

3. The debriefing shall not include point-by-point comparisons of the debriefed offeror's proposal with those of other offerors. Moreover, the debriefing shall not reveal any information prohibited from disclosure by FAR 24.202 or exempt from release under the Freedom of Information Act (5 U.S.C. 552) including:

- Trade secrets;

- Privileged or confidential manufacturing processes and techniques;

- Commercial and financial information that is privileged or confidential, including cost breakdowns, profit, indirect cost rates, and similar information; and

- The names of individuals providing reference information about an offeror's past performance.

deductive change

A change resulting in a reduction in contract price because of a net reduction in the contractor's work.

default

1. The actual or anticipated failure of a contractor to fulfill the terms and conditions of the contract, thus giving the contracting officer the right to terminate the contract.

2. The failure to perform a legal obligation or duty.

defect

1. The absence of something necessary for completeness or perfection.

2. A deficiency in something essential to the proper use for the purpose for which a thing is to be used.

3. Some structural weakness in a part or component that is responsible for damage.

4. Any condition or characteristic in any supplies or services furnished by the contractor under the contract that is not in compliance with the requirements of the contract.

defective certification

A certificate that alters or otherwise deviates from the language in the *Federal Acquisition Regulation* or that is not executed by a person duly authorized to bind the contractor with respect to the claim. Failure to certify shall not be deemed to be a defective certification.

defective cost or pricing data

Certified cost or pricing data subsequently found to have been inaccurate, incomplete, or not current as of the effective date of the certificate.

defective specifications

Mistakes and omissions in the requirements set forth are generally identified in this way. This area is frequently the basis for claims and litigation between contracting parties.

deficiency

A material failure of a proposal to meet a government requirement or a combination of significant weaknesses in a proposal that increases the risk of unsuccessful contract performance to an unacceptable level.

definite-quantity contract

A contractual instrument that provides for a definite quantity of supplies or services to be delivered at some later, unspecified date.

definitize

To make definite. Often used in contracting methods like letter contracts, which authorize contractors to begin work before reaching a final agreement on contract terms. To control costs and schedules, the contract terms must be definitized.

delegation

Conferring authority, from one government agency or representative to another, to accomplish contract administrative tasks. Such authority may be shared or recalled.

delinquency

The actual or potential failure by the contractor to meet or maintain the contract delivery or performance schedule.

delivery

1. Transfer of possession. A "delivery order" directs an established source to transfer possession of goods from the source to the ordering activity. Applied to shipping, delivery occurs when a bill of lading is surrendered and title of goods passes to the receiver or consignee.

2. Constructive or actual delivery; the performance of services for the customer or requisitioner; accessorial services, when they are normally recorded in the billing and collection cycle immediately following performance.

delivery incentives

Should be considered when improvement from a required delivery schedule is a significant government objective. It is important to determine the buyer's primary objectives in a given contract (e.g., earliest possible delivery or earliest quantity production).

delivery order contract

A delivery order is a written order to a contractor pursuant to an indefinite-delivery type contract, which then becomes the basic obligating document for the transaction. A delivery order contract is a contract for supplies that does not procure or specify a firm quantity of supplies (other than a minimum or maximum quantity) and that provides for the issuance of orders for the delivery of supplies during the period of the contract.

design statement of work (design SOW)

Most often used when the buyer requires a specific manufactured good. Design SOWs are extremely detailed, and usually define all required materials, production processes, and specifications such as size, shape, color, tolerances, etc.

design-to-cost (DTC)

1. A concept that establishes cost elements as management goals to achieve the best balance between life cycle cost, acceptable performance, and schedule. Under this concept, cost is a design constraint during the design and development phases and a management discipline throughout the acquisition and operation of the system or equipment.

2. A management concept that historically emphasized cost-effective design (minimizing cost while achieving performance) and targeting an average unit procurement cost. DTC concentrated on the contractors' activities associated with tracking/controlling costs and performing cost-performance analyses/tradeoffs. Cost as an independent variable (CAIV) has refocused DTC to consider cost objectives for the total life cycle of the program and to view CAIV with the understanding it may be necessary to trade off performance to stay within cost objectives and constraints. DTC is now those actions that are undertaken to meet cost objectives through explicit design activities. Contractual implementation of DTC should go beyond simply incentivizing the contractor to meet cost commitments—it should also incentivize the contractor to seek out additional cost reduction opportunities.

determination and findings (D&F)

A document signed by an authorized government official justifying a decision to take a certain action; expressed in terms of meeting the regulatory requirements of the situation. The determination is a conclusion or decision supported by the findings. The findings are statements of fact or rationale essential to support the determination and must cover each requirement of the statute or regulation.

determination of responsibility

The process by which a contractor is determined to be a responsible bidder/offeror.

direct costs

1. Costs specifically identifiable with a contract requirement, including but not restricted to costs of material and/or labor directly incorporated into an end item.

2. Those costs that are assignable to a specific product, primarily classified as "direct labor cost," "direct material cost," or "purchased cost." These costs are usually treated as variable and do not include general overhead or common cost allocations.

direct labor

1. All labor that is obviously related and specifically and conveniently traceable to specific products.

2. Labor specifically identified with a particular final cost objective. Manufacturing direct labor includes fabrication, assembly, inspection, and test for constructing the end product. Engineering direct labor consists of engineering labors such as reliability, quality assurance, test, design, etc., that are readily identified with the end product.

direct material

Material, including raw material, purchased parts, and subcontracted items, directly incorporated into an end item, which is identifiable to a contract requirement.

directed change

Most contracts contain a "changes" clause that gives the buyer the right to direct changes during contract performance. The clause describes what type of changes the buyer can direct, the procedure for ordering the change, and a provision for equitable adjustment to the contract amount or period of performance if there is a resultant change in cost or schedule. A directed change usually must be within the original scope of the contract.

discharge of a contract

Results when the obligations incurred by the parties when they entered into the agreement are excused, and the parties are no longer bound to perform as promised.

disclosure statement

An official statement in which persons or firms are required to describe their contract cost accounting practices by providing data responsive to the requirements of the government's Cost Accounting Standards.

discussion

Any verbal or written communication between the government and an offeror other than communications conducted for the purpose of minor clarification, whether or not initiated by the government, that involves information essential for determining the acceptability of a proposal, or provides the offeror an opportunity to revise or modify its proposal. When negotiations are conducted in a competitive acquisition, they take place after establishment of the competitive range and are called discussions.

draft request for proposal (DRFP)

1. Usually sent out to prospective industry offerors authorized by the government to receive it in advance of a final request for proposal. Solicits offerors' recommendations to add, delete, or modify requirements, and gives them advance notice of the government's requirements.

2. A tentative solicitation submitted to prospective offerors for review and comment.

earned value management system (EVMS)

1. Industry developed set of 32 standards adopted for use in 1996 for evaluation of contractor management systems. The EVMS replaced the Cost/Schedule Control Systems Criteria (C/SCSC) that contained 35 standards for evaluation of contractor management systems.

2. A project management system that combines schedule performance and cost performance to answer the question, "What did we get for the money we spent?" The EVMS guidelines incorporate best business practices to provide strong benefits for program or enterprise planning and control. The processes include:

   • Integration of program scope, schedule, and cost objectives;

   • Establishment of a baseline plan for accomplishment of program objectives; and

   • Use of earned value techniques for performance measurement during the execution of a program.

The system provides a sound basis for problem identification, corrective actions, and management replanning, as may be required.

3. A project (investment) management tool that effectively integrates the investment scope of work with schedule and cost elements for optimum investment planning and control. The qualities and operating characteristics of an EVMS are described in American National Standards Institute/Electronic Industries AllianceStandard-748-1998, "Earned Value Management Systems," approved May 19, 1998. It was reaffirmed on August 28, 2002.

economic order quantity (EOQ)

This concept holds that the appropriate quantity to order may be the one that tends to minimize all the costs associated with the order-carrying costs,

acquisition costs, and the cost of the material itself. The EOQ formula states that EOQ occurs when annual carrying cost (CC) = annual acquisition cost (AC) (i.e., CC = AC).

economic price adjustment (EPA)

An alteration permitted and specified by contract provisions for the upward or downward revision of a stated contract price upon the occurrence of certain specifically defined contingencies.

economic purchase quantity

A supply acquisition quantity that produces economic benefit to the government. Evaluation should consider the costs related to purchasing and holding the supply item.

elements of a contract

Elements that must be present in a contract if the contract is to be binding. These include the following:

• An offer,

• Acceptance,

• Consideration,

• Execution by competent parties,

• Legality of purpose, and

• Clear terms and conditions.

elements of cost

Those cost categories that directly or indirectly influence the cost of producing material or providing services and that can be apportioned to the contract.

end item

An assembled whole system or equipment ready for its intended use.

end product

Supplies delivered under a line item of a contract.

engineering change proposal (ECP)

1. A document proposing any design change requiring revision to contract specifications or engineering drawings. It may be originated by either party to a contract. It requires detailed documentation and an evaluation of technical, cost, and schedule effects.

2. A proposal to the responsible authority recommending that a change to an original item of

equipment be considered, and the design or engineering change be incorporated into the article to modify, add to, delete, or supersede original parts.

engineering data
Engineering documents such as specifications, drawings, standards, lists, or other information prepared by a design activity relating to the design, performance, manufacture, test, or inspection of items and services.

environmentally preferable purchasing (EPP)
Ensures that environmental considerations are included in purchasing decisions, along with traditional factors such as product price and performance. The EPP program provides guidance for federal agencies to facilitate purchases of goods and services that pose fewer burdens on the environment.

equitable adjustment
1. The compensation or price adjustment to which a contractor is entitled upon the occurrence of a contract change or special event.

2. The courts and boards have recognized four methods for pricing equitable adjustment claims:

   - Total cost,
   - Modified total cost,
   - Jury verdict, and
   - Actual costs.

equitable remedies
Include an order of specific performance, restitution, and rescission. In the case of goods or real property, an order of specific performance can require the breaching party to perform in accordance with the contract.

established catalog price
A price that is regularly maintained by a manufacturer or vendor, published or made available for inspection by customers, and which states prices at which sales are currently, or were last, made to a significant number of buyers constituting the general public.

established government source
Government and nongovernment sources of supplies, equipment, and services that are designated by law or regulation as mandatory sources in a set order of priority for particular items and services.

established market price
A current price, established in the usual and ordinary course of trade between buyers and sellers free to bargain, which can be substantiated from sources independent of the manufacturer or vendor.

estimating system
The contractor's policies, procedures, and practices for generating cost estimates and other data included in proposals submitted to customers in the expectation of receiving contract awards. Components include the contractor's:

- Organizational structure;
- Established lines of authority, duties, and responsibilities;
- Internal controls and managerial reviews;
- Flow of work, coordination, and communications; and
- Estimating methods, techniques, accumulation of historical costs, and other analyses used to generate cost estimates.

evaluation factors
Factors that will be considered in evaluating proposals tailored to each acquisition and which have an impact on the source selection decision. Price or cost to the government shall be included as an evaluation factor in every source selection. Quality shall also be addressed in every source selection. Quality may be expressed in terms of technical excellence, management capability, personnel qualifications, prior experience, past performance, and schedule compliance. Any other relevant factors, such as cost realism, may also be included.

evaluation standards
A predetermined level of merit against which proposals are measured. Standards are usually a statement of the minimum level of compliance with a requirement that must be offered for a proposal to be considered acceptable.

excess funds
Funds relating to a specific line item or deliverable that was not performed on a contract. These funds are de-obligated by contract modification.

excess reprocurement costs
The contractor is liable to the government for any excess costs incurred by the government to repurchase supplies or services similar to those terminated for default.

excusable delay

1. A contractual provision designed to protect the contractor from sanctions for late performance. To the extent that it has been excusably delayed, the contractor is protected from default termination, liquidated damages, or excess costs of reprocurement or completion. Excusable delays also may lead to recovery of additional compensation if the government constructively accelerates performance.

2. Protects contractors from penalties for delays that are beyond their control. Examples of excusable delay include:

   - Acts of God or the public enemy,
   - Acts of the government in either its sovereign or contractual capacity,
   - Fire,
   - Flood,
   - Quarantines,
   - Strikes,
   - Epidemics,
   - Unusually severe weather, and
   - Freight embargoes.

executed contract

A written document, signed by both parties and mailed or otherwise furnished to each party, which expresses the requirements, terms, and conditions to be met by both parties in the performance of the contract.

executory contract

A contract that has not yet been fully performed by one or more parties.

expedited procedure

Procedure under the Contract Disputes Act whereby an appellant before an agency board of contract appeals can elect, for claims of $100,000 or less, to have a decision issued on a claim within four months after making the election. (*See* FAR 33.211.)

express contract

A contract in which the terms of the contract are stated in words, either written or spoken.

express warranty

A written statement arising out of a sale to the consumer of a consumer good, pursuant to which the manufacturer, distributor, or retailer undertakes to preserve or maintain the utility or performance of the consumer good or provide compensation if there is a failure in utility or performance. It is not necessary to the creation of an express warranty that formal words such as "warrant" or "guarantee" be used, or that a specific intention to make a warranty be present. For commercial contracts, an express warranty must be included in the contract by addendum.

extended overhead

This concept was devised as a means of recovering management and other fixed costs during a period of delay where the overhead during the period will not be fully recovered by the formula of overhead as a "markup" on direct costs. Equity requires that the government pay for the additional management attention given to the project during delays. In such cases, contractors need to recover their fixed overhead costs using a different formula than overhead as a "markup" on direct costs.

extraordinary contractual relief

Form of relief for contractors under federal law giving the president the power to authorize federal agencies to enter into contracts or amendments or modifications of contracts without regard to other provisions of law relating to the making, performance, amendment, or modification of contracts when the president believes the action will facilitate national defense.

fact finding

The process of identifying and obtaining information necessary to complete the evaluation of proposals. This may include fact-finding sessions with offerors.

factory overhead

All factory costs other than direct labor and direct material. (Also known as "factory burden," "indirect manufacturing costs," and "manufacturing overhead.")

fair and reasonable

A subjective evaluation of what each party deems as equitable consideration in areas such as terms and conditions, cost or price, assured quality, and timeliness of contract performance, and/or any other areas subject to negotiation.

fair and reasonable price

A price that is fair to both the buyer and the seller, considering the agreed-upon conditions, promised quality, and timeliness of contract performance. Although generally a fair and reasonable price is a function of the law of supply and demand, there are statutory, regulatory, and judgmental limits on the concept.

fast payment procedure

A procedure utilized with small purchases that provides payment to the contractor immediately upon receipt of its invoice (and before inspection and acceptance has taken place), provided the contractor certifies that the supplies have been delivered to a "point of first receipt" (such as a common carrier) and are as ordered.

federal assistance (grants and cooperative agreements)

1. The furnishing of assistance (anything of value) by the federal government by grant or cooperative agreement to a recipient to accomplish a public purpose. Different from procurement in that it is not an acquisition of products or services for the direct benefit or use of the federal government.

2. Refers to federal financing for public purposes through transfer of funds to state or local governments or to other recipients. The principal distinction between an assistance arrangement and procurement is found in the purpose of the funding. If the purpose is to sponsor property or to support services not for the government's express use or benefit, assistance arrangements are used. Within the category of assistance, there are two principal types of instruments: the grant and the cooperative agreement. The distinction between the grant and the cooperative agreement relates to management: Grants have little or no federal involvement in management, whereas cooperative agreements involve collaborative management from the sponsoring agency.

Federal Supply Schedule (FSS) Program

Directed and managed by the General Services Administration, it provides federal agencies with a simplified process for obtaining commonly used supplies and services at prices associated with volume buying. There are four types of Federal Supply Schedules:

- Single Award,
- Multiple Award,
- New Item Introductory, and
- International.

Schedules are designated as mandatory- or optional-use for specific government agencies.

fee

1. An agreed-to amount of reimbursement beyond the initial estimate of costs.

2. The term "fee" is used when discussing cost-reimbursement contracts, whereas "profit" is used in relation to fixed-price contracts.

fiduciary

A person who handles another person's money or property in a capacity that involves a confidence or trust. Examples of fiduciaries are executors or guardians of the estates of minors or deceased persons.

final cost objective

A cost objective that has allocated to it both direct and indirect costs and, in the contractor's accumulation system, is one of the final accumulation points.

final decision

For purposes of the Contract Disputes Act, this is a contracting officer's unilateral adjudication of a contract claim that is a prerequisite to jurisdiction over the claim by a board of contract appeals or federal court.

final indirect cost rate

The indirect cost rate established and agreed upon by the government and the contractor as not subject to change. It is usually established after the close of the contractor's fiscal year (unless the parties decide upon a different period) to which it applies. For cost-reimbursement research and development contracts with educational institutions, it may be predetermined; that is, established for a future period on the basis of cost experience with similar contracts, together with supporting data.

firm bid rule

A rule that prohibits the bidder from withdrawing its bid for the period specified in the invitation for bids; usually 60 days after bid opening.

firm-fixed-price (FFP) contract

A contract that provides for a price that is not subject to any adjustment by reason of costs experienced by the contractor in the performance of the contract.

firm-fixed-price, level-of-effort (FFP-LOE) contract

Requires the contractor to provide a specified level of effort over a stated period of time on work that can be stated only in general terms. Also requires the buyer to pay the contractor a fixed dollar amount.

first article and first article testing (FAT)

1. Preproduction models, initial production samples, test samples, first lots, or pilot samples submitted for testing and evaluation for conformance with specified contract requirements before or in the initial stages of production.

2. First article testing and approval is used by the federal government to ensure that the vendor can furnish a product that conforms to all contract requirements for acceptance. This procedure, although costly, can be a significant contributor to risk reduction. Assuming that more than one product is to be built, the risk to the remaining products is minimized based on the lessons learned during the first article inspection.

fixed cost

1. A cost which, for a given period of time and range of activity, called the "relevant range," does not change in total but becomes progressively smaller on a per-unit basis as volume increases.

2. Operating expenses that are incurred to provide facilities and organization that are kept in readiness to do business without regard to actual volumes of production and sales. Examples of fixed costs consist of rent, property tax, and interest expense.

fixed price

A form of pricing that includes a ceiling beyond which the buyer bears no responsibility for payment.

fixed-price award fee (FPAF)

Award-fee provisions may be used in fixed-price contracts when the government wishes to motivate a contractor and other incentives cannot be used because contractor performance cannot be measured objectively. Such contracts shall establish a fixed price (including normal profit) for the effort. This price will be paid for satisfactory contract performance. Award fee earned (if any) will be paid in addition to that fixed price.

fixed-price contract with retroactive price redetermination

Provides for a fixed ceiling price and a retroactive price determination within the ceiling after completion of the contract.

fixed-price-incentive (FPI) contract

A type of contract that provides for adjusting profit and establishing the final contract price by application of a formula based on the relationship of total final negotiated cost to total target cost. The final price is subject to a price ceiling, negotiated at the outset. There are two types of FPI contracts:

- "Fixed-price-incentive (firm target) contract" (FPIF): Specifies a target cost, target profit, price ceiling (but not a profit ceiling or floor), and a profit adjustment formula. These elements are all negotiated at the outset.

- "Fixed-price-incentive (successive target) contract" (FPIS): Specifies the following elements, all of which are negotiated at the outset: an initial target cost, initial target profit, and initial profit adjustment formula. These targets and formula are used to establish:

  o The firm target profit, including a ceiling and floor for the firm target profit;

  o The production point at which the firm target cost and firm target profit will be negotiated (usually before delivery or shop completion of the first item); and

  o A ceiling price that is the maximum that may be paid to the contractor, except for any adjustment under other contract clauses providing for equitable adjustment or other revision of the contract price under stated circumstances.

fixed-price, level-of-effort (FPLOE) contract

A contract suitable for investigation or study in a specific research and development area. The product of the contract is usually a report showing the results achieved through application of the required level of effort. However, payment is based on the effort expended rather than on the results achieved. This type of contract requires:

- The contractor to provide a specified level of effort, over a stated period of time, on work that can be stated only in general terms; and

- The government to pay the contractor a fixed dollar amount.

fixed-price prospective price redetermination

A contract that provides for a firm-fixed-price for an initial period of contract deliveries or performance and prospective redetermination (at a stated time or times during performance) of the price for subsequent periods of performance.

Pfixed-price redeterminable (FPR) contract

A fixed-price type contract that contains provisions for subsequently negotiated adjustment, in whole or in part, of the initially negotiated base price.

fixed-price with economic price adjustment (FPEPA) contract

A fixed-price contract that permits an element of cost to fluctuate to reflect current market prices. Economic price adjustments may be based on established prices, actual costs of labor or material, or cost indexes of labor or material.

flexible progress payments

A method of making progress payments used by the Department of Defense for certain negotiated contracts performed in the United States. It tailors the progress payment rate to more closely match the contractor's cash needs for financing contract performance.

flow down

The transfer and translation of prime contract requirements to subcontracts.

forbearance

An intentional failure of a party to enforce a contract requirement, usually done for an act of immediate or future consideration from the other party. It is sometimes referred to as a "nonwaiver" or as a "one-time waiver," but not as a relinquishment of rights.

formal contract

A contract that requires a special form or method of formation (creation) in order to be enforceable.

forward buying

The practice of buying materials in a quantity exceeding specified current requirements, but not beyond the actual foreseeable requirements. Even though not known with precision, it is reasonably certain that a longer-term production need for the material does exist. Any purchases beyond this point fall into the speculative buying category. Forward buying can be used in stable markets or in unstable markets where prices appear to be rising. One potential hazard in forward buying, however, is the possible price risk involved, depending on the volatility of the market in which the purchase is made. The buyer must also consider the additional inventory carrying costs and the attendant tie-up of working capital that accompany forward buys.

forward pricing

Action involving negotiations and a resultant agreement between a contractor and the buyer to use certain rates and/or indices for a specified future period of time in pricing contracts or contract modifications.

forward pricing rate agreement (FPRA)

A written agreement negotiated between a contractor and the government to make certain rates available during a specified period for use in pricing contracts or modifications. Such rates represent reasonable projections of specific costs that are not easily estimated for, identified with, or generated by a specific contract, contract end item, or task. These projections may include rates for such things as labor, indirect costs, material obsolescence and usage, spare parts provisioning, and material handling.

Four Corners Doctrine

A theory of contract interpretation that the contract itself should include all of the terms and conditions that the parties wish to be part of the agreement; the notion that the agreement should be contained within the "four corners" of the document.

framework pricing arrangement

A contract that is definitive in all respects except pricing. The agreement or contract specifies a predetermined index, formula, or algorithm (i.e., the "framework") for the calculation of price at the point of sale.

free on board (FOB)

This term is used in conjunction with a physical point to determine the responsibility and basis for payment of freight charges and, unless otherwise agreed, the point at which title for goods passes to the buyer or consignee:

- "FOB origin": The seller places the goods on the conveyance by which they are to be transported. Cost of shipping and risk of loss are borne by the buyer.

- "FOB destination": The seller delivers the goods on the seller's conveyance at destination. Cost of shipping and risk of loss are borne by the seller.

full and open competition

All responsible sources are permitted to compete.

functional statement of work (functional SOW)

Describes requirements in terms of the end purpose, expected result, or final objective rather than in terms of how the work effort is to be performed. The functional SOW is the least restrictive of the three basic SOW types.

futures contract

A contract for the purchase or sale and delivery of commodities at a future date, primarily used as a hedging device against market price fluctuations or unforeseen supply shortages.

gap-fillers

Interim agreements that define the rights and obligations of the parties, and establish the basis for the conduct of business prior to the establishment of a long-term contractual relationship. Includes memorandums of understanding, letter contracts, teaming agreements, and other short-term agreements.

general and administrative (G&A) expenses

1. Indirect expenses related to the overall business. Expenses for a company's general and executive offices, executive compensation, staff services, and other miscellaneous support purposes.

2. Any indirect management, financial, or other expense that is not assignable to a program's direct overhead charges for engineering manufacturing, material, etc., but is routinely incurred by or allotted to a business unit; and is for the general management and administration of the business as a whole.

general provisions

A collection of contract clauses that are not specific to a given procurement, but are part of a common contract language.

global sourcing

The procurement of goods or services outside the continental limits of the United States. In many firms, the term "global" infers the development of a longer-term, planned continuing relationship with international suppliers.

go/no-go decision

A determination to proceed with or abandon a plan or project. In quality control, "go" denotes that a product conforms to the specifications; when it does not, it is "no go."

government purchase card

Authorized for use in making and/or paying for purchases of supplies, services, or construction. The card may be used by contracting officers and other designated individuals. The card may be used only for purchases that are otherwise authorized by law or regulation. The card may be used to make micro-purchases; place a task or delivery order (if authorized in the basic contract, basic ordering agreement, or blanket purchase agreement); or make payments when the contractor agrees to accept payment by the card.

governmentwide acquisition contract (GWAC)

1. A contract available to multiple buyers that provides for an indefinite quantity, within stated limits, of supplies or services during a fixed period. The buyer places orders for individual requirements. The quantity may be stated as number of units or as dollar values.

2. A task-order or delivery-order contract for information technology established by one agency for governmentwide use that is operated by an executive agent designated by the Office of Management and Budget pursuant to 40 U.S.C. 11302(e).

grandfather clause

A contractual or legal provision that protects the existing interests of affected parties.

grants

An award of financial assistance, the principal purpose of which is to transfer a thing of value from a federal agency to a recipient to carry out a public purpose of support or stimulation authorized by a law of the United States (see 31 U.S.C. 6101(3)). A grant is distinguished from a contract, which is used to acquire property or services for the federal government's direct benefit or use.

gratuity

Something of monetary value, freely given to someone else with no explicit expectation of return or reward. In actual practice, the motive behind dispensing a gratuity is often suspect, as if the giver were bribing or buying special consideration.

green contracting

Contract actions, including task and delivery orders, for products and services meeting environmentally preferred requirements, such as being energy-efficient, water-efficient, bio-based, non-ozone-depleting, or containing recovered materials. Procured products should also be nontoxic or less toxic than alternatives.

identical bids
Bids for the same line item that are determined to be identical as to unit price or total line item amount, with or without the application of evaluation factors (e.g., transportation cost).

implied acceptance
In the case of a bilateral contract, acceptance of an offer need not be expressed, but it may be shown by any words or acts indicating the offeree's assent to the proposed bargain.

implied contract
A contract (sometimes called an "implied-in-fact contract") in which the terms of the contract are wholly or partly inferred from the conduct (as opposed to the words) of the parties or surrounding circumstance. In order to establish an implied contract:

- The seller must have furnished some service or property to the buyer,

- The seller must have reasonably expected to be paid and the buyer knew or should have known that a reasonable person in the seller's shoes would have expected to be paid for the service or property rendered by the seller, and

- The buyer must have had the opportunity to reject the services or property and failed to do so.

implied warranty
A promise arising by operation of law that something that is sold shall be merchantable and fit for the purpose for which the seller has reason to know that it is required. Some types of implied warranties are as follows: implied warranty of fitness for a particular purpose, implied warranty of merchantability, implied warranty of title, and implied warranty of wholesomeness.

importing
The purchase of commodities by one country from a source in a foreign country for trade or resale by the purchaser.

imprest fund
A cash fund of a fixed amount established by advance of funds, without charge to an appropriation, from an agency finance or disbursement officer to a duly appointed cashier, for disbursement as needed from time to time in making payment in cash for relatively small purchases.

improper payment
Any payment that should not have been made or that was made in an incorrect amount under statutory, contractual, administrative, or other legally applicable requirements.

in-scope
Phrase used to denote that an action performed or requested to be performed by a contractor for the buyer could reasonably be considered to be within the requirements of the contract.

"in writing," "writing," or "written"
Any worded or numbered expression that can be read, reproduced, and later communicated, and includes electronically transmitted and stored information.

incentive
Motivating the contractor in calculable monetary terms to turn out a product that meets significantly advanced performance goals, improve on the contract schedule up to and including final delivery, substantially reduce costs of the work, or complete the project under a weighted combination of some or all of these objectives.

incentive contract
Appropriate when a firm-fixed-price contract is not appropriate and the required supplies or services can be acquired at lower cost and, in certain instances, with improved delivery or technical performance by relating the amount of profit or fee payable under the contract to the contractor's performance. Incentive contracts are designed to obtain specific acquisition objectives by establishing reasonable and attainable targets that are clearly communicated to the contractor efforts that might not otherwise be emphasized, and to discourage contractor inefficiency and waste.

incremental funding
1. The obligation of funds to a contract (which contains a total price or estimated cost) in periodic installments as the work progresses, rather than a lump sum.

2. The provision (or recording) of budgetary resources for a program or project based on obligations estimated to be incurred within a fiscal year when such budgetary resources will

cover only a portion of the obligations to be incurred in completing the program or project as programmed. This differs from full funding, where budgetary resources are provided or recorded for the total estimated obligations for a program or project in the initial year of funding. Most commonly used for research and development, as opposed to production, which must be fully funded.

indefinite delivery/indefinite quantity (IDIQ) contract

Contracts that provide for an indefinite quantity within stated limits of supplies or services to be furnished within a fixed period with deliveries or performance to be scheduled by placing orders with the contractor. Examples of these contracts are delivery order, task order, definite quality, requirements, and indefinite quantity.

independent contractor

People such as doctors, dentists, veterinarians, lawyers, accountants, contractors, subcontractors, public stenographers, or auctioneers who are in an independent trade, business, or profession in which they offer services. The following elements are essential to establish the relationship of an independent contractor to its client, as contrasted with the relationship of an agent to its principal. In order to be considered an independent contractor, one must:

- Exercise independent judgment as to the means used to accomplish the result,

- Be free from control orders from any other person, and

- Be responsible only under the contract with the client for the result obtained.

independent government cost estimate (IGCE)

A cost estimate developed by the government technical activity based on the requirements (statement of work, statement of objectives, etc.) and without the influence of potential contractors' (marketing) efforts. Properly developed IGCEs provide acquisition managers with an essential part of their structured management process that should be used to think through, develop, and document their acquisition. Acquisition managers can use IGCE documentation to justify, defend, make tradeoff decisions, and manage their acquisitions throughout the life cycle of the requirement.

independent research and development (IR&D)

The cost of effort that is neither sponsored by a grant nor required in performing a contract, and which falls within any of the following four areas:

- Basic research,

- Applied research,

- Development, and

- Systems and other concept formulation studies.

indirect cost

Any cost not directly identifiable with a specific cost objective, but subject to two or more cost objectives.

indirect cost rate

The percentage or dollar factor that expresses the ratio of indirect expense incurred in a given period to direct labor cost, manufacturing cost, or another appropriate base for the same period.

indirect labor

All labor that is not specifically associated with or cannot be practically traced to specific units -of output.

ineligible

Excluded from government contracting (and subcontracting, if appropriate) pursuant to statutory, executive order, or regulatory authority other than the Federal Acquisition Regulation and its implementing and supplementing regulations (e.g., pursuant to the Davis-Bacon Act and its related statutes and implementing regulations, the Service Contract Act, the Equal Employment Opportunity Acts and executive orders, the Walsh-Healey Public Contracts Act, the Buy American Act, or the Environmental Protection Acts and executive orders).

informal contract

A contract that does not require a specified form or method of formation in order to be valid.

information other than cost or pricing data

Any type of information required to determine price reasonableness or cost realism that does not require offeror certification as accurate, complete, and current in accordance with Federal Acquisition Regulation 15.406-2. It may include pricing, sales, or cost information. It includes cost or pricing data for which certification is determined inapplicable after submission.

inherently governmental function

A function that is so intimately related to the public interest as to mandate performance by government employees. This definition is a policy determination, not a legal determination. An inherently governmental function includes activities that require either the exercise of discretion in applying government authority or the making of value judgments in making decisions for the government.

inspection

The examination (including testing) of supplies and services (including, when appropriate, raw materials, components, and intermediate assemblies) to determine whether the supplies and services conform to the contract requirements.

intellectual property

Includes inventions, trademarks, patents, industrial designs, copyrights, and technical information including software, data designs, technical know-how, manufacturing information and know-how, techniques, technical data packages, manufacturing data packages, and trade secrets.

inter-agency contracting

Commonly conducted through indefinite-delivery contracts, such as task and delivery order contracts. The indefinite-delivery contracts used most frequently to support inter-agency acquisitions are Federal Supply Schedules, governmentwide acquisition contracts, and multi-agency contracts.

interested party

An actual or prospective bidder or offeror whose direct economic interest would be affected by the award of the contract or by failure to award the contract. A protest may only be filed by an interested party.

interveners

Awardees of the protested procurement or all other offerors who had a "reasonable prospect" of receiving an award.

invitation for bids (IFB)

The method of solicitation for the sealed bid process. The IFB must describe the requirements of the government clearly, accurately, and completely. Unnecessarily restrictive specifications or requirements that might unduly limit the number of bidders are prohibited. The IFB includes all documents (whether attached or incorporated by reference) furnished by prospective bidders for the purpose of bidding.

invoice

A contractor may submit an invoice (a bill) to the government for payment for contract performance. Such invoice payments are not made for the purpose of financing work in process. Invoice payments are made for the purpose of honoring a contractual obligation to pay for work accepted. Under cost-reimbursement contracts, contractors may submit two types of invoices: interim vouchers and final vouchers. Interim vouchers are submitted prior to completion of the contract. Final vouchers are submitted when the contract is completed.

issue in controversy

A material disagreement between the buyer and the contractor that may result in a claim; or is all or part of an existing claim.

joint venture

The parties jointly own and manage either a partnership or a corporation established for the express purpose of entering into a contract with the customer. Neither party alone enjoys direct privity of contract with the customer; only the joint venture itself has direct privity.

jury verdict basis

A means of pricing equitable adjustments used when the two parties rely on different costing approaches. This technique is not limited to use in court; it can also be used during negotiations. It requires compromise. The evidence is presented by both parties, the information is evaluated, and the "jury verdict" method is used to determine a reasonable claim amount.

justification and approval (J&A)

A document to justify procurement using other than full and open competition. This document is required prior to commencing negotiation for a contract resulting from an unsolicited proposal or any other contract award that does not provide for full and open competition.

kickbacks

1. Payment back of a portion of the purchase price to a buyer or public official by the seller to induce purchase or to improperly influence future purchases or leases. A federal statute makes kickbacks a criminal offense in connection with a contract for construction or repair of a public building or a building financed by loans from the government.

2. Any money, fee, commission, credit, gift, gratuity, thing of value, or compensation of any kind that is provided, directly or indirectly, to any prime contractor, prime contractor employee, subcontractor, or subcontractor employee for the purpose of improperly obtaining or rewarding favorable treatment in connection with a prime contractor in connection with a subcontract relating to a prime contract.

labor hour contract

1. A contract that provides for reimbursement of the contractor's labor costs at a fixed hourly rate.

2. A variation of the time-and-materials contract, differing only in that materials are not supplied by the contractor.

labor surplus area

A geographic area identified by the Department of Labor in accordance with 20 C.F.R. 654, Subpart A, as an area of concentrated unemployment or underemployment or an area of labor surplus.

labor surplus area concern

A concern that together with its first-tier subcontractors will perform substantially in labor surplus areas. Performance is substantially in labor surplus areas if the costs incurred under the contract on account of manufacturing, production, or performance of appropriate services in labor surplus areas exceed 50 percent of the contract price.

late bid

A bid received in the office designated in the invitation for bids after the exact time set for opening.

lead time

The period of time from the date of a purchase order to the date of delivery of the order.

leader-follower concept

A government contractual relationship for the delivery of an end item through a prime or subcontract relationship or to provide assistance to another company. Variants include:

- A prime contract awarded to an established source (leader) who is obligated to subcontract to and assist another source (follower);

- A contract is awarded requiring the leader to assist the follower, who has the prime contract for production; or

- A prime contract awarded to the follower for production, and the follower is obligated to subcontract with a designated leader for assistance (the leader may be producing under another contract).

lease

1. When used with reference to tangible personal property, "lease" means a contract by which the owner of such property grants another the right to possess, use, and enjoy it for a specified period of time in exchange for periodic payment of a stipulated price.

2. A legal contract between two parties—the lessor, who owns the asset, and the lessee, who uses the asset.

lease or buy decision

The decision concerning whether to contract for the possession and use of an asset owned by another party for a period of time in return for lease payments, as opposed to purchasing the asset.

letter contract

A written preliminary contractual instrument that authorizes the immediate commencement of activity under its terms and conditions, pending definitization of a fixed-price or cost-reimbursement pricing arrangement for the work to be done. Includes specifications of the buyer's maximum liability and must be superseded by a definite contract within a specified time.

letter of credit

1. An international business document that assures the seller that payment will be made by the bank issuing the letter of credit upon fulfillment of the sales agreement.

2. A contract between the banks representing the exporter and the importer and including all the terms and conditions of the sale.

letter of intent (LOI)

An obligation instrument that can be used to protect price and availability of long-lead-time items and for other purposes.

level of effort (LOE)

The devotion of talent or capability to a predetermined level of activity, over a stated period of time, on the basis of a fixed-price or cost-reimbursement pricing arrangement; payment is usually based on effort expended rather than results achieved.

level unit pricing

The requirement in most multiyear contracts to price each year's deliveries at the same unit price.

life cycle

The entire duration of a contract, from beginning to end. Contracts follow a life cycle typically comprising the following stages:

- Requirements,
- Requisition,
- Tender,
- Evaluation,
- Contract administration, and
- Contract closure.

life cycle cost (LCC)

The total cost of a system, building, or other product computed over its useful life. It includes all relevant costs involved in acquiring, owning, operating, maintaining, and disposing of the system or product over a specified period of time, including environmental and energy costs.

liquidated damages

1. A contract provision providing for the assessment of damages on the contractor for its failure to comply with certain performance or delivery requirements of the contract. Used when the time of delivery or performance is of such importance that the buyer may reasonably expect to suffer damages if the delivery or performance is delinquent.

2. A stipulation in a contract on monetary amount that must be paid by the contractor if the contractor fails to deliver supplies or perform services as specified in the contract or any modification. Payments are in lieu of actual damages related to the failure. The rate (e.g., dollars per day of delay) is fixed in the contract and must be reasonable considering probable actual damages related to any failure in contract performance.

liquidation

A term used when the contractor pays back or reimburses the government for contractor financing or a loan given in the form of progress payments. (A "progress payment" is a financing method to support the future delivery of a product.) When the product is delivered and accepted by the government, the progress payments are liquidated or offset against the delivery price. At delivery, instead of paying the full line-item price, the government will subtract from the line-item price a percentage (the "liquidation rate") as payback for the financing. Generally, the liquidation rate is the same percentage as the progress payment rate.

lowest price technically acceptable

This source selection process is appropriate when best value is expected to result from selection of the technically acceptable proposal with the lowest evaluated price. When using the lowest price technically acceptable process, the following apply:

- The evaluation factors and significant subfactors that establish the requirements of acceptability shall be set forth in the solicitation. Solicitations shall specify that award will be made on the basis of the lowest evaluated price of proposals meeting or exceeding the acceptability standards for non-cost factors. If the contracting officer documents the file pursuant to *Federal Acquisition Regulation* (*FAR*) 15.304(c)(3)(iii), past performance need not be an evaluation factor in lowest price technically acceptable source selections. If the contracting officer elects to consider past performance as an evaluation factor, it shall be evaluated in accordance with FAR 15.305. However, the comparative assessment in FAR 15.305(a)(2)(i) does not apply. If the contracting officer determines that a small business' past performance is not acceptable, the matter shall be referred to the Small Business Administration for a Certificate of Competency determination, in accordance with the procedures contained in FAR 19.6.

- Tradeoffs are not permitted.

- Proposals are evaluated for acceptability but not ranked using the non-cost/price factors.

- Exchanges may occur.

lump sum

A lot price or a fixed-total price paid in one sum.

mailbox rule

The idea that the acceptance of an offer is effective when deposited in the mail if the envelope is properly addressed.

make-or-buy program

That part of a contractor's written plan for the development or production of an end item outlining the subsystems, major components, assemblies, subassemblies, and parts intended to be manufactured, test-treated, or assembled by the contractor (make) and those the contractor intends to procure from another source (buy).

margin pricing
A pricing method where price is based on the relationship between cost and profit.

mark-up pricing
Establishing prices based on estimated direct cost or total cost plus a percentage mark-up.

market research
The process used for collecting and analyzing information about the entire market available to satisfy the minimum agency needs to arrive at the most suitable approach to acquiring, distributing, and supporting supplies and services.

master agreements
Business arrangements in which the parties determine the underlying commercial arrangement governing the relationship (e.g., terms and conditions) but defer specific negotiation of elements of the contract to specific events or transactions (e.g., price).

master solicitation
A document containing special clauses and provisions that have been identified as essential for the acquisition of a specific type of supply or service that is acquired repetitively.

may
Denotes the permissive. However, the words "no person may" mean that no person is required, authorized, or permitted to do the act described.

mediation
A private, informal process in which the parties are assisted by one or more neutral third parties in efforts to achieve settlement. Mediators do not judge or arbitrate; they advise and consult impartially with the parties in an attempt to bring about a mutually agreeable resolution.

memorandum of agreement (MOA)/ memorandum of understanding (MOU)
1. The documentation of mutually-agreed-to statements of facts, intentions, procedures, and parameters for future actions and matters of coordination.

2. An MOU may express mutual understanding of an issue without implying commitments by parties to the understanding.

3. MOUs are bilateral agreements between two parties that include policy statements regarding a specific commodity, service, or area of trade.

method of procurement
The process employed for soliciting offers, evaluating offers, and awarding a contract. In federal contracting, contracting officers use one of the following methods for any given acquisition:

- Simplified acquisitions,
- Sealed bidding,
- Negotiation, or
- Two-step sealed bidding.

micropurchase
Acquisition of supplies or services, the aggregate amount of which does not exceed the micropurchase thresholds as defined in Federal Acquisition Regulation 2.101.

mistake
Mistakes in a contractor's proposal that are disclosed after award shall be processed substantially in accordance with the procedures for mistakes in bids at Federal Acquisition Regulation 14.407-4, which states: "When a mistake in a contractor's bid is not discovered until after award, the mistake may be corrected by contract modification if correcting the mistake would be favorable to the government without changing the essential requirements of the specifications."

mistake in bid
A procedure that enables a bidder to correct or withdraw its bid when a mistake has been made in preparing the bid.

modified total cost basis
A means of pricing equitable adjustments. Under this approach, information on specific costs incurred is included in addition to a total cost portion of the claim. This is probably the most frequently used of all costing approaches in claims preparation.

modular contracting
A contracting approach under which the need for a system is satisfied in successive acquisitions of interoperable increments. Each increment complies

with common or commercially acceptable standards applicable to information technology so that the increments are compatible with the other increments of IT comprising the system.

Multiple Award Schedule (MAS)

Contracts made with multiple suppliers, pursuant to the Federal Supply Schedule Program, for relatively the same items at varying prices for delivery within the same geographic area.

multiyear contract

1. A method of procuring known requirements for supplies or services for more than one year, even though the total funds obligated are not *available* at the time of entering into the contract.

2. A fixed-price contract, lasting up to five years, that is funded on a yearly basis with cancellation costs being paid to the seller if the contract is canceled before completion.

3. A procurement of more units of products than can be funded by the buyer in a single year. The total purchase is divided into annual segments that are negotiated at one time. Under multiyear considerations, the buyer pays lower unit prices due to larger buys; however, the seller is protected from annual cancellations through clauses in the contract.

mutual assent

Consists of an offer made by one party and the unconditional acceptance of that offer by another party.

mutual mistake

A mistake made by both parties regarding the same material subject of a contract, which may warrant voiding the contract.

negotiable instrument

A transferable, signed document that promises to pay the bearer a sum of money at a future date or on demand. Examples include checks, bills of exchange, and promissory notes.

negotiated ceiling

Maximum negotiated value for which the buyer is liable for payment to the seller.

negotiated contract cost

The estimated cost negotiated in a cost-plus-fixed-fee contract, or the negotiated contract target cost in either a fixed-price-incentive or cost-plus-incentive-fee contract.

negotiation

1. A process between buyers and sellers seeking to reach mutual agreement on a matter of common concern through fact-finding, bargaining, and persuasion.

2. Government acquisition of supplies or services, including construction, by other-than-sealed-bidding procedures.

3. Exchanges, in either a competitive or sole-source environment, between the government and offerors, that are undertaken with the intent of allowing the offeror to revise its proposal. These negotiations may include bargaining. Bargaining includes persuasion, alteration of assumptions and positions, and give-and-take, and may apply to price, schedule, technical requirements, type of contract, or other terms of a proposed contract. When negotiations are conducted in a competitive acquisition, they take place after establishment of the competitive range and are called "discussions."

negotiation objectives

Determining the issues to be negotiated and the minimum and maximum positions for each issue. They address strategies that provide the overall framework that will guide the conduct of the negotiation. They include both win-lose and win-win strategies and all tactics and counter-tactics necessary to achieve the desired result.

no-cost cancellation

A type of quasi-termination that usually occurs shortly after contract execution, often because the seller realizes that it will be unable to perform. If both parties agree, no debts or obligations are due, and if the buyer can obtain performance from other sources, a no-cost cancellation can be a quick and efficient way to sever a contractual relationship.

nonbinding arbitration

Involves an evidentiary hearing before a third party, composed of one or more arbitrators, that draws conclusions regarding the issues in dispute. These hearings typically include broad fact-finding activities, which assist in educating the third party about the matters in dispute. Upon completion of presentations by each party, the third party renders its decision. The parties are not bound by the arbitrator's decision, and either or both sides may reject it. The intent of nonbinding arbitration is to predict the likely adjudicated outcome of the case as an aid to settlement.

nonconforming services/supplies

Services/supplies that do not conform in all respects to contract requirements.

nondevelopmental item (NDI)

1. Any previously developed item of supply used exclusively for governmental purposes by a federal agency, a state or local government, or a foreign government with which the United States has a mutual defense cooperation agreement.

2. Any item described in (1.) of this definition that requires only minor modification or modifications of a type customarily available in the commercial marketplace in order to meet the requirements of the procuring department or agency.

3. Any item of supply being produced that does not meet the requirements of (1.) or (2.) of this definition solely because the item is not yet in use.

nondisclosure agreement (NDA)

A legally binding document setting forth the conditions under which proprietary information is offered and received between the parties.

nonrecurring costs

Costs that are generally incurred on a one-time basis. For example, nonrecurring production costs could include such costs as plant or equipment relocation, plant rearrangement, special tooling and special test equipment, preproduction engineering, initial spoilage and rework, and specialized workforce training.

normal costing

A type of product costing that applies to units produced (as costs of production), the actual direct materials consumed, the actual direct labor used, and an estimated, predetermined portion of overhead calculated on the basis of a normal or average schedule of production.

not-to-exceed (NTE) price

1. A maximum price that the contractor may not exceed while negotiations are underway to establish the final price. Permits the contractor to perform the contract while negotiations are being conducted and protects the government (buyer) from excessive expenditures.

2. A ceiling for a particular cost element in a cost reimbursable contract.

notice of award

A notification to the lowest, responsive construction contractor that it must obtain a performance bond and a payment bond before it can be awarded a contract.

notice of termination

A written notice to the contractor that the contract is being terminated for convenience or default.

novation agreement

A legal instrument executed by the contractor (transferor), the successor in interest (transferee), and the government (buyer) by which, among other things, the transferor guarantees performance of the contract, the transferee assumes all obligations under the contract, and the government (buyer) recognizes the transfer of the contract and related assets.

obligation

1. A legal requirement for the disbursement of funds based on orders placed, contracts awarded, services received, or other contractual documents.

2. A duty to make a future payment of money. The duty is incurred as soon as an order is placed, or a contract is awarded for the delivery of goods and the performance of services. The placement of an order is sufficient. An obligation legally encumbers a specified sum of money, which will require outlay(s) or expenditures in the future.

obligation of funds

Legally binding commitments, such as contract awards, made by federal agencies during a given period that will require outlays during the same or some future period.

offer

1. A legally binding promise, made by one party to another, to enter into a contractual agreement if the offer is accepted. In sealed bidding, offers made in response to invitations for bids are called "bids." In negotiated acquisitions, offers made in response to requests for proposals are called "proposals."

2. A proposal to make a contract. It is made verbally, in writing, or by other conduct, and it must contain the terms legally necessary to create a contract. Acceptance of the proposal creates the contract.

3. A response to a solicitation that, if accepted, would bind the offeror to perform the resultant contract.

4. The manifestation of willingness to enter into a bargain, so made as to justify another person in understanding that his or her assent to that bargain is invited and will conclude it.

5. An unequivocal and intentionally communicated statement of proposed terms made to another party. An offer is presumed revocable unless it specifically states that it is irrevocable. Once made, an offer will be open for a reasonable period of time and is binding on the offeror unless revoked by the offeror before the other party's acceptance.

offeror
Any person who has submitted an offer in response to a request for proposal.

open end contract
An agreement for the supply of goods or services that contains varying limits, or no limit, on time and quantity, and which usually involves recurring orders and changes of various types.

open market
The collective name for private, commercial business sources of supplies and services. For example, in government simplified acquisitions, open market sources can be used under two conditions: if no mandatory sources can meet the need, or if the open market can provide the same supplies or services at substantial savings.

operation and maintenance (O&M) costs
Costs associated with equipment, supplies, and services required to train, operate, and maintain forces in a recipient country, including the cost of spare parts other than concurrent spares and initial stockages, ammunition and missiles used in training or replacements for such items expended in training or operations, rebuild and overhaul costs (excluding modernization) of equipment subsequent to initial issue, training and other services that do not constitute investment costs, and administrative costs associated with overall program management and administration.

option
A unilateral right in a contract by which, for a specified time, the buyer may elect to purchase additional quantities of the supplies or services called for

in the contract, or may elect to extend the period of performance of the contract.

order of precedence
1. A solicitation provision that establishes priorities so that contradictions within the solicitation can be resolved.

2. A contract clause that specifies the sequential hierarchy of documents for the interpretation and resolution of any conflicting terms.

3. For government contracts, the order of precedence is established in Federal Acquisition Regulation 52.215-8, "Order of Precedence— Uniform Contract Format."

organizational conflict of interest (OCI)
1. Exists when the nature of the work to be performed under a proposed contract may, without some restriction on future activities, result in an unfair competitive advantage to the contractor or impair the contractor's objectivity in performing the contract work.

2. Because of other activities or relationships with other persons, a person is unable or potentially unable to render impartial assistance or advice to the government, the person's objectivity in performing the contract work is or might be otherwise impaired, or a person has an unfair competitive advantage.

original equipment manufacturer (OEM)
1. A company whose products are used as components in another company's product.

2. A company that buys a product and incorporates or re-brands it into a new product under its own name.

other direct cost (ODC)
Labor hours, materials and subcontracts, and travel costs are considered "direct costs"; that is, they are costs directly incurred in design, manufacturing, testing, or production of the product itself. Added to these direct costs is the category "other direct costs," which includes such elements as computer services, reproduction services, and training.

outsourcing
(1.) A version of the make-or-buy decision in which a firm elects to purchase an item that was previously made in-house (commonly utilized for services.) (2.) A contractual process of obtaining another party

to provide goods and/or services that were previously done internal to an organization.

overhead
An accounting cost pool that generally includes general indirect expenses that are necessary to operate a business but not directly accountable to a specific good or service produced. Some examples are building rent, utilities, salaries of corporate officers, janitorial services, office supplies and furniture, etc.

partial payment
1. A payment authorized under a contract, to be made upon completion of the delivery of one or more complete units called for, delivered, and accepted by the buyer under the contract.

2. A payment made against a termination claim upon prior approval before final settlement of the total termination claim.

partial set-aside
When small business sources cannot satisfy the government's entire requirement at a reasonable price (i.e., a total set-aside is not appropriate), the contracting officer may elect to set aside only a portion of the acquisition for small businesses.

partial termination
The termination of a part, but not all, of the work that has not been completed and accepted under a contract.

pass-through charges
Costs (i.e., indirect costs, profit) added by the prime contractor or higher-tier subcontractors on work performed by subcontractors.

past performance
An offeror's or contractor's performance on active and physically completed contracts.

past performance evaluation
One indicator of an offeror's ability to perform the contract successfully. The currency and relevance of the information, source of the information, context of the data, and general trends in contractor's performance shall be considered. This comparative assessment of past performance information is separate from the responsibility determination required under *Federal Acquisition Regulation (FAR)* 9.1. (*See* FAR 15.305(a)(2).)

payment
The amount payable under the contract supporting data required to be submitted with invoices, and other payment terms such as "time for payment" and "retention."

performance
1. The execution of the terms of a contract. If a buyer offers to purchase from a supplier, the supplier performs by furnishing the buyer's requirements.

2. An informal means of accepting an offer.

performance-based acquisition (PBA)
1. A documented business arrangement in which the buyer and seller agree to use a performance work statement, performance-based metrics, and a quality assurance surveillance plan to ensure contract requirements are met or exceeded.

2. An acquisition structured around the results to be achieved as opposed to the manner by which the work is to be performed. A performance-based contract is a contract that is structured around the purpose of the work to be performed as opposed to either the manner in which the work is to be performed or a broad statement of work. Typically, a performance work statement is used to describe the requirement.

performance incentives
May be considered in connection with specific product characteristics (e.g., a missile range, an aircraft speed, an engine thrust, or vehicle maneuverability) or other specific elements of the contractor's performance. These incentives should be designed to relate profit or fee to results achieved by the contractor compared with specified targets.

performance statement of work (performance SOW)
Defines requirements in terms that relate to the minimum acceptable standards or ranges of acceptable performance. A performance SOW may require a particular approach or a particular type of product, but it leaves most of the "how" decisions to the contractor. Performance SOWs are less restrictive than design SOWs.

post-award conference/orientation
1. A meeting of buyer and supplier personnel held soon after contract award to ensure that everyone understands the contract requirements.

2. A post-award meeting, conference, letter, or other form of written communication between government and contractor representatives after award of a contract and prior to commencement of work to discuss significant elements of administering the contract, including any unusual or significant contract requirements, and to identify and resolve potential problems.

pre-award inquiry

Questions and comments from prospective offerors about specifications, terms, and conditions in a solicitation received prior to the opening date of the invitation for bids or closing date of the request for proposals.

pre-award process (buyer)

Process by which buyers develop a comprehensive plan for fulfilling requirements for products or services in a timely manner at a reasonable price. Includes developing an overall strategy for the purchase, which is accomplished through researching the marketplace, developing strategies, initiating the procurement, and selecting a supplier.

pre-award process (seller)

Process by which sellers develop and execute a strategy for obtaining the award of a contract, including market strategies, pricing strategies, and responding to the procurement.

pre-award survey

An evaluation of a prospective contractor's ability to perform a specific contract, performed by the contract administration office or the purchasing office, with assistance from an audit organization at the request of either office. The evaluation addresses the physical, technical, managerial, and financial capability of the prospective contractor. Also addressed is the adequacy of the contractor's systems and procedures and past performance record.

pre-bid conference

A conference held with prospective bidders in sealed-bid procurements prior to the submission of a bid to clarify any ambiguous situations, answer bidder questions, and ensure that all bidders have a common basis of understanding regarding the supplies or services required. (Also known as a "pre-proposal conference" in a negotiated procurement.)

pre-contract costs

Costs incurred before the effective date of the contract directly pursuant to the negotiation and in anticipation of the contract award when such incurrence is necessary to comply with the proposed contract delivery schedule.

pre-performance meeting

This meeting can help avoid problems during contract performance and can set the foundation for good communication between the buyer and seller. When conducted, this meeting should be chaired by contracting professionals from the buyer and seller and include appropriate managers and staff personnel from the buyer's organization (i.e., the customer who will interface with and receive the benefits from the contractor's work) and appropriate managers and staff personnel from the seller's organization (i.e., the contactor's resources that will interface with and perform work for the customer).

pre-proposal conference

A meeting held with contractors after the request for proposals in negotiated procurements have been sent out. The goal is to promote uniform interpretation of work statements and specifications by all prospective contractors.

pre-qualification

A buyer's announcement of interest, including criteria for selecting proposals, and selecting offerors capable of meeting the requirements.

pre-solicitation conference

A meeting held with potential contractors or subcontractors prior to a formal solicitation to discuss technical and other problems connected with a proposed procurement. The conference is also used to elicit the interest of prospective contractors in pursuing the task, such as a research and development effort.

price

1. A monetary unit given, received, or asked for in exchange for supplies or services.

2. The amount of money or equivalent paid or charged for supplies or services, including cost and profit or fee.

3. Cost plus any fee or profit applicable to the contract type.

price analysis

1. The process of examining and evaluating a prospective price without evaluation of the separate cost elements and proposed profit of the individual offeror.

2. Evaluates an offer by comparing it with indicators of reasonableness. Primary comparisons include competitive analysis and published prices. Secondary comparisons include:

- Comparative analysis (previous contracts, prior quotations);
- Market data;
- Price index;
- Cost estimating relationships;
- Government price lists;
- Government estimates; and
- Discounts.

Auxiliary techniques include value analysis and visual analysis.

price negotiation memorandum (PNM)
The document that relates the story of the negotiation. A sales document establishing the reasonableness of the agreement reached with the successful offeror, as well as a permanent record of the decisions made by the negotiator in establishing that the price was fair and reasonable.

price-related factors
Elements that can be quantified and used with price to determine the most advantageous bid for the government. They include:

- Foreseeable costs or delays to the government resulting from such factors as differences in inspection, locations of supplies, and transportation;
- Changes made, or requested by the bidder, in any of the provisions of the invitation for bids, if the change does not constitute a ground for bid rejection;
- Advantages or disadvantages to the government that might result from making more than one award;
- Federal, state, and local taxes; and
- Origin of supplies, and, if foreign, the application of the Buy American Act or any other prohibition on foreign purchases.

pricing
The process of establishing a reasonable amount or amounts to be paid for supplies or services.

pricing arrangement
An agreed-to basis between contractual parties for the payment of amounts for specified performance; usually expressed in terms of a specific cost-reimbursement or fixed-price type arrangement.

prime contract
1. A contract or contractual action entered into by two or more parties for the purpose of obtaining supplies, materials, equipment, or services of any kind. This term is generally used to differentiate the main (i.e., "prime") contract with any subcontract(s) that may be entered into to support the execution of the main (prime) contract's requirements. A prime contract is held either by the owner of a project or by a main or primary contractor having full responsibility for the job.
2. A contract awarded directly by the federal government.

prime contractor
1. Also simply called the "prime," a prime contractor is the owner of a project or the main or primary contractor having full responsibility for the contract requirements.
2. The entity with whom an agent of the United States enters into a prime contract for the purpose of obtaining supplies, materials, equipment, or services of any kind.

privity of contract
1. The direct legal (contractual) relationship that exists between parties that allows either party to enforce contractual rights against the other party and seek remedy directly from the other party with whom this relationship exists.
2. The legal relationship between two parties to the same contract. The government has privity of contract with the prime contractor. Therefore, the government's relationship with subcontractors is indirect in nature. Government involvement with subcontractors is channeled through prime contractor–directed activities; only the prime contractor is authorized to direct the subcontractor.

pro forma invoice
A document prepared in advance of a sale to provide evidence of the final form and amount of invoice.

procurement administrative lead time (PALT)

The time interval between the initiation of procurement and the receipt into the supply system of material purchased as a result of such action.

procurement authorization

A document that establishes the approved material procurement program and authorizes and directs the action to be taken to place the approved material program under procurement.

procurement integrity

A set of rules of conduct, contained in the 1989 amendments to the Office of Federal Procurement Policy Act (41 U.S.C. 423), that were formalized for the purpose of upholding the integrity of the government procurement process. The rules are implemented by *Federal Acquisition Regulation* 3.104.

procurement package

All information required to obtain bids or proposals; the technical information necessary to accurately describe the item to be procured.

procurement request (PR)

Document that describes the required supplies or services so that a procurement can be initiated. Some procuring activities actually refer to the document by this title; others use different titles such as "procurement directive." Combined with specifications, the statement of work, and the contract data requirements list, it is called the "PR package," a basis for solicitation.

profit

1. The difference between total cost and revenue.

2. The amount realized by a contractor after the cost of performance (both direct and indirect) are deducted from the amount to be paid under the terms of the contract.

3. The net proceeds from selling a product or service when costs are subtracted from revenues. May be positive (profit) or negative (loss).

4. Represents that element of the potential total remuneration that contractors may receive for contract performance over and above allowable costs. Both the government and contractors should be concerned with profit as a motivator of efficient and effective contract performance. Negotiations aimed merely at reducing prices by reducing profit, without proper recognition of the function of profit, are not in the government's interest. Negotiation of extremely low profits, use of historical averages, or automatic application of predetermined percentages to total estimated costs do not provide proper motivation for optimum contract performance.

profit objective

The part of the estimated contract price objective that the contracting officer concludes is appropriate for the procurement at hand. Developed after a thorough review of proposed contract work and all available knowledge regarding an offeror, as well as an analysis of the offeror's cost estimate and a comparison of it with the government's estimate or projection of cost.

progress payment

1. A payment made as work progresses under a contract on the basis of percentage of completion accomplished, or for work performed at a particular stage of completion.

2. An interim payment for delivered work in accordance with contract terms; generally tied to meeting specified performance milestones.

progressive down-selection

A type of down-selection strategy for a phased acquisition. In this method, a single solicitation is issued for all phases of the program. The initial phase contracts are awarded and the contractors for subsequent phases are expected to be chosen through a down-selection from among the preceding phase contractors. In each phase, progressively fewer contracts are awarded until a single contractor is chosen for the final phase. Normally, all down-selections are accomplished without issuing a new, formal solicitation.

proposal

1. An offer in response to a request for proposals.

2. Normally, a written offer by a seller describing its offering terms. Proposals may be issued in response to a specific request or may be made unilaterally when a seller feels there may be an interest in its offer (which is also known as an "unsolicited proposal").

proposal evaluation

1. An assessment of both the proposal and the offeror's ability (as conveyed by the proposal) to successfully accomplish the prospective contract. An agency shall evaluate competitive proposals solely on the factors specified in the solicitation.

2. Evaluations may be conducted using any rating method or combination of methods, including color or adjectival ratings, numerical weights, and ordinal rankings. The relative strengths, deficiencies, significant weaknesses, and risks supporting proposal evaluation shall be documented in the contract file.

prospective pricing
A pricing decision made in advance of performance, based on analysis of comparative prices, cost estimates, past costs, or combinations of such considerations.

protest
A written objection by an interested party to a solicitation by an agency for offers for a proposed contract for the acquisition of supplies or services, or a written objection by an interested party to a proposed award or the award of such a contract.

provisioning
The process of determining or meeting the range and quantity of items required to support and maintain or function for a set period of time.

prudent businessperson concept
A phrase used as a measure of reasonableness in assessing an offer, counter-offer, or other action taken under a contract. Related to making a procurement decision based on sound fiduciary or business principles.

public-private partnership (PPP)
A contractual agreement between a public agency (federal, state, or local) and a private-sector entity. Through this agreement, the skills and assets of each sector (public and private) are shared in delivering a service or facility for the use of the general public. In addition to the sharing of resources, each party shares in the risks and rewards potential in the delivery of the service and/or facility.

purchase card
A credit card issued to authorized organizational personnel to acquire and to pay for supplies and services on behalf of the organization.

purchase description
1. A description of the essential physical characteristics and functions required to meet the buyer's minimum needs.

2. A simplified specification that is used when an item is purchased infrequently.

purchase order (PO)
A document, signed by a contracting officer and addressed to a contractor, requesting the future delivery of supplies, equipment, or material, or the future performance of nonpersonal services in accordance with certain terms in exchange for a promise by the government to pay the stated price. Considered an offer to contract rather than an acceptance of contract.

purchase request (PR)
An exact description of a product or service used in invitations for bids, requests for proposals, and contracts to tell prospective suppliers precisely what is required. (Also known as a "purchase description.")

purchase requisition (PR)
A written or computerized request to the purchasing department for a procurement of goods or services from suppliers.

purchasing
1. The process of buying supplies and services utilizing a variety of contractual arrangements.

2. In government, the process of buying readily available supplies and services utilizing procedures such as purchase orders, blanket purchase agreements, and pre-negotiated schedules.

qualification requirement
A buyer requirement for testing or other quality assurance demonstration that must be completed before award of a contract.

qualified bidders list (QBL)
A list of bidders who have had their products examined and tested and who have satisfied all applicable qualification requirements for that product or have otherwise satisfied all applicable qualification requirements.

qualified manufacturers list (QML)
A list of manufacturers who have had their products examined and tested and who have satisfied all applicable qualification requirements for that product.

qualified product
An item that has been examined and tested for compliance with specification requirements and qualified for inclusion in a qualified products list.

qualified products list (QPL)

A list of products that have been examined, tested, and have satisfied all applicable qualification requirements.

quality assurance surveillance plan (QASP)

The method by which federal employees will supervise in-house or contract performance to ensure that the standards of the performance work statement are met within the costs bid.

quality control (QC)

1. The process of measuring quality performance, comparing it with the standard, and acting on the difference.

2. All those tasks done within an organization to improve the quality of its output. This would include inspection systems set up by a contractor to monitor its own output at key intervals in the contracting process.

quantity discount

1. Voluntary price reduction offered by a firm to customers acquiring quantities of a product. Unit prices normally decline as volume increases, primarily because fixed costs are being divided by an increasing number of units.

2. A price reduction given to a buyer for purchasing increasingly larger quantities of materials. A quantity discount is normally offered for:

   - Purchasing a specific quantity of items at one time,

   - Purchasing a specified dollar total at one time, or

   - Purchasing a specified dollar total over an agreed-upon time period.

quasi contract

Obligations imposed by law to prevent the unjust enrichment of one person at another's expense. Sometimes called "implied in law."

quick closeout

A faster method of completing the closeout process for a cost-reimbursement contract. Final indirect rates are negotiated on a contract basis rather than by fiscal year, as in regular closeout methods. Quick closeout can only be done in limited circumstances, such as if the contract is physically complete, the amount of unsettled indirect costs to be allocated to the contract is relatively insignificant, and an agreement can be reached on a reasonable estimate for allocable dollars.

quotation

A statement of price, either written or verbal, which may include, among other things, a description of the product or service; the terms of sale, delivery, or period of performance; and payment. Such statements are usually issued by sellers at the request of potential buyers. In government procurement, quotations do not constitute an offer that can be accepted to form the basis of a binding contract. Rather, quotations are solicited to obtain market information for planning purposes.

ratification

In a broad sense, the confirmation of a previous act done either by the party itself or by another, as confirmation of a voidable act. The affirmance by a person of a prior act that did not bind the person, but which was done or professedly done on his or her account, whereby the act, as to some or all persons, is given the effect as if originally authorized by the person.

rating/scoring system

A method of rating/scoring an evaluation factor in relationship to its corresponding standard such as numerical, adjective, color, etc. The source selection plan establishes the factors against which all proposals will be evaluated, the weights to be assigned to each factor, and the applicable rating system. A rating system may be based on colors, points, or adjectives. An example of a color-based rating system is as follows: blue = exceptional, green = acceptable, yellow = marginal, and red = unacceptable. An example of an adjective-based rating system is "excellent," "very good," "good," "fair," and "poor."

reasonable cost

1. A cost is reasonable if, in its nature and amount, it does not exceed that which would be incurred by a prudent person in the conduct of competitive business.

2. A business decision reached jointly by a buyer and seller; a product of judgment influenced by bargaining strength and economic realities dictated by the marketplace.

reasonable or competitive prices

The expected range of prices resulting from experience obtained through the competitive free enterprise system for like or similar activities. Determinations are to be made by the contracting officer.

recurring costs

Costs that are required to operate and maintain an operation and that vary or occur with the quantity being produced, and occur repeatedly during the life cycle of a program, system, product, or service.

regular dealer

A person that owns, operates, or maintains a store, warehouse, or other establishment in which the materials, supplies, articles, or equipment of the general character described by the specifications and required under the contract are bought, kept in stock, and sold to the public in the usual course of business.

request for deviation

A specific written authorization to depart from a particular requirement of an item's current approved configuration documentation for a specific number of units or a specified period of time. It differs from an engineering change since a deviation does not affect a change to a configuration document.

request for equitable adjustment (REA)

A letter or proposal from a contractor requesting a change to the contract price or schedule.

request for information (RFI)

1. A document used to obtain price, delivery, other market information, or capabilities for planning purposes when the government does not presently intend to issue a solicitation.

2. A formal invitation to submit general and/or specific information concerning the potential future purchase of goods and/or services.

request for proposals (RFP)

1. Used in negotiated acquisitions to communicate government requirements to prospective contractors and to solicit proposals. RFPs for competitive acquisitions shall, at a minimum, describe the following:

   - The government's requirement;

   - The anticipated terms and conditions that will apply to the contract:

     o The solicitation may authorize offerors to propose alternative terms and conditions, including the contract line item number (CLIN) structure; and

     o When alternative CLIN structures are permitted, the evaluation approach should consider the potential impact on other terms and conditions or the requirement;

   - Information required to be in the offeror's proposal; and

   - Factors and significant subfactors that will be used to evaluate the proposal and their relative importance.

2. Solicitation document used in negotiated procurement when the buyer reserves the right to award without further verbal or written negotiation. Only the acceptance of the buyer is required to create a binding contract. Of course, the buyer can choose to negotiate further at its option.

3. A formal invitation that contains a scope of work and seeks a formal response (proposal), describing both methodology and compensation, to form the basis of a contract.

request for quotations (RFQ)

1. The solicitation form normally used in simplified acquisitions or negotiated procurement when award will be made after negotiation with the offeror. Since the prospective subcontractor's quotation is not a formal offer, the prime contractor and subcontractor must reach a bilateral negotiated agreement before a binding contract exists.

2. A formal invitation to submit a price for goods and/or services as specified.

request for technical proposals

Solicitation document used in two-step sealed bidding. Normally in letter form, it asks only for technical information; price and cost breakdowns are forbidden.

required sources of supplies and services

The U.S. government buyer must first examine sources offered from or through the government before fulfilling the requirement with an outside source. Federal Acquisition Regulation Part 8 details the required sources of supplies and services and their order of priority.

requirements

1. Technical requirements specify what the product should do and how the seller will support it.

2. Administrative requirements specify how the customer/buyer relationship will work.

requirements contract

1. An indefinite-delivery contract that provides for filling all actual purchase requirements of designated government activities for supplies

or services during a specified contract period, with deliveries or performance to be scheduled by placing orders with the contractor.

2. A type of contract that provides for the filling of all actual purchase requirements of specific supplies or services for a designated activity during a specified contract period.

requisition
A request for supplies or services originating from the party actually requiring them.

rescission
The unmaking of a contract, or an undoing of it from the beginning. Not merely a termination. It may be effected by mutual agreement of parties, or by one of the parties declaring rescission of contract without consent of the other if a legally sufficient ground therefore exists. An action of equitable nature in which a party seeks to be relieved of its obligations under a contract on the grounds of mutual mistake, fraud, impossibility, etc.

research and development (R&D) contract
A contract for basic research (directed toward increasing knowledge); applied research (directed toward improving or expanding new scientific discoveries, technologies, materials, processes, or techniques); or development (directed production of, or improvements in, useful products to meet specific performance requirements through the systematic application of scientific knowledge).

responsible contractor
A capable party that has the financial resources, personnel, facilities, integrity, and overall capability to fulfill specific contractual requirements satisfactorily.

responsive
1. Describes a bid that meets, without any material deviation, the expressed requirements of a solicitation.

2. When a bidder fully complies with and does not materially deviate from the terms, conditions, and specifications set forth in an invitation for bids (sealed-bid method), it is deemed " responsive."

3. When an offeror materially complies with a solicitation and is capable of being made compliant through discussions, it is deemed "responsive."

restitution
Seeks to restore the nonbreaching party to the position he, she, or it was in before the formation of the contract.

retroactive pricing
A pricing decision made after some or all of the work specified under contract has been completed, based on a review of performance and recorded cost data.

return on investment (ROI)
A measure of income or profit divided by the investment required to help obtain the income or profit. That is, given the same risks, for any given amount of resources required, the investor wants the maximum income.

reverse auction (RA)
A single buyer of a single item (or lot of items) receives decreasing offers from prospective sellers. The auction ends at a predetermined time, and the item is purchased from lowest offeror for the lowest offer price.

rights in technical data
The right for the government to acquire technical data. If the government has funded or will fund a part of or the entire development of the item, component, or process, then the government is entitled to unlimited rights in the technical data. However, if the item is developed by a contractor or subcontractor exclusively at private expense, the government is entitled to limited rights. Such data must be unpublished and identified as limited rights data.

rollover of unearned award fee
The process of transferring unearned award fee, which the contractor had an opportunity to earn, from one evaluation period to a subsequent evaluation period, thus allowing the contractor an additional opportunity to earn that previously unearned award fee.

royalties
Any costs or charges in the nature of royalties, license fees, patent or license amortization costs, or the like that are paid for the use of or for rights in patents and patent applications in connection with performing a contract or subcontract.

scope
A general statement defining the parameters or boundaries of expected actions, required

performance, or products required. Scope statements can be viewed as the "fenced-in area" in which the contractor performs.

sealed bid
Document enclosed in a glued (sealed) envelope and submitted in response to an invitation for bids. Sealed bids received up to the deadline date are generally opened at a stated time and place (usually in the presence of anyone who may wish to be present) and evaluated for award of a contract.

sealed-bid procedure
1. An acquisition method in which the government issues an invitation for bids (IFB). The IFB is publicized by distributing it to prospective bidders and posting it in public places and on the FedBizOpps website. Sufficient time must be allowed between the time the IFB is publicized and bids are opened publicly to enable prospective bidders to prepare and submit bids. An IFB should describe the government's requirements clearly, accurately, and completely. Unnecessarily restrictive specifications or requirements that might unduly limit the number of bidders are prohibited. The invitation includes all documents (whether attached or incorporated by reference) furnished to prospective bidders for bidding purposes. Agencies must use a fixed-price contract for sealed bidding.

2. A method of contracting that employs competitive bids, public bid opening, and awards. Award is made to that responsible bidder whose bid, conforming to the invitation for bids, will be most advantageous to the government considering only price and price-related factors included in the invitation.

sealed bidding
Procurement by obtaining sealed bids and awarding the contract to the lowest-priced responsible bidder whose bid is responsive.

second source
An acquisition strategy that establishes two or more producers for the same part, system, or service for the purpose of increasing competition or broadening the industrial base.

sequestration
Across-the-board cuts in budget resources of all programs within a category (new budget authority, unobligated balances, direct spending authority,

and obligation limitations). The term has been adapted by Congress in more recent years to describe a new fiscal policy procedure originally provided for in the Gramm- Rudman-Hollings Deficit Reduction Act of 1985. If Congress cannot agree on ways to reduce the deficit or does not pass a new, higher budget resolution, then an "automatic" form of spending cutback takes place. This automatic spending cut is called "sequestration." Under sequestration, an amount of money equal to the difference between the cap set in the budget resolution and the amount actually appropriated is "sequestered" by the Treasury and not handed over to the agencies to which it was originally appropriated by Congress.

service contract
1. A contract for the time and services of individuals or organizations in support of a government objective.

2. A contract that directly engages the time and effort of a contractor whose primary purpose is to perform an identifiable task rather than furnish an end item of supply.

set-aside
1. A kind or class of procurement reserved for contenders that fit a certain category (e.g., business size, region, minority status).

2. Can be total or partial, or a class set-aside (whereby a class of acquisitions of selected products or services may be set aside for exclusive participation by small business concerns).

severable contract
A contract divisible into separate parts; a default of one section does not invalidate the whole contract.

shall
The imperative.

should
An expected course of action or policy that is to be followed unless inappropriate for a particular circumstance.

should cost
1. An estimate of what an item or system should cost based upon an evaluation by independent reviewers of all applicable contractor business methods (contrasting more efficient methods with present contractor methods). This evaluation should include subcontractor procedures when subcontracting is part of the proposal.

The result is utilized to develop realistic price objectives for contract negotiation purposes.

2. An estimate of contract price that reflects reasonably achievable contractor economy and efficiency. It is accomplished by a government team of procurement, contract administration, audit, and engineering representatives performing an in-depth cost analysis at the contractor's and subcontractor's plants. Its purpose is to develop a realistic price objective for negotiation purposes.

3. A specialized form of cost analysis. A should-cost review differs from traditional evaluation methods because it does not assume that a contractor's historical costs reflect efficient and economical operation. Instead, the review evaluates the economy and efficiency of the contractor's existing workforce, methods, materials, facilities, operating systems, and management.

show cause letter
A written delinquency notice informing a contractor of failure to perform within the specified terms of the contract, and advising that the government is considering termination for default. Affords the contractor the opportunity to show cause why it should not be terminated.

simplified acquisition
A less rigorous method for entering into relatively low-dollar-threshold contracts. Simplified acquisition usually occurs without the elaborate and formal solicitation techniques required by sealed bidding and negotiation. Very small purchases should be made using simplified acquisition tools such as charge cards.

simplified procedures
1. Methods for entering into contracts without using elaborate and formal solicitation techniques (i.e., invitations for bids and requests for proposals). Restricted to purchases under the simplified acquisition threshold.

2. Means the methods prescribed in Federal Acquisition Regulation Part 13 for making purchases of supplies or services.

Single Award Schedule (SAS)
Contracts made with one supplier, pursuant to the Federal Supply Schedule Program, to cover delivery to one geographic area.

single source
One source among others in a competitive marketplace that, for justifiable reason, is found to be most advantageous for the purpose of contract award.

single-source negotiation
Negotiation with a single provider, because either the provider is the sole supplier of the product or service, or the relationship with the provider is of strategic importance based on long-term relationships and built on mutual trust. (Also called "sole-source negotiation.")

small business concern
A business that is independently owned and operated, and is not dominant in its field; a business concern meeting government size standards for its particular industry type.

small business set-aside
A set-aside acquisition reserved exclusively for small businesses. A small business set-aside may be open to all small businesses. It may also relate to a single acquisition or a class of acquisitions and may be total or partial. For federal government contacts, all acquisitions within a certain dollar range are automatically set-aside for small businesses. Small business set-asides may be withdrawn by the contracting officer if award would be detrimental to the public interest (e.g., paying more than a fair market price).

smart cards
Purchase cards defined as "plastic cards the size of standard credit cards containing a microchip that can store user data, provide security features, and provide computational capability." The government uses purchase cards such as these as part of its simplified acquisition process.

sole-source acquisition
A contract for the purchase of supplies or services that is entered into or proposed to be entered into after soliciting and negotiating with only one source.

solicitation
1. Any request to submit offers or quotations to the government. Solicitations under sealed-bid procedures are called "invitations for bids." Solicitations under negotiated procedures are called "requests for proposals." Solicitations under simplified acquisition procedures may require submission of either a quotation or an offer.

2. A document requesting or inviting offerors to submit offers. Solicitations basically consist of a draft contract and provisions on preparing and submitting offers.

solicitation provision
A term or condition used only in solicitations and applying only before contract award.

source selection
The process wherein the requirements, facts, recommendations, and policies relevant to an award decision in a competitive procurement of a system/ project are examined and the decision made.

source selection authority (SSA)
The person who makes the final source selection in a competition. The SSA is responsible for ensuring that the entire source selection process is properly and efficiently conducted. While the SSA may use reports and analyses prepared by others, the source selection decision must represent the SSA's independent judgment.

source selection decision
The source selection decision is made by the source selection authority (SSA) and shall be based on a comparative assessment of proposals against all source selection criteria in the solicitation. While the SSA may use reports and analyses prepared by others, the source selection decision shall represent the SSA's independent judgment. The source selection decision shall be documented, and the documentation shall include the rationale for any business judgments and tradeoffs made or relied on by the SSA, including benefits associated with additional costs. Although the rationale for the selection decision must be documented, that documentation need not quantify the tradeoffs that led to the decision.

specification
1. A document intended primarily for use in acquisition that clearly describes the essential technical requirements for items, materials, or services, including the criteria for determining that requirements have been met.

2. A description of the technical requirements for a material, product, or service that includes the criteria for determining that the requirements have been met.

3. There are generally three types of specifications used in government contracting:

- "Detailed/design specifications": prescribe the design requirements, such as how the item is to be fabricated or what materials must be used. A specification that contains both performance and prescriptive requirements is still considered a detailed specification.

- "Functional specification": A purchase description that describes the deliverable in terms of performance characteristics and intended use, including those characteristics that at minimum are necessary to satisfy the intended use.

- "Performance-based specifications": define an item's functional requirements or capabilities, the environment in which the item must operate, the item's interface and interchangeability characteristics, and the criteria for verifying the item's compliance. These specifications do not describe how a requirement is to be achieved, nor do they require the use of specific materials or parts or give detailed design or construction requirements beyond those needed to ensure interchangeability with existing items.

spot purchase
A one-time purchase made in the open market.

standard
A document that establishes engineering and technical limitations and applications of items, materials, processes, methods, designs, and engineering practices. It includes any related criteria deemed essential to achieve the highest practical degree of uniformity in materials or products, or interchangeability of parts used in those products.

standards
1. Used in competitive negotiations to evaluate a proposal. It includes both the maximum acceptable value and the minimum acceptable value for all selected evaluation criteria.

2 A predetermined level of merit against which proposals are measured. Standards are usually a statement of the minimum level of compliance with a requirement that must be offered for a proposal to be considered acceptable. Standards may be qualitative or quantitative.

start date
1. The date when a cost comparison begins, generally defined as the date that a local study

team is formed and actual work on the performance work statement, management plan, and in-house cost estimate begins.

2. May refer to the actual date work is scheduled to begin under a contract, as provided in the solicitation.

statement of objectives (SOO)

1. A government-prepared document incorporated into the solicitation that states the overall performance objectives. It is used in solicitations when the government intends to provide the maximum flexibility to each offeror to propose an innovative approach.

2. That portion of a contract that establishes a broad description of the government's required performance objectives.

statement of work (SOW)

1. That portion of a contract describing the actual work to be done by means of specifications or other minimum requirements, quantities, performance date, and a statement of the requisite quality.

2   The SOW for the project should reflect all work to be performed. The SOW communicates the work scope requirements for a program and should define the requirements to the fullest extent practicable. It is a basic element of control used in the processes of work assignment and establishment of program schedules and budgets.

stop work order

A request for interim stoppage of work, such as when a work stoppage is required for reasons such as advancements in the state of the art, production or engineering breakthroughs, or realignment of programs.

storyboarding

A conceptual planning tool used to help proposal writers plan each proposal section before drafting text. It contains assignments, requirements, strategies, preliminary visuals, and content.

subcontract

1. A contract or contractual action entered into by a prime contractor or subcontractor for the purpose of obtaining supplies, materials, equipment, or services of any kind under a prime contract.

2. Any agreement (other than one involving an employer-employee relationship) entered into by a government prime contractor or subcontractor calling for supplies and/or services required for performance of the contract, contract modification, or subcontract.

3. A contract between a buyer and a seller in which a significant part of the supplies or services being obtained is for eventual use in a government (prime) contract.

subcontracting management

Describes the role a prime contractor has in ensuring a subcontractor performs in accordance with its contract with the prime. In a subcontract, the prime contractor delegates some of the required work to another company, the subcontractor. Subcontracting usually occurs where the contracted work, such as the construction of a building, requires a variety of skills. Responsibility for fulfilling the original contract remains with the original contracting party, the prime contractor.

subcontracting plan

These plans are required for government acquisitions expected to exceed specific thresholds (see Federal Acquisition Regulation 19.7) that have subcontracting possibilities. They must contain goals for both small businesses and small disadvantaged businesses. The goals are stated in terms of percentages of dollars awarded, and are negotiated with the contracting officer or the agency's small and disadvantaged business utilization specialist prior to contract award. The negotiated plan is subsequently incorporated into the contract by reference. Small businesses themselves are exempt from the requirement to submit a subcontracting plan.

subcontractor

A contractor that enters into a contract with a prime contractor or a subcontractor of the prime contractor.

substantial performance

1. Performance that deviates only in minor respects from contract requirements.

2. Doctrine that prohibits termination of a contract for default if a contractor's performance deviates only in minor respects from the contract's requirements.

substantially as follows

When used in the prescription and introductory text of a provision or clause, it means that authorization is granted to prepare and utilize a variation of that provision or clause to accommodate requirements that are peculiar to an individual acquisition; provided that the variation includes the salient features of the original provision or clause and is not inconsistent with the intent, principle, and substance of the original provision or clause or related coverage of the subject matter.

supplemental agreement

1. Any contract modification that is accomplished by the mutual action of the parties.

2. Bilateral written modification to a contract by which the government and the contractor settle price and/or performance adjustments to the basic contract.

supplier

The individual or concern actually performing services, or manufacturing, producing, and shipping any supplies required by the contract or subcontract.

supplier goods/services

Management of any contract, agreement, or purchase order (and any preliminary contractual instrument other than a prime contract) calling for the performance of any work or the making or furnishing of any material required for the performance of a prime contract; includes managing the purchase of supplies that are consumed in use or become incorporated in other property, thus losing identity.

supplier rating system

A system used to evaluate and rate suppliers' performance, which generally involves quality, service, delivery, and price. Rating formulas vary depending on the nature of the item being purchased, the quality required, and competition within the supplying industry.

supplies

All property except land or interest in land. It includes (but is not limited to):

- Public works, buildings, and facilities;

- Ships, floating equipment, and vessels of every type, character, and description, together with parts and accessories;

- Aircraft and aircraft parts, accessories, and equipment;

- Machine tools; and

- The alteration or installation of any of the foregoing.

supply chain management (SCM)

Managing supply chain activities to improve customer value and establish a competitive advantage. It is a means to run supply chains in the most effective and efficient ways possible.

surety

An individual or corporation legally liable to the debt, default, or failure of a principal to satisfy a contractual obligation.

suspension

Action taken by a suspending official to disqualify a contractor temporarily from government contracting and subcontracting.

synopsis

A brief summary or a condensed version.

system acquisition process

The sequence of acquisition activities starting from an organization's delineation of its requirement needs with its capabilities, priorities, and resources, and extending through the introduction of a system into operational use.

systems contract

A contract that authorizes designated employees of the buying firm, using a predetermined release system, to place orders directly with the supplier for specified materials during a given contract period. One principal objective of systems contracting is to reduce the buyer's inventories to a level as low as is consistent with assured continuity of supply; thus, systems contracting is sometimes referred to as "stockless purchasing." Order releases under systems contracts should usually be made by personnel from the using department.

target cost

1. Final agreed-upon cost that serves as a basis for computing cost savings in incentive-type contracts.

2. The estimated cost of a contract as initially negotiated, adjusted for any change in contract requirements.

target fee

The fee initially negotiated on the assumption that a contract would be performed for a cost equal to the estimated cost initially negotiated, adjusted for any change in contract requirements.

task order (TO)
An order for services placed against an established contract or with government sources.

task order contract
A services contract that does not procure or specify a firm quantity of services (other than a minimum or maximum quantity) and that provides for the issuance of orders for the performance of tasks during the period of the contract.

teaming agreement
1. An agreement of two or more firms to form a partnership or joint venture to act as a potential prime contractor.
2. An agreement by a potential prime contractor to act as a subcontractor under a specified acquisition program.
3. An agreement for a joint proposal resulting from a normal prime contractor-subcontractor, licensee-licenser, or leader company relationship.

technical analysis
1. The technical analysis should examine the types and quantities of material proposed and the need for the types and quantities of labor hours and the labor mix. Any other data that may be pertinent to an assessment of the offeror's ability to accomplish the technical requirements or to the cost or price analysis of the service or product being proposed should also be included in the analysis. The contracting officer may request that personnel having specialized knowledge, skills, experience, or capability in engineering, science, or management perform a technical analysis of the proposed types and quantities of materials, labor, processes, special tooling, equipment, real property, the reasonableness of scrap and spoilage, and other associated factors set forth in the proposal(s) in order to determine the need for and reasonableness of the proposed resources, assuming reasonable economy and efficiency.
2. Evaluation, ordinarily conducted by engineering, technical, or specialized personnel, of the technical and managerial qualifications of a contractor to perform a particular contract requirement, and applicability/sufficiency of the technical solution proposed to fulfill contemplated contract requirements.

technical data package
Those documents, drawings, reports, manuals, revisions, technical orders, or other submissions as set forth as a contract data requirements list line item to be delivered as required by contract.

technical direction
An interpretation of statement of work (SOW) requirements provided by a representative of the contracting officer. Representatives of the contracting officer have no authority to alter the SOW. The SOW can only be altered through use of a contract modification signed by the contracting officer.

technical evaluation factors
1. Factors other than price-related factors used in evaluating offers for award. Examples include technical excellence, management capability, personnel qualifications, prior experience, past performance, and schedule compliance.
2. Descriptions of the technical aspects of an offer used to evaluate the merit of the proposed technical approach and/or work to be performed (e.g., technical approach, understanding of the requirement, and compliance with requirement).

technical leveling
Helping an offeror to bring its proposal up to the level of other proposals through successive rounds of discussion, such as by pointing out weaknesses resulting from the offeror's lack of diligence, competence, or inventiveness in preparing the proposal.

technical proposal
An unpriced proposal that sets forth in detail that which a vendor proposes to furnish in response to a solicitation.

technical specification
Specifications that establish the material and performance requirements of goods and services.

technical transfusion
Disclosing technical information pertaining to a proposal that results in improvement of a competing proposal.

technology transfer
The process by which federal scientific research and development is transformed into commercially viable products and services.

term contract

Normally covers a 12-month period or may cite another specific time to complete the project or service.

term contracting

A technique by which a source of supply is established for a specific period of time. Term contracts are established based on indefinite quantities to be ordered "as needed," although such contracts can specify definite quantities with deliveries extended over the contract period.

term form

A form of cost-plus-fixed-fee contract that describes the scope of work in general terms and obligates the contractor to devote a specified level of effort for a stated time period. If contract performance is considered satisfactory by the government, the fixed-fee is payable at the expiration of the agreed-upon period, upon contractor statement that the level-of-effort specified in the contract has been expended in performing the contract work. Renewal for further periods of performance is a new acquisition that involves new cost and fee arrangements.

terminated portion of the contract

The portion of a contract that the contractor is not to perform following a partial termination.

termination

An action taken pursuant to a contract clause in which the contracting officer unilaterally ends all or part of the work; can be a "termination for convenience," in which the ending of work is in the best interest of the government, or a "termination for default," in which the contractor has not performed according to the terms of the contract.

termination by mutual consent

Commonly used in the commercial contracting environment, termination by mutual consent is a bilateral agreement indicating that the parties no longer wish to be bound by the contract, and terminating both parties' respective rights and obligations. Termination by mutual consent clauses are sometimes included in the basic contract, though they can also be negotiated and executed during the period of performance.

termination claim

Any claim or demand by a prime contractor for compensation because of the termination before completion of any contract or subcontract for the convenience of the government.

termination contracting officer (TCO)

The contracting officer assigned responsibility for settling terminations for default or convenience, and in some cases settling claims and actions involving extraordinary relief.

termination for convenience (T4C)

In government contracting, the government always has the unilateral right to terminate a contract for the convenience of the government when the contract no longer serves the best interests of the government. Terminations for convenience often result from a change in government priorities, program termination or downsizing, or other significant events that were not anticipated at the time of contract formation. When the government pursues a termination for convenience, a termination settlement is negotiated with the seller.

termination for default (T4D)

Also referred to as "termination for cause," it is normally a right of law as well as a right vested as the result of the inclusion of appropriate terms and conditions in the contract. Termination for default can result from one party's failure to perform one or more actions required by the contract.

terms and conditions (T's and C's)

All language in a contract, including time of delivery, packing and shipping, applicable standard clauses, and special provisions. The primary function of terms and conditions is to eliminate or reduce the risk of contract ambiguity; often the source of disputes and misunderstandings.

testing

1. The determination by technical means of the physical and chemical properties or elements of materials, supplies, or components involving not so much the element of personal judgment as the application of established scientific principles and procedures.

2. An element of inspection.

time and materials (T&M) contract

A type of contract providing for a fixed hourly rate, including overhead and profit and material at cost plus handling charges. Used when it is impossible to estimate schedule and costs at the time of contract award.

total cost

Sometimes called "all-in costs." In purchasing, total cost generally includes the price of the purchase and transportation cost, plus indirect handling, inspection, quality, rework, maintenance, incremental operations, and all other follow-on costs associated with the purchase.

total cost basis

1. A means of pricing equitable adjustments when the costs associated with a claim are not clearly identifiable. Using the total cost approach, an equitable adjustment is calculated as the difference between the contractor's proposed price on the original contract and the actual total cost of performing the contract as changed.

2. This method assumes that all costs expended by the contractor were caused by the change, and the contractor's original estimate was correct and reasonable.

total set-aside

When the entire amount of an acquisition is reserved for small businesses.

tradeoff

The selection among alternatives with the intent of obtaining optimal, achievable system configuration. Often, a decision is made to opt for less of one parameter in order to achieve a more favorable overall system result.

tradeoff process

1. In a negotiated acquisition, a procedure that permits consideration of tradeoffs among cost or price and non-cost factors and allows the government to accept other than the lowest-priced proposal. The perceived benefits of the higher-priced proposal must merit the additional cost and the rationale for tradeoffs must be documented in the contract file.

2. Appropriate when it may be in the best interest of the government to consider award to other than the lowest-priced offeror or other than the highest technically rated offeror. When using a tradeoff process, the following apply:

   - All evaluation factors and significant subfactors that will affect contract award and their relative importance shall be clearly stated in the solicitation, and

   - The solicitation shall state whether all evaluation factors other than cost or price, when combined, are significantly more important than, approximately equal to, or significantly less important than cost or price.

3. Selection among alternatives with the intent of obtaining the optimal, achievable system configuration. Often, a decision is made to opt for less of one parameter in order to achieve a more favorable overall system result.

unallowable cost

Any cost that, under the provisions of any pertinent law, regulation, or contract, cannot be included in prices, cost-reimbursements, or settlements under a government contract to which it is allocable.

unauthorized commitment

A nonbinding agreement because the government representative who made it lacked authority to do so. Government employees are prohibited from committing or obligating funds in excess of those available. Doing so results in an unauthorized commitment. In order to convert an unauthorized commitment to a binding agreement, it must be ratified by authorized government representatives.

unbalanced pricing

May increase performance risk and could result in payment of unreasonably high prices. Unbalanced pricing exists when, despite an acceptable total evaluated price, the price of one or more contract line items is significantly over or understated as indicated by the application of cost or price analysis techniques. The greatest risks associated with unbalanced pricing occur when:

- Startup work, mobilization, first articles, or first article testing are separate line items;

- Base quantities and option quantities are separate line items; or

- The evaluated price is the aggregate of estimated quantities to be ordered under separate line items of an indefinite-delivery contract.

undefinitized contract action

Any contract action for which the terms, specifications, or price are not agreed upon before performance is begun under the action. Examples are letter contracts, orders under basic ordering agreements, and provisioned item orders, for which the price has not been agreed upon before performance has begun. Letter contracts await negotiation to definitize prices.

unenforceable contract

An otherwise valid contract rendered unenforceable by some statute or law (e.g., a verbal contract that, due to the passage of time, must be in writing to be enforceable).

unilateral
Means that the contracting officer (buyer) does something without the concurrence of the contractor. For example, a unilateral modification would be a change to a contract that the procuring contracting officer signs but the contractor does not. Unilateral modifications are used for the following:

- Making administrative changes;

- Issuing change orders;

- Making changes authorized by clauses other than the changes clause (e.g., options clause, property clause, etc.); and

- Issuing termination notices.

unilateral nonperformance
Termination of a contract by one of the parties. The right to terminate, notice required, and procedures for termination are typically specified in the contract. Most commonly, this is available as a remedy for the seller's nonperformance or the buyer's failure to pay.

unit cost
A total cost divided by some related base, such as labor hours, machine-hours, or units of product.

unrestricted procurement
Those acquisitions available to all contractors, and not reserved to satisfy social or economic programs of the federal government.

unsettled contract change
Any contract change or contract term for which a definitive modification is required but has not been executed.

unsolicited proposal
1. A written proposal for a new or innovative idea that is submitted to an agency on the initiative of the offeror for the purpose of obtaining a contract with the government, and that is not in response to a request for proposals, broad agency announcement, Small Business Innovation Research topic, Small Business Technology Transfer research topic, program research and development announcement, or any other government-initiated solicitation or program.

2. A research or developmental proposal that is made by a prospective contractor without prior formal or informal solicitation from a purchasing activity.

3. A written proposal that is submitted to an agency on the submitter's initiative for the purpose of obtaining a contract with the government, and which is not in response to a formal or informal request.

valid contract
A contract satisfying all of the contract requisites (agreement, consideration, capacity, legal purpose, assent, and form).

validation
Acceptance by auditors of reported cost reduction savings and cost reduction reports, based on a selective review of cost reduction reports and supporting documentation.

value analysis
A systematic and objective evaluation of the function of a product and its related cost; a pricing tool that provides insight into the inherent worth of a product. Value analysis assumes that value is a function of three variables:

- Demand,

- Use, and

- Aesthetics.

value engineering (VE)
An organized effort directed at analyzing the function of systems, subsystems, equipment, facilities, procedures, and supplies for the purpose of achieving the required function at the lowest total cost consistent with performance, reliability, quality, maintainability, and producibility.

value engineering change proposal (VECP)
A proposal that requires a change to the contract to implement and results in reducing the overall projected cost to the agency without impairing essential functions or characteristics, provided that it does not involve a change in deliverable end item quantities, research and development quantities, or the contract type.

value engineering proposal
An in-house, agency-developed proposal, or a proposal developed by a contractor under contract to

provide value engineering services, to provide value engineering studies for a government project/program.

variable cost
(1.) A cost that changes with the rate of production of goods or performance of services.
(2.) Costs associated with production that change directly with the amount of production; e.g., the direct material or labor required to complete the build or manufacturing of a product.

vendor
An individual, partnership, corporation, or other entity from which items are acquired in the performance of a contract.

void contract
A contract having no legal force or binding effect (e.g., a contract entered into for an illegal purpose).

voidable contract
An otherwise valid contract that may be legally avoided, cancelled, or annulled at the option of one of the parties (e.g., a contract entered into under duress or under false pretenses).

waiver
1. The voluntary relinquishment by a person of a right that he or she has.
2. Acceptance by the buyer of a minor nonconformity that does not degrade the function of the item.
3. A written authorization to accept a configuration item or other designated item, which, during production, or after having been submitted for inspection, is found to depart from specified requirements, but nevertheless is considered suitable "as is" or after rework by an approved method.
4. Decision to not require certain criteria to be met for certain reasons, such as national security.

warranty
A promise or affirmation given by a seller to a buyer regarding the nature, usefulness, or condition of the supplies or performance of services furnished under the contract. Generally, a warranty's purpose is to delineate the rights and obligations for defective items and services, and to foster quality performance.

weakness
A flaw in the proposal that increases the risk of unsuccessful contract performance. A "significant weakness" in the proposal is a flaw that appreciably increases the risk of unsuccessful contract performance.

chapter five

NCMA Certification Examinations

Certification is a reflection of your professional strength. Certification is a mark of distinction and serves to reflect professionalism attained though experience, education, training, and knowledge.

The NCMA Salary Surveys have consistently shown those with an NCMA certification typically earn more per year than those with no certification. However, those with a certification and higher salary realize professionalism does not rest solely on certification. Employers want people who can make quick and accurate decisions, and can solve problems with less-than-perfect information.

Professional contract managers must be proficient at solving complex problems and providing sound business advice. In addition, they must know how to influence multifunctional teams to achieve organizational goals (whether in charge of the team or not), and must be able to establish long-term partnerships with those inside and outside the organization.

Whether you are a buyer or a seller, you are expected to perform at a high standard, and certification can serve as evidence of your professional development. However, certification is not the culmination of professional development—it is the beginning.

A means of validating the depth and breadth of a contract manager's education, training, and experience is through an examination process. NCMA certification examinations are mapped to *CMBOK* competencies. The Certified Professional Contracts Manager (CPCM) examination is mapped directly to the *CMBOK*, the Certified Federal Contracts Manager (CFCM) examination is mapped directly to the *Federal Acquisition Regulation* (*FAR*), while the Certified Commercial Contracts Manager (CCCM) examination is mapped directly to the Uniform Commercial Code (UCC).

When a certification candidate passes the relevant certification examination and meets the established requirements for education, training, and experience, NCMA is confident the contract manager has met the standards of professionalism required for the specific certification. In conjunction with the CMBOK, FAR, and UCC updates, NCMA makes appropriate changes to its certification examinations to ensure they are reflective of actual practice.

Examination Format

The NCMA examination format consists of multiple-choice questions. Many people assume multiple-choice questions are easy to answer because they have had experience with tests that are not "psychometrically sound" (i.e., every test question has undergone the full rigor of educational and statistical testing necessary to ensure it elicits the exact response desired, that it is unambiguous, and that it has only one correct answer). However, three other plausible possible answers will separate those who know and understand the material from those who don't. Furthermore, multiple-choice testing can test more than simple recall of facts and recognition of words. It can test for understanding of content and for responses that indicate application of principles to a situation.

The benefits of multiple-choice examination lie in the objective assessment of question answers. There is no scope for alternative interpretation of results. That is not to say that every question is perfect. Rather, the multiple-choice format has the flexibility that allows NCMA, working in conjunction with psychometricians or test developers, to change the examination and make every question fair, valid, and reliable.

Using a computer-based multiple-choice examination allows NCMA to provide candidates with their results before they leave the testing site. In addition, multiple-choice questions allow for a wider sampling of the body of knowledge. On the one hand, this means that candidates are bound to find areas with which they are familiar; on the other hand, it means that candidates may be unsure exactly where to concentrate their study. However, candidates should feel confident that the examination will ask only those questions that determine whether a contract manager has the knowledge to be a good practitioner. NCMA will not be testing on extraneous or trivial matters.

The computer has hastened the acceptance of multiple-choice examinations. Familiarity with this style of testing begins as early as elementary school. Because the future contract management community is in the hands of the demographic strata of the population that has either grown up with or grown familiar with computers, this style of testing will gain even wider acceptance. Furthermore, because multiple-choice examinations lend themselves to computer delivery, test developers can readily discern trends and make judgments about the examination or the underlying practice. In either case, the examination can be changed to correct or reflect the practice.

The Anatomy of a Multiple-Choice Question

A multiple-choice question has its own terminology. The question itself is called the "stem." The stem should contain all the information needed to provide the correct answer. The stem should be phrased in clear, unambiguous language that will leave no doubt as to what is being asked. A knowledgeable candidate should be able to discern the correct answer upon reading only the stem.

The answers also have specific terminology. The correct answer is the "key," and the other possible answers are the "distracters." The key is the only correct answer. The distracters are plausible to those who are unsure about the correct answer.

How to Study

Given that the examinations sample a wider slice of the body of knowledge, how should a candidate prepare? First of all, candidates should relax. Examinations do not include "everything but the kitchen sink." Rather, the examinations will reflect the sum of the eligibility requirements and current contract management practice.

Self-assessment is the first step to a study program. Does the candidate work well in a group or alone? Given the *CMBOK*, are there areas about which the candidate has little or no knowledge? Are there areas that the candidate is confident enough to teach others? In a review program, the areas where the candidate is confident would be areas of less intense concentration.

Even working alone, it is good to have a study plan. For example, candidates might plan to study one hour on a weekend for the next eight weeks, or three hours per week for the next six weeks. Even as little as half an hour of study can help candidates gain knowledge and increase comprehension.

An alternative study method would be to join a group—for example, a group of office colleagues or a study group at the chapter level. NCMA chapters have provided study groups to hundreds of examination candidates. Study groups successfully allow for multiple points of view, as well as for sharing

information and resources. Furthermore, chapter study group sessions are often led by experts in the field. In terms of time spent, expert information beats informed research almost any day. Candidates may contact their local chapters for study group information. Chapters may be accessed through the NCMA website by clicking on the "Membership" button and selecting "Chapter Information" from the menu list.

Test Specifications for Certification Examination Certification candidates must take and pass examinations consisting of multiple-choice questions. The distribution of certification examination questions is explained as follows. The NCMA Certification and Accreditation Board developed this distribution with the aid of a team of psychometricians and from the results of the body of knowledge revision. This includes research, the input of subject matter experts, and the results of surveys.

The answers to the questions in the examination are based on common terms and concepts found in publications, including this guide, readily available and normally found in public libraries, websites, or through NCMA. When constructing an examination, the number of items or questions devoted to a task or topic is determined by the relative importance of a task or topic.

How to Approach the Certification Examinations For the mental side of examinations, here are a few good test-taking techniques:

- Relax. The examination is based on your profession.

- Read the questions carefully, answering those you can easily and quickly answer. It is usually a good idea to go with your first impression when answering a question; second-guessing can cause you to change a correct answer to an incorrect one.

- Skip over or flag questions that appear too difficult and return to them later.

- Don't stop. Keep going. Keep reading questions until you find one you can answer. The questions you've read will be in the back of your mind; when you return to them, you'll have a fresh perspective. Avoid overanalyzing and second-guessing the question. Choose the correct answer for the question as it is written. Do not make assumptions about what the question means. Don't regard questions as being "trick questions" or concentrate on the exceptions to normal practice.

- Keep an eye on the clock. Judge the time you have so you don't spend a lot of time puzzling over one question to the detriment of being able to answer several others. Flag questions you are having trouble with and move on.

- Don't try to "game" the system by choosing answers to ensure that an equal number of A's, B's, C's and so on are selected. In the long run (over a lifetime), this may be a good technique, but in the short run (for one examination) the statistical underpinning for this myth has not been proven.

- Try to answer the question in your mind before you read the choices. Good test questions are constructed to allow the knowledgeable examination candidate to do this.

- If you can't readily identify the correct answer, make an educated guess. Eliminate the choices you know to be false and select from those remaining.

- Look over your answers, if time permits. However, avoid trying to second-guess your answers.

- Don't worry about the examination. You may feel wrung out and exhausted at the end of the examination, but that is not an indication of how well or how poorly you may have performed.

Lifetime Certification

For those currently certified individuals who have been continuously certified for a period of at least 20 years, or who reach the age of 60 during their recertification period, a "Lifetime Certification" is available. Applicants for Lifetime Certification based on age alone must submit verification of age in addition to their application and application processing fee.

Once awarded Lifetime Certification, the designee is no longer required to meet the five-year recertification requirements. This improvement allows those who maintain their certification over a 20-year period to apply for Lifetime Certification regardless of age.

Contract Management Curricula Models

The *Contract Management Body of Knowledge* (*CMBOK*) provides the knowledge areas and competencies that are integral to the contract management process and the contract management profession. NCMA has established the *CMBOK* as the recommended guidance for how colleges and universities should align their contract management curricula.

Contract management is moving from the backroom to the boardroom. It is recognized as a corporate asset and is used as a competitive advantage. There is an art and science in bringing buyers and sellers together in the marketplace and crafting long-term relationships between them. Partnering is difficult. Also, there is a challenge in crafting a mutually beneficial contract. Getting a "win-win" situation is difficult. Contract management is increasingly seen as a strategic core competency and successful organizations recognize that if you don't have control of your contracts, you don't have control of your business.

Since contract management is comprised of many business administration and public administration competencies (i.e., management, marketing, operations management, financial analysis, accounting, economics, information science, and leadership), it is traditionally not a first career choice for professionals. Organizations want to quickly identify, hire, and train energetic and capable professionals to be able to deal with current economic threats and opportunities.

In this section, NCMA provides curricula models for bachelor and master degrees. NCMA recommends these guidelines for colleges and universities in developing or updating contract management curricula. The presented curricula specialize in federal contract management. However, though a college, university, or any other organization may use and abide by these curricula, the course titles are merely indicators as to the course content. Also, the courses will likely include more *CMBOK* competencies than are presented in the models.

Sample Curriculum for *Bachelor of Business Administration*

CMBOK Section	*CMBOK* Competency	Course Title
5.1	Management	Introduction of Management
5.1	Management	Business Communications
5.1	Management	Organizational Theory & Behavior
5.1	Management	Business Policy & Strategy
5.4	Operations Management	Production & Operations Management
5.6	Accounting	Principles of Accounting I & II
5.4 5.5	Operations Management Financial Analysis	Business Statistics
5.4 5.5 5.6	Operations Management Financial Analysis Accounting	Budgeting
5.7	Economics	Principles of Macro Economics
5.7	Economics	Principles of Micro Economics
5.5	Financial Analysis	Business Finance
5.8	Information Science/Technology	Computer Applications in Business
5.8	Information Science/Technology	Management Information Systems
5.3	Marketing	Introduction to Business
5.3	Marketing	Introduction to Marketing Management
1.1	Laws and Regulations	Legal Environment of Business
1.1 1.8 2.7 3.6	Laws and Regulations Intellectual Property Protests Contract Interpretation and Disputes	Federal Procurement Law

1.1	Laws and Regulations	Federal Acquisitions System
1.3	Standards of Conduct	Business Ethics
2.1	Acquisition Planning, Market Research, and Marketing	Purchasing & Materials Management
4.8	Supply Chain Management	
2.1	Acquisition Planning, Market Research, and Marketing	Effective Contract Writing
1.6	Contracting Methods	Formation of Government Contracts
1.5	Contract Types	
4.5	Service Contracts	
3.1	Contract Management	Contract Administration
3.2	Quality Assurance	
3.4	Contract Changes and Modifications	
3.7	Contract Closeout	
3.8	Contract Termination and Excusable Delay	
2.4	Cost and Price Analysis	Cost & Price Analysis
2.6	Source Selection and Contract Award	
5.5	Financial Analysis	
2.1	Acquisition Planning, Market Research, and Marketing	Contract Negotiation
2.5	Negotiation	
5.0	Business Competencies	
4.6	International Contracting	International Business Elective

Sample Curriculum for *Master of Business Administration*

CMBOK Section	CMBOK Competency	Course Title
5.1	Management	Strategic Management
5.1	Management	Organizational Behavior & Human Resources
5.4	Operations Management	Managing Projects
5.4	Operations Management	Management Accounting & Controls
5.5	Financial Analysis	
5.6	Accounting	
5.7	Economics	Management Economics
2.4	Cost and Price Analysis	Advanced Pricing Concepts
5.5	Financial Analysis	
5.6	Accounting	
5.8	Information Science/Technology	Management Information Systems
1.1	Laws and Regulations	Government Contract Law
1.3	Standards of Conduct	
1.8	Intellectual Property	
2.7	Protests	
3.6	Contract Interpretation and Disputes	

Sample Curriculum for *Master of Business Administration* (continued)

CMBOK Section	CMBOK Competency	Course Title
3.1	Contract Management	Advanced Contract Management & Administration
3.2	Quality Assurance	
3.4	Contract Changes and Modifications	
3.7	Contract Closeout	
3.8	Contract Termination and Excusable Delay	
2.1	Acquisition Planning, Market Research, and Marketing	Business Development & Proposal Preparation
2.2	Drafting Solicitations	
2.3	Responding to Solicitations	
3.3	Subcontract Management	Subcontracts
2.1	Acquisition Planning, Market Research, and Marketing	Negotiation Principles & Practices
2.5	Negotiation	
5.0	Business Competencies	

CMBOK Syllabus Options

	15-week semester contract focused	15-week semester Full CMBOK	Trimester
1.0 Pre-Award Competencies			
1.1 Laws and Regulations	Week 1	Week 1	Week 1
1.2 Contract Principles			
1.3 Standards of Conduct	Week 2		
1.4 Socioeconomic Programs			
1.5 Contract Types		Week 2	Week 2
1.6 Contracting Methods	Week 3		
1.7 Contract Financing			
1.8 Intellectual Property			
2.0 Acquisition Planning/ Strategy Competencies			
2.1 Acquisition Planning, Market Research, and Marketing	Week 4	Week 3	Week 3
2.2 Drafting Solicitations			
2.3 Responding to Solicitations	Week 5		
2.4 Cost and Price Analysis			
2.5 Negotiation	Week 6	Week 4	Week 4
2.6 Source Selection and Contract Award			
2.7 Protests			
	Midterm Week 7		

CMBOK Syllabus Options (continued)

3.0 Post-Award Competencies			
3.1 Contract Management	Week 8	Week 5	Week 5
3.2 Quality Assurance	Week 8	Week 5	Week 5
3.3 Subcontract Management	Week 9	Week 5	Week 5
3.4 Contract Changes and Modifications	Week 9	Week 5	Week 5
			Midterm
3.5 Transportation	Week 10	Week 6	Week 6
3.6 Contract Interpretation and Disputes	Week 10	Week 6	Week 6
3.7 Contract Closeout	Week 11	Week 6	Week 6
3.8 Contract Termination and Excusable Delay	Week 11	Week 6	Week 6
		Midterm Week 7	
4.0 Specialized Knowledge Area Competencies			
4.1 Research and Development	Week 12	Week 8	Week 7
4.2 Architect-Engineer Services and Construction	Week 12	Week 8	Week 7
4.3 Information Technology	Week 12	Week 8	Week 7
4.4 Major Systems	Week 13	Week 9	Week 7
4.5 Service Contracts	Week 13	Week 9	Week 7
4.6 International Contracting	Week 13	Week 9	Week 7
4.7 State and Local Government	Week 14	Week 10	Week 8
4.8 Supply Chain Management	Week 14	Week 10	Week 8
4.9 Government Property	Week 14	Week 10	Week 8
4.10 Other Specialized Areas	Week 14	Week 10	Week 8
	Week 15 Final Exam		
5.0 Business Competencies			
5.1 Management		Week 11	Week 9
5.2 Leadership Skills		Week 11	Week 9
5.3 Marketing		Week 12	Week 9
5.4 Operations Management		Week 12	Week 9
5.5 Financial Analysis		Week 13	Week 10
5.6 Accounting		Week 13	Week 10
5.7 Economics		Week 14	Week 10
5.8 Information Science/Technology		Week 14	Week 10
		Week 15 Final Exam	Final Exam

Other Recommended Master Courses:

- Advanced Financial Management
- Business Ethics
- Conducting Critical Conversations
- Information Management
- Intercultural Communication
- Leadership
- Marketing Management
- Public Speaking
- Program Management
- Quantitative Methods
- Strategic Purchasing & Logistics
- Supply Chain Management

appendices

Appendix A. *UCC* Table of Contents

Uniform Commercial Code—Article 1

Part 1. General Provisions

Part 2. General Definitions and Principles of Interpretation

Part 3. Territorial Applicability and General Rules

Uniform Commercial Code—Article 2

Part 1. Short Title, General Construction, and Subject Matter

Part 2. Form, Formation, and Readjustment of Contract

Part 3. General Obligation and Construction of Contract

- 2A-516. Effect of Acceptance of Goods; Notice of Default; Burden of Establishing Default After Acceptance; Notice of Claim or Litigation to Person Answerable Over.

- 2A-517. Revocation of Acceptance of Goods.

- 2A-518. Cover; Substitute Goods.

- 2A-519. Lessee's Damages for Non-Delivery, Repudiation, Default, and Breach of Warranty in Regard to Accepted Goods.

- 2A-520. Lessee's Incidental and Consequential Damages.

- 2A-521. Lessee's Right to Specific Performance or Replevin.

- 2A-522. Lessee's Right to Goods on Lessor's Insolvency.

C. Default by Lessee

- 2A-523. Lessor's Remedies.

- 2A-524. Lessor's Right to Identify Goods to Lease Contract.

- 2A-525. Lessor's Right to Possession of Goods.

- 2A-526. Lessor's Stoppage of Delivery in Transit or Otherwise.

- 2A-527. Lessor's Rights to Dispose of Goods.

- 2A-528. Lessor's Damages For Non-Acceptance, Failure to Pay, Repudiation, or Other Default.

- 2A-529. Lessor's Action for The Rent.

- 2A-530. Lessor's Incidental Damages.

- 2A-531. Standing to Sue Third Parties for Injury to Goods.

- 2A-532. Lessor's Rights to Residual Interest.

Uniform Commercial Code—Article 3

Part 1. General Provisions and Definitions

- 3-101. Short Title.

- 3-102. Subject Matter.

- 3-103. Definitions.

- 3-104. Negotiable Instrument.

- 3-105. Issue of Instrument.

- 3-106. Unconditional Promise or Order.

- 3-107. Instrument Payable in Foreign Money.

- 3-108. Payable on Demand or at Definite Time.

- 3-109. Payable to Bearer or to Order.

- 3-110. Identification of Person to Whom Instrument is Payable.

- 3-111. Place of Payment.

- 3-112. Interest.

- 3-113. Date of Instrument.

- 3-114. Contradictory Terms of Instrument.

- 3-115. Incomplete Instrument.

- 3-116. Joint and Several Liability; Contribution.

- 3-117. Other Agreements Affecting Instrument.

- 3-118. Statute of Limitations.

- 3-119. Notice of Right to Defend Action.

Part 2. Negotiation, Transfer, and Indorsement

- 3-201. Negotiation.

- 3-202. Negotiation Subject to Rescission.

- 3-203. Transfer of Instrument; Rights Acquired by Transfer.

- 3-204. Indorsement.

- 3-205. Special Indorsement; Blank Indorsement; Anomalous Indorsement.

- 3-206. Restrictive Indorsement.

- 3-207. Reacquisition.

Part 3. Enforcement of Instruments

- 3-301. Person Entitled to Enforce Instrument.

- 3-302. Holder in Due Course.

- 3-303. Value and Consideration.

- 3-304. Overdue Instrument.

- 3-305. Defenses and Claims in Recoupment.

- 3-306. Claims to an Instrument.

- 3-307. Notice of Breach of Fiduciary Duty.

- 3-308. Proof of Signatures and Status as Holder in Due Course.

- 3-309. Enforcement of Lost, Destroyed, or Stolen Instrument.

- 3-310. Effect of Instrument on Obligation for Which Taken.

- 3-311. Accord and Satisfaction by Use of Instrument.

Uniform Commercial Code—Article 4

Part 1. General Provisions And Definitions

Part 2. Collection of Items: Depositary and Collecting Banks

Part 3. Execution of Sender's Payment Order by Receiving Bank

Part 4. Payment

Part 5. Miscellaneous Provisions

Uniform Commercial Code—Article 5

Uniform Commercial Code—Article 6

Alternative A

Alternative B

Part 1. Subject Matter and Definitions

Uniform Commercial Code—Article 7

Part 1. General

Part 2. Warehouse Receipts: Special Provisions

Part 3. Bills of Lading: Special Provisions

Part 4. Warehouse Receipts and Bills of Lading:

General Obligations

Part 5. Warehouse Receipts and Bills of Lading: Negotiation and Transfer

Part 6. Warehouse Receipts and Bills of Lading:

Miscellaneous Provisions

Uniform Commercial Code—Article 8

Part 1. Short Title and General Matters

- 8-101. Short Title.
- 8-102. Definitions.
- 8-103. Rules for Determining Whether Certain Obligations and Interests are Securities or Financial Assets.
- 8-104. Acquisition of Security or Financial Asset or Interest Therein.
- 8-105. Notice of Adverse Claim.
- 8-106. Control.
- 8-107. Whether Indorsement, Instruction, or Entitlement Order is Effective.
- 8-108. Warranties in Direct Holding.
- 8-109. Warranties in Indirect Holding.
- 8-110. Applicability; Choice of Law.
- 8-111. Clearing Corporation Rules.
- 8-112. Creditor's Legal Process.
- 8-113. Statute of Frauds Inapplicable.
- 8-114. Evidentiary Rules Concerning Certificated Securities.
- 8-115. Securities Intermediary and Others Not Liable to Adverse Claimant.
- 8-116. Securities Intermediary as Purchaser for Value.

Part 2. Issue and Issuer

- 8-201. Issuer.
- 8-202. Issuer's Responsibility and Defenses; Notice of Defect or Defense.
- 8-203. Staleness as Notice of Defect or Defense.
- 8-204. Effect of Issuer's Restriction on Transfer.
- 8-205. Effect of Unauthorized Signature on Security Certificate.
- 8-206. Completion or Alteration of Security Certificate.
- 8-207. Rights and Duties of Issuer With Respect to Registered Owners.
- 8-208. Effect of Signature of Authenticating Trustee, Registrar, or Transfer Agent.
- 8-209. Issuer's Lien.
- 8-210. Overissue.

Part 3. Transfer of Certificated and Uncertificated Securities

- 8-301. Delivery.
- 8-302. Rights of Purchaser.
- 8-303. Protected Purchaser.
- 8-304. Indorsement.
- 8-305. Instruction.
- 8-306. Effect of Guaranteeing Signature, Indorsement, or Instruction.
- 8-307. Purchaser's Right to Requisites For Registration of Transfer.

Part 4. Registration

- 8-401. Duty of Issuer to Register Transfer.
- 8-402. Assurance that Indorsement or Instruction is Effective.
- 8-403. Demand that Issuer not Register Transfer.
- 8-404. Wrongful Registration.
- 8-405. Replacement of Lost, Destroyed, or Wrongfully Taken Security Certificate.
- 8-406. Obligation to Notify Issuer of Lost, Destroyed, or Wrongfully Taken Security Certificate.
- 8-407. Authenticating Trustee, Transfer Agent, and Registrar.

Part 5. Security Entitlements

- 8-501. Securities Account; Acquisition of Security Entitlement from Securities Intermediary.
- 8-502. Assertion of Adverse Claim against Entitlement Holder.
- 8-503. Property Interest of Entitlement Holder in Financial Asset Held by Securities Intermediary.
- 8-504. Duty of Securities Intermediary to Maintain Financial Asset.
- 8-505. Duty of Securities Intermediary With Respect to Payments and Distributions.
- 8-506. Duty of Securities Intermediary to Exercise Rights as Directed by Entitlement Holder.
- 8-507. Duty of Securities Intermediary to Comply With Entitlement Order.
- 8-508. Duty of Securities Intermediary to Change Entitlement Holder's Position to Other Form of Security Holding.

Uniform Commercial Code—Article 9

Part 1. General Provisions

[Subpart 1. Short Title, Definitions, and General Concepts]

[Subpart 2. Applicability of Article]

Part 2. Effectiveness of Security Agreement; Attachment of Security Interest; Rights of Parties to Security Agreement

[Subpart 1. Effectiveness and Attachment]

[Subpart 2. Rights And Duties]

Part 3. Perfection and Priority

[Subpart 1. Law Governing Perfection and Priority]

Temporary Perfection Without Filing or Transfer of Possession.

- 9-313. When Possession by or Delivery to Secured Party Perfects Security Interest Without Filing.

- 9-314. Perfection by Control.

- 9-315. Secured Party's Rights on Disposition of Collateral and in Proceeds.

- 9-316. Continued Perfection of Security Interest Following Change in Governing Law.

[Subpart 3. Priority]

- 9-317. Interests That Take Priority Over or Take Free of Unperfected Security Interest or Agricultural Lien.

- 9-318. No Interest Retained in Right to Payment That is Sold; Rights and Title of Seller of Account or Chattel Paper With Respect to Creditors and Purchasers.

- 9-319. Rights and Title of Consignee With Respect to Creditors and Purchasers.

- 9-320. Buyer of Goods.

- 9-321. Licensee of General Intangible and Lessee of Goods in Ordinary Course of Business.

- 9-322. Priorities Among Conflicting Security Interests in and Agricultural Liens on Same Collateral.

- 9-323. Future Advances.

- 9-324. Priority of Purchase-Money Security Interests.

- 9-325. Priority of Security Interests in Transferred Collateral.

- 9-326. Priority of Security Interests Created by New Debtor.

- 9-327. Priority of Security Interests in Deposit Account.

- 9-328. Priority of Security Interests in Investment Property.

- 9-329. Priority of Security Interests in Letter-of-Credit Right.

- 9-330. Priority of Purchaser of Chattel Paper or Instrument.

- 9-331. Priority of Rights of Purchasers of Instruments, Documents, and Securities Under Other Articles; Priority of Interests in Financial Assets and Security Entitlements Under Article 8.

- 9-332. Transfer of Money; Transfer of Funds from Deposit Account.

- 9-333. Priority of Certain Liens Arising by Operation of Law.

- 9-334. Priority of Security Interests in Fixtures and Crops.

- 9-335. Accessions.

- 9-336. Commingled Goods.

- 9-337. Priority of Security Interests in Goods Covered by Certificate of Title.

- 9-338. Priority of Security Interest or Agricultural Lien Perfected by Filed Financing Statement Providing Certain Incorrect Information.

- 9-339. Priority Subject to Subordination.

[Subpart 4. Rights Of Bank]

- 9-340. Effectiveness of Right of Recoupment or Set-Off Against Deposit Account.

- 9-341. Bank's Rights and Duties with Respect to Deposit Account.

- 9-342. Bank's Right to Refuse to Enter into or Disclose Existence of Control Agreement.

Part 4. Rights of Third Parties

- 9-401. Alienability of Debtor's Rights.

- 9-402. Secured Party Not Obligated on Contract of Debtor or in Tort.

- 9-403. Agreement Not to Assert Defenses Against Assignee.

- 9-404. Rights Acquired by Assignee; Claims and Defenses Against Assignee.

- 9-405. Modification of Assigned Contract.

- 9-406. Discharge of Account Debtor; Notification of Assignment; Identification and Proof of Assignment; Restrictions on Assignment of Accounts, Chattel Paper, Payment Intangibles, and Promissory Notes Ineffective.

- 9-407. Restrictions on Creation or Enforcement of Security Interest in Leasehold Interest or in Lessor's Residual Interest.

- 9-616. Explanation of Calculation of Surplus or Deficiency.
- 9-617. Rights of Transferee of Collateral.
- 9-618. Rights and Duties of Certain Secondary Obligors.
- 9-619. Transfer of Record or Legal Title.
- 9-620. Acceptance of Collateral in Full or Partial Satisfaction of Obligation; Compulsory Disposition of Collateral.
- 9-621. Notification of Proposal to Accept Collateral.
- 9-622. Effect of Acceptance of Collateral.
- 9-623. Right to Redeem Collateral.
- 9-624. Waiver.

[Subpart 2. Noncompliance With Article]

- 9-625. Remedies for Secured Party's Failure to Comply with Article.
- 9-626. Action in Which Deficiency or Surplus is in Issue.
- 9-627. Determination of Whether Conduct was Commercially Reasonable.
- 9-628. Nonliability and Limitation on Liability of Secured Party; Liability of Secondary Obligor.

Part 7. Transition

- 9-701. Effective Date.
- 9-702. Savings Clause.
- 9-703. Security Interest Perfected Before Effective Date.
- 9-704. Security Interest Unperfected Before Effective Date.
- 9-705. Effectiveness of Action Taken Before Effective Date.
- 9-706. When Initial Financing Statement Suffices to Continue Effectiveness of Financing Statement.
- 9-707. Amendment of Pre-Effective-Date Financing Statement.
- 9-708. Persons Entitled to File Initial Financing Statement or Continuation Statement.
- 9-709. Priority.

Appendix B. *Federal Acquisition Regulation* (*FAR*) General Structure and Subparts as of FAC 2005–65

Subchapter A—General

Part 1—Federal Acquisition Regulation System

Part 2—Definitions of Words and Terms

Part 3—Improper Business Practices and Personal Conflicts of Interest

Part 4—Administrative Matters

Subchapter B—Competition and Acquisition Planning

Part 5—Publicizing Contract Actions

Part 6—Competition Requirements

Part 7—Acquisition Planning

Part 8—Required Sources of Supplies and Services

Part 9—Contractor Qualifications

Part 10—Market Research

Part 11—Describing Agency Needs

Part 12—Acquisition of Commercial Items

Subchapter C—Contracting Methods and Contract Types

Part 13—Simplified Acquisition Procedures

Part 14—Sealed Bidding

Part 15—Contracting by Negotiation

Part 16—Types of Contracts

Part 17—Special Contracting Methods

Part 18—Emergency Acquisitions

Subchapter D—Socioeconomic Programs

Part 19—Small Business Programs

Part 20—[Reserved]

Part 21—[Reserved]

Part 22—Application of Labor Laws to Government Acquisitions

Part 50—Extraordinary Contractual Actions And The Safety Act

Part 51—Use of Government Sources by Contractors

Subchapter H—Clauses and Forms

Part 52—Solicitation Provisions and Contract Clauses

Part 53—Forms

Appendix

Appendix C. Task List from Job Analysis Study for Contract Managers

Domain 1: Identify Needs

1.1 Perform Needs Assessment

1.2 Conduct Preliminary Market Research for Capability

1.3 Shape Customer Requirements (e.g., Work with Requiring Activity/Program Office)

1.4 Determine Achievability

1.5 Refine Needs Assessment

Domain 2: Plan Contracting

2.1 Conduct Detailed Market Research Regarding Potential Suppliers

2.2 Conduct A Pre-Proposal Conference

2.3 Select Proper Contract Type

2.4 Formulate Contracting Strategy

2.5 Document Acquisition Plan, Including Supporting Documents (e.g., Justification and Approvals, Determinations and Findings)

2.6 Formulate Proposal Evaluation Plan

2.7 Perform Contract Portfolio Management (e.g., Evaluate Alternative Solutions to Support Requirements, Review Customer Requirements, Return on Investment)

2.8 Perform Requirements Analysis

2.9 Perform Spend Analysis

2.10 Perform Risk Analysis (Identification, Probability, Impact, Mitigation)

2.11 Make Teaming Decisions

2.12 Negotiate Nondisclosure Agreements (NDAs)

2.13 Negotiate Teaming Agreements

2.14 Assess Competition

2.15 Manage Potential Organizational Conflicts of Interest (OCIs), Fraud Identification

2.16 Conduct Bid/No Bid Analysis

2.17 Develop Win Strategies

2.18 Determine Appropriate Clauses and Provisions

2.19 Determine Need for any Pre-Award Reviews (e.g., Integrated Baseline Review, Financial Survey, etc.) and Analyze Results

Domain 3: Select Source

3.1 Prepare Solicitations

3.2 Advertise Solicitations

3.3 Amend Solicitations (When Necessary)

3.4 Respond to Questions from Potential Sources

3.5 Review Solicitations in Order to Understand Unique/Special Requirements

3.6 Review Solicitation and Write Request for Proposal Abstract/Compliance Matrix

3.7 Develop Pricing Strategy

3.8 Write Proposal

3.9 Prepare Independent Government Cost Estimate (IGCE)

3.10 Participate in Pre-Proposal Conference

3.11 Submit Proposal and Verify Receipt

3.12 Conduct Compliance Review of Proposals

3.13 Submit Proposals to Appropriate Audit Agency for Review (e.g., Defense Contract Management Agency [DCMA]/Defense Contract Audit Agency [DCAA]) (if Required)

3.14 Analyze Audits of Proposals (Both Technical and Cost)

3.15 Respond to Audit Questions and Support Position

3.16 Perform Cost Analysis

3.17 Perform Price Analysis

3.18 Prepare/Respond to Clarification Requests/ Deficiency Reports

3.18 Conduct Negotiations

3.20 Request/Prepare Final Proposal Revision

3.21 Evaluate Submitted Proposals in Accordance with Evaluation Factors

3.22 Select Source

3.23 Prepare Contract Document

3.24 Review/Approve the Contract Document and Contract File

3.25 Document Selection Process in Contract File (e.g., Price Memorandum, Evaluation Comments)

3.26 Notify Unsuccessful Offerors

3.27 Manage Protests and Appeals

3.28 Execute Contract Document

3.29 Capture, Document, and Share Lessons Learned

Domain 4: Manage Contract

4.1 Debrief Offerors

4.2 Conduct Post-Award Conference Meeting

4.3 Monitor Contract Performance

4.4 Prepare Contract Modifications

4.5 Execute Contract Modifications

4.6 Obtain Consent to Subcontract (if Required)

4.7 Execute Contract Agreements (e.g., Subcontracts, Teaming Arrangements)

4.8 Manage Subcontracts

4.9 Monitor Contractor's Subcontract Management

4.10 Manage Contract Changes (e.g., Modifications, Negotiated Changes, Post-Award Audits, Configuration Control)

4.11 Analyze and Respond to Audit Findings

4.12 Conduct Performance Reviews

4.13 Conduct Contractor Systems Reviews (e.g., Contractor Purchasing Systems, Earned Value Management System [EVMS])

4.14 Deliver Contract Requirements (e.g., Contract Data Requirements List, Contract Line Item Number, Products and Services)

4.15 Inspect and Accept Contract Requirements (e.g., Contract Data Requirements List, Contract Line Item Number, Products and Services)

4.16 Maintain Contract Documentation/Files

4.17 Ensure Compliance with Contract Terms and Conditions

4.18 Track Project Funding and Contract Value

4.19 Manage Contract Payment Process (Submission/Payment of Invoices, Progress Payments, Vouchers, etc.)

4.20 Manage Key Personnel Changes

4.21 Require/Submit a Truth in Negotiations Act (TINA) Certification (When Appropriate)

4.22 Manage Government/Contractor-Furnished Property, Equipment, Information

4.23 Maintain Communications with Requiring Activity/Program Office

4.24 Compile and Maintain Contractors' Past Performance Data

4.25 Reclaim or Rebut Past Performance Information Data

Domain 5: Close Contract

5.1 Verify Contract Completion

5.2 Prepare Contract Completion Documents

5.3 Make Final Payment

5.4 Manage Disposition of Government/Contractor-Furnished Property/Equipment

5.5 Reconcile Contracts (e.g., Funding, Deliverables, Inventories, Payments, Modifications)

5.6 Capture, Document, and Share Lessons Learned Knowledge Domains From Job Analysis Study

Appendix D. Knowledge Domains from Job Analysis Study for Contract Managers

Content Area 1
Pre-Award Knowledge of:

K1.1 Requirements Identification Techniques

K1.2 Market Research Techniques and Tools to Understand the Competitive Environment, Markets, and Available Information Sources

K1.3 Elements of Planning (e.g., Acquisition Streamlining Techniques, Sources of Supply, Competition, Socioeconomic Policies)

K1.4 Risk Analysis and Mitigation Strategies

K1.5 Portfolio (i.e., Collection of Programs Management Principles

K1.6 Roles and Responsibilities in Program Management

K1.7 Industry—Commercial Contracting Considerations (e.g., Uniform Commercial Code [UCC], Teaming Agreements, NDAs, Pricing Strategies)

K1.8 Organizational and Personal Conflict of Interest Identification and Mitigation Strategies

K1.9 Methods to Solicit or Invite Offers

K1.10 Contract Incentives (e.g., Cost, Performance, Delivery)

K1.11 Other Contracts, Agreements, and Arrangements (e.g., Basic Agreements, Letter Contracts, Indefinite Delivery/Indefinite Quantity Contacts)

K1.12 Contract Financing Options

K1.13 Elements of a Solicitation Package (e.g., Statement of Work, Contract Type and Method, Terms and Conditions)

K1.14 Elements of a Subcontract Package

K1.15 Government Requirements for Publicizing Solicitations

K1.16 Proposal Evaluation Factors (e.g., Price/Cost, Technical Capabilities, Past Performance)

K1.17 Proposal Evaluation Techniques (e.g., Rating Scales and Weights, Separate Evaluation of Technical and Price/Cost Proposals)

K1.18. Contract Negotiation Strategies and Tactics

K1.19 Pre-Award Practices Unique to Federal Contracting

K1.20 Pricing and Payments (e.g., Prelists, Payment Structures, Milestone Payments, Incentives)

K1.21 Price and Cost Analysis

K1.22 Flow-Down Contract Requirements and Clauses

K1.23 Legal Entity Structures (e.g., Joint Venture, Teaming Agreements)

K1.24 Federal Government Uniform Contract Format

K1.25 Award Practices Unique to Federal Contracting (e.g., Pre and Post-Award Notification, Debriefing, Mistakes and Protests, Small Business Programs, Inspection, Acceptance, Title, Warranties)

K1.26 Appropriate Documentation Techniques to Mitigate Protests

K1.27 Subcontract Flow Down and Applicable Provisions

Content Area 2
Post-Award Knowledge of:

K2.1 Types of Contract Changes (e.g., Directed, Constructive, Cardinal)

K2.2 Change Management (e.g., Scope Creep, Configuration Control)

K2.3 Subcontract Management Techniques (e.g., Flow Down of Changes)

K2.4 Alternate Dispute Resolution Methods

K2.5 Legal Dispute Resolution (e.g., Claims, Remedies)

K2.6 Forms of Contract Termination (e.g., Termination for Cause, Termination by Mutual Consent, Termination for Convenience)

K2.7 Post-Award Practices Unique to Federal Contracting (e.g., Treatment of Property, Contract Financing Methods and Preferences)

K2.8 Contract Close-Out Procedures

K2.9 Inspection and Acceptance

K2.10 Quality Management Principles

Content Area 3
Business Knowledge of:

K3.1 Oral and Written Communication Techniques

K3.2 Team Leadership Techniques

K3.3 Electronic Contracting Tools

K3.4 Generally Accepted Accounting Principles (e.g., Balance Sheets, Profit and Loss, Cash Flow)

K3.5 Cost Principles (e.g., Overhead, General and Administrative [G&A] Rates, Wrap Rate Calculations)

K3.6 Economic Principles (e.g., Supply and Demand, Forecasting, Inflation, Trade-Offs, Economic Price Adjustments)

K3.7 Principles of Marketing (e.g., Product/ Service Planning, Promotion, Pricing)

K3.8 Customer Relationship Management (CRM) Techniques

K3.9 Business Advisory Roles of the Contract Manager

K3.10 Knowledge Management (e.g., Lessons Learned, Benchmarking, Best Practices)

K3.11 Types of Audits (e.g., Pre-Award Surveys, Close-Out, Operations, Financial, Floor Check)

K3.12 Suspension and Debarment Procedures

K3.13 Networking Techniques

K3.14 Life Cycle Management

K3.15 Management Tools (e.g., Earned Value Management Systems [EVMS])

Content Area 4
Legal/Regulatory/Professional Knowledge of:

K4.1 Forms of Legal Relationships (e.g., Consortia, Teaming Agreements, Joint Venture, Memorandum of Agreement [MOA]/ Memorandum of Understanding)

K4.2 *Federal Acquisition Regulation* (*FAR*) and Supplements

K4.3 Article 2 of the UCC

K4.4 Non-FAR Transactions (e.g., Financial Assistance, Grants, Other Transactions)

K4.5 Cost Accounting Standards (CAS)

K4.6 Sarbanes-Oxley Act

K4.7 Laws Related to International Contracting

K4.8 K4.8 Professional Standards of Conduct and Codes of Ethics

K4.9 K4.9 Classes of Agents (e.g., Universal, General, Special)

K4.10 Basis of Authority of Agents to Act (i.e., Expressed, Implied, Apparent)

K4.11 Labor Law (e.g., Service Contract Act, Walsh-Healy Public Contracts Act, Davis-Bacon Act)

K4.12 Appropriations/Fiscal Law as it Relates to Contract Funding (e.g., Color of Money, Bona Fide Needs Rule, Antideficiency Act)

K4.13 Intellectual Property (e.g., Patent, Copyright, Data) and its Legal Treatment (e.g., Licensing, Royalties, Nondisclosure Agreements)

K4.14 Roles of Different Branches of Government in Contract Oversight

Domain 5
Specialized Knowledge of:

K5.1 Research and Development

K5.2 Architect, Engineering, and Construction Services

K5.3 Information Technology

K5.4 Contracting for Services

K5.5 Performance-Based Acquisition

K5.6 Contracts with State and Local Governments

K5.7 Supply Chain Management

K5.8 International Contracting (e.g., Export/Import Control/Offsets, Foreign Corrupt Practices Act)

K5.9 International Traffic in Arms Regulation (ITAR)/ Export Administration Regulation (EAR)

K5.10 Government Property

K5.11 Security (e.g., Industrial, Physical, Personal, Information Assurance)

K5.12 Contingency Contracting

K5.13 Spend Analysis

K5.14 Environmental Contracting

K5.15 Inter-Agency Contracting (e.g., Federal Supply Schedules, Government-wide Acquisition Contracts, Multi-Agency Contracts)

K5.16 Contractor System Reviews (e.g., Earned Value Management Systems, Contractor Purchasing System Reviews)

K5.17 Foreign Military Sales

K5.18 Government Purchase Card (GPC)

K5.19 Undefinitized Contract Action (UCA)

American Council of Engineering Companies, "The Brooks Act: How to Use Qualifications-Based Selection" (Originally produced by the Texas Society of Architects), *available at* www.acec.org/advocacy/committees/brooks2.cfm.

"Benefits of Performance-Based Acquisition," *available at* www.acquisition.gov/sevensteps/introduction.html.

Henry Campbell Black and Bryan A. Garner, *Black's Law Dictionary, Pocket Edition, Fourth Edition.* (West, 2011).

Louis E. Boone and David L. Kurtz, *Contemporary Business, thirteenth ed.* (John Wiley & Sons, Inc., 2009).

Max Chafkin, "How to Compete in a Reverse Auction," *Inc. Magazine* (May 2007).

John Cibinic Jr. and Ralph C. Nash Jr., *Formation of Government Contracts, Third Edition* (Wolters Kluwer, 1998).

John Cibinic Jr. and Ralph C. Nash Jr., *Administration of Government Contracts, Fourth Edition* (Wolters Kluwer, 2006).

Contract Management Institute, *Metrics for the Contract Management Discipline* (Vienna, Virginia: NCMA, 2002).

Council of Supply Chain Management Professionals, "CSCMP's Definition of Logistics Management," *available at* http://cscmp.org/about-us/supply-chain-management-definitions.

Council of Supply Chain Management Professionals, "Logistics Management—Boundaries and Relationships," *available at* http://cscmp.org/about-us/supply-chain-management-definitions.

Deputy Director of Defense Procurement and Acquisition Policy (Cost, Pricing, and Finance), *Contract Pricing Reference Guide, volume 4* (Washington, DC: Department of Defense, 2012).

Margaret G. Rumbaugh and John W. Wilkinson, *Desktop Guide to Basic Contracting Terms, seventh edition* (Ashburn, Virginia: NCMA, 2012).

Cole Ehmke, Joan Fulton, and Jayson Lusk; "Marketing's Four P's: First Steps for New Entrepreneurs"; Purdue University; Purdue Extension EC-730 (March 2007).

Lita Epstein and Susan Myers, *Small Business Accounting* (John Wiley & Sons, Inc., 2009).

Federal Accounting Standards Advisory Board (FASAB), *FASAB Handbook of Federal Accounting Standards* (Norwalk: FASAB, 2012).

Federal Accounting Standards Advisory Board (FASAB), *Managerial Cost Accounting* (Norwalk: FASAB, 2012).

Roger Fisher, William Ury, and Bruce Patton; *Getting to Yes, Second Edition* (Penguin Group, 2011).

S.M. Flynn, *Eyeing the Four Basic Market Structures* (New York: John Wiley & Sons, 2013).

Government Accountability Office, "Electronic Government Act: Agencies Have Implemented Most Provisions But Key Areas of Attention Remain" (2012).

Robert K. Herdman, "The Roles of the SEC and the FASB in Establishing GAAP," Testimony Before the House Subcommittee on Capital Markets, Insurance, and Government Sponsored Enterprises, Committee on Financial Services (May 14, 2012).

W. Noel Keyes and Steven W. Feldman, *Government Contracts in a Nutshell, Fifth Edition* (West, 2011)

D.L. Kurtz and L.E. Boone, *Contemporary Business* (Fort Worth, Texas: Harcourt College Publishers, 2002).

W. Gregor Macfarlan, "The Buyer as a Business Manager?" *Contract Management* Magazine (August 2000).

M. Mandel, Economics: *The Basics* (New York: McGraw-Hill, 2012).

David Marshall, Wayne McManus, and Daniel Viele; *Accounting: What the Numbers Mean; 9/e* (McGrawHill, 2011).

Microsoft, "E-Procurement" (2013), *available at* www.microsoft.com/about/companyinformation/

procurement/process/en/us/online.aspx.
Microsoft, "Microsoft Templates" (2013), *available at* http://office.microsoft.com/en-us/templates/word-templates-FX102825522.aspx.

J.F. Newhart, "Service With A Smile," *Contract Management* Magazine (December 2003).

Catherine Z. Remley and Robert A. Ludvik, *Guide to the Contract Management Body of Knowledge (CMBOK), Third Edition* (Ashburn, VA: NCMA, 2011).

Margaret G. Rumbaugh, *Understanding Government Contract Source Selection* (Management Concepts, 2010).

Roberta S. Russell and Bernard W. Taylor, *Operations Management: Creating Value Along the Supply Chain* (Hoboken, New Jersey: John Wiley & Sons Inc., 2009).

Securities and Exchange Commission, "Beginner's Guide to Financial Statements" (2013), *available at* www.sec.gov/investor/pubs/begfinstmtguide.htm.

Small Business Administration, "Marketing" (2012), *available at* www.sba.gov/category/navigation-structure/starting-managing-business/managing-business/running-business/marketing.

Symplicity Corporation, *FedBizOpps Vendor Guide* (Washington, DC: FedBizOpps, 2012).

"The Primary Colors of Leadership," interview with Dr. David Pendleton, *Contract Management* Magazine (June 2013).

USLegal.com, "Royalties Law and Legal Definition," *available at* http://definitions.uslegal.com/r/royalties/.

U.S. Patent and Trademark Office, "General Information Concerning Patents," *available at* www.uspto.gov/patents/resources/general_info_concerning_patents.jsp#.

Diane K. Whitmoyer, "Managing Organizational Conflicts of Interest," *Contract Management* Magazine (June 2004).

Jeff Wolf, "Leadership in Crisis: Take 8 Steps to Avoid Pitfalls," *available at* www.wolfmotivation.com/articles/leadership-in-crisis-take-8-steps-to-avoid-pitfalls.

World Intellectual Property Organization, "Licensing of Intellectual Property Rights; a Vital Component of the Business Strategy of Your SME," *available at* www.wipo.int/sme/en/ip_business/licensing/licensing.htm.

The CMBOK is an independent publication and is not affiliated with, nor has it been authorized, sponsored, or otherwise approved by Microsoft Corporation.